聞いて覚える英単語
キクタン
TOEFL® TEST
【頻出編】

ITP&iBT両対応

田中真紀子 監修・解説

英語は聞いて覚える！
アルク・キクタンシリーズ

「読む」だけでは、言葉は決して身につきません。私たちが日本語を習得できたのは、赤ちゃんのころから日本語を繰り返し「聞いて」きたから──『キクタン』シリーズは、この「当たり前のこと」にこだわり抜いた単語集・熟語集です。「読んでは忘れ、忘れては読む」──そんな悪循環とはもうサヨナラです。「聞いて覚える」、そして「読んで理解する」、さらに「使って磨く」──英語習得の「新しい1歩」が、この1冊から必ず始まります！

付属CDについて
- 弊社制作の音声CDは、CDプレーヤーでの再生を保証する規格品です。
- パソコンでご使用になる場合、CD-ROMドライブとの相性により、ディスクを再生できない場合がございます。ご了承ください。
- パソコンでタイトル・トラック情報を表示させたい場合は、iTunesをご利用ください。iTunesでは、弊社がCDのタイトル・トラック情報を登録しているGracenote社のCDDB（データベース）からインターネットを介してトラック情報を取得することができます。
- CDとして正常に音声が再生できるディスクからパソコンやmp3プレーヤー等への取り込み時にトラブルが生じた際は、まず、そのアプリケーション（ソフト）、プレーヤーの製作元へご相談ください。

Preface
TOEFL® テスト過去問題を徹底分析。
全セクションで通用する頻出単語800選です!

監修・解説 田中真紀子

**1日わずか10語、
1分でも大丈夫。
TOEFL®テストハイスコア
を目指すための必須語彙を
80日間で効率よく学習!**

本書は過去にアルク社から出版された『TOEFL®テスト完全攻略 英単語』を底本とし、聞いて覚える英単語「キクタンシリーズ」として再編されたものです。TOEFL ハイスコアを目指すために最低限必要な語彙を800語に絞り、基本語彙200語と自然科学／人文科学関連の教養語600語で構成されています。

改編に際し、1日の学習量を10語に限定し、80日間で確実に覚えられるように構成しています。また、楽しい音楽に乗りながら耳からも語彙を定着させる「チャンツCD」を2枚用意しています。効果的に「覚える」ためには「耳」からの学習は不可欠です。ぜひ、目だけでなく、耳も使って語彙を定着させましょう。

**Reading Section
対策に必須!
確実に得点するための、
重要例文を厳選。
語彙の運用力アップで
リスニング、文法力も増強。**

TOEFL テストの Reading Section で扱われる内容の英文にならって、各見出し語の例文を作成しました。テストに出題される英文に慣れるだけでなく、見出し語に関連した分野の語彙の増強や知識の蓄積に役立つ例文を厳選しています。

見出し語の解説中の定義や同義語、例文中の語彙を学習すれば、2000語近い語句が習得できるように配慮されています。「単に見出し語800だけではなく、例文をしっかり勉強してこそ効率よく語彙力がつく」ことを念頭におきましょう。本書を勉強することで身につけた語彙力は、読解問題だけでなく、リスニングや文法のセクションを解く際にも必ず強い味方となります。

Contents

1日10語、80日間で
TOEFL® 頻出厳選語彙800語をマスター

Chapter 1

基本語彙 200語

Page15 ▶ 70

Day 1-5　動詞 ①〜⑤
Day 6-10　名詞 ①〜⑤
Day 11-15　形容詞 ①〜⑤
Day 16-20　副詞 ①〜⑤

復習テスト
動詞　▶ 26
名詞　▶ 38
形容詞 ▶ 50
副詞　▶ 62
基本語彙　総復習テスト ▶ 64

Chapter 2

自然科学 300語

Page71 ▶ 151

Day 21-23　宇宙 ①〜③
Day 24-26　気象 ①〜③
Day 27-29　地学 ①〜③
Day 30-32　環境 ①〜③
Day 33-35　生物 ①〜③
Day 36-38　動物 ①〜③
Day 39-41　生理学 ①〜③
Day 42-44　健康 ①〜③
Day 45-47　化学 ①〜③
Day 48-50　物理 ①〜③

復習テスト
宇宙 ▶ 78　　動物　▶ 118
気象 ▶ 86　　生理学 ▶ 126
地学 ▶ 94　　健康　▶ 134
環境 ▶ 102　　化学　▶ 142
生物 ▶ 110　　物理　▶ 150

Chapter 3
社会・人文科学300語
Page153 ▶ 233

Day 51-53 政治 **1**〜**3**
Day 54-56 経済 **1**〜**3**
Day 57-59 社会 **1**〜**3**
Day 60-62 法律 **1**〜**3**
Day 63-65 教育 **1**〜**3**
Day 66-68 心理 **1**〜**3**
Day 69-71 文学語学 **1**〜**3**
Day 72-74 歴史 **1**〜**3**
Day 75-77 文化 **1**〜**3**
Day 78-80 芸術 **1**〜**3**

復習テスト

政治	▶160	心理	▶200
経済	▶168	文学語学	▶208
社会	▶176	歴史	▶216
法律	▶184	文化	▶224
教育	▶192	芸術	▶232

Preface
Page3

TOEFL® テストとは
Page 6 ▶ 9

本書の構成と特徴
Page 10 ▶ 11

本書とCDの利用法
Page 12 ▶ 13

復習テスト解答・訳例
Page 234 ▶ 250

Index
Page 251 ▶ 264

【記号説明】
・( )：省略可能・用語の解説
　例）メートル（法）の
　　→メートルの、メートル法の
・[ ]：代替可能
　例）研究室 [所]
　　→研究室、研究所
・〈 〉：語の用法
　例）exploit〈資源などを〉開発する
・**動名形副**：順に動詞、名詞、形容詞、副詞を表します。
・**反熟関**：順に反意語、熟語、関連語を表します。

TOEFL® テストとは

TOEFL テストとは

TOEFL（Test of English as a Foreign Language）テストとは、その名称が示すように、外国語としての英語力判定テストである。アメリカの非営利教育団体 Educational Testing Service（ETS）により開発運営されている TOEFL テストは、主にアメリカやカナダの大学院、大学・短大で、留学志願者の英語力が授業についていくのに必要な基準に達しているかを測るための目安として使われてきた。最近では、アメリカ、カナダのみならずイギリス、オーストラリア、ニュージーランドを含む英語圏各国において、8500 を超える大学・短大が、英語が母語でない留学生に対して、必要な英語力の基準を、TOEFL テストのスコアで提示し、入学要件のひとつとしている（TOEFL テストとともに他の英語力判定テストのスコアを採用している大学もある）。現在では、Internet-Based Testing（以下 iBT）と呼ばれるインターネットを利用して行われる TOEFL テストが実施されており、従来の Paper-Based Testing（PBT）はすでに中止されている（便宜的に実施される可能性はある）。

TOEFL iBT の概要

TOEFL iBT は、リーディング、リスニング、スピーキング、ライティングの 4 つのセクションに分かれている。リーディングとリスニングは選択式で、選択肢や文中の語などをマウスでクリックする解答方式となっている。スピーキングは設問に対する自分の考えを述べたり、提示される内容を要約して話したりする方式で、ライティングはタイピングによって解答する。テスト時間の合計は約 4 時間半、問題数合計は Pretest（採点されないといわれている設問）が含まれるため78〜115問となっている。各セクショ

ンでメモを取ることが許されている。

〈リーディングセクション〉（試験時間：60〜80分／問題数：36〜56問）
3〜4つのパッセージを読み設問に答えるセクション。このセクションでは1パッセージ約700語の文章を20分程度で読む必要があるので、かなりの速読能力が求められる。出題範囲が広いため、普段からさまざまな分野のトピックやニュースを英語で読んでおくことが重要である。

〈リスニングセクション〉（試験時間：60〜90分／問題数：34〜51問）
2〜3つの会話、4〜6つの講義や討論を聞き設問に答えるセクション。このセクションでは「適切なメモを取る力」と「高度なリスニング能力」が求められる。会議や講義、討論は非常に長いので、ポイントを押さえたメモをとる練習が必要となる。

〈スピーキングセクション〉（試験時間：約20分／問題数：6タスク）
受験者はマイク付ヘッドセットをつけ、パソコン画面に表示されるタスクに対してマイクを通して英語で解答する。1つのタスクにつき、解答時間は45〜60秒。短時間で思考をまとめ、論理的にスピーチを行う能力が求められるので、日頃からスピーチの練習をしておく必要がある。

〈ライティングセクション〉（試験時間：50分／問題数：2タスク）
3分間でパッセージを読み、その後2分程度の短い講義を聞いて設問に答える統合型問題（Integrated Task）と、あるトピックについての意見をまとめる形式の問題（Independent Task）とが出題される。正しい文法の知識、文章構成能力、タイピング技術はもちろん、統合型問題では読解力、リスニング能力も求められる。

TOEFL ITP とは

TOEFL ITP（Institutional Testing Program）は、TOEFL テスト作成・運営元である ETS が提供する TOEFL の団体向けテストプログラムのことである。主に教育機関において大学・短期大学、高校でのクラス分けや大学院入試などに利用されている。交換留学の選考で求められることも多いが、TOEFL ITP スコアは試験実施団体内でのみ有効で、公的には認められない。そのため交換留学以外で留学を希望する場合は、本試験として実施されるTOEFL iBTを受験する必要がある。問題は2種類ある。ひとつは PBT TOEFL で過去に出題された試験問題を再利用して出題される Level 1 TOEFL、もうひとつは Level 1 TOEFL の難易度を下げた Level 2 Pre-TOEFL である。本書では Level 1 TOEFL を対象としている。試験内

容は、リスニング、文法、リーディングの３つのセクションから成り、TOEFL iBTで実施されるライティング、スピーキングセクションは出題されない。すべて４者択一の試験問題で解答はマークシート方式。メモをとることは禁止されている。

〈リスニングセクション〉（試験時間：約35分／問題数：50問）
短い会話、長い会話、講義の一部などを聞き、その内容に関する設問に答えるセクション。短い会話は30、長い会話は２つ、講義の一部などは３つ読まれ、それぞれに対して30問、8問、12問が出題される。

〈文法セクション〉（試験時間：25分／問題数：40問）
英文の空所に適切な語句を補充するStructureと、英文中の間違いを指摘するWritten Expressionが出題される。問題数はそれぞれ15問と25問。

〈リーディングセクション〉（試験時間：55分／問題数：50問）
200語から300程度の英文を読み、その内容および本文中の語彙に関する設問に答えるセクション。出題される英文は５つ程度。

スコアについて

TOEFL iBTのスコアは、リーディング、リスニング、スピーキング、ライティングの４つのセクション別に０～30点の間で算出され、その合計が全体のスコアとなる。つまり最低スコアが０点、最高スコアは120点となる。TOEFL ITPでは、リスニング、文法、リーディングの全セクションの合計スコアは、最高677、最低310。セクションごとに正解数を変換し、セクション別のスコアが算出される。それらを合計して10を掛け、３で割った数でスコアが表される。

TOEFLテストのスコアは英語圏の多くの大学で英語力の判定材料とされ、大学、短大によって要求されるスコアは異なる。目安として、アメリカの場合、コミュニティーカレッジと呼ばれる２年制大学ではTOEFL iBTで46～61、TOEFL ITPで450～500、学部留学ではiBT: 61～80、ITP: 500～550、大学院留学ではiBT: 80～100、ITP: 550～600が目標とされている。しかし入学のための競争が激し

【iBT／ITPテストスコア換算表】

iBT	120	105	100	92	88	80	68	61	45	32	0-8
ITP	677	620	600	580	570	550	520	500	450	400	310

い学校や、高い英語能力が要求される専攻分野などでは、要求スコアがこの目安よりも高めに設定されている場合がある。

受験手続きについて

TOEFL ITP は団体が実施する試験であるため、個人での受験申込みはできない。学校や企業など所属団体に問い合わせ、そこから申し込む必要がある。ここでは一般に公開されている TOEFL iBT の受験手続きの方法を紹介する。

まず、Information Bulletin（以下 Bulletin）と呼ばれる受験要項を入手する。Bulletin には、受験手続きから、教材の購入方法まで、TOEFL テストに関する諸注意がこと細かに説明されている。情報のほとんどが英語で書かれているため、全部を読みこなすのはたいへんだが、TOEFL テスト受験の第一歩と考え挑戦してみよう。Bulletin は、国際教育交換協議会（CIEE）日本代表部のウェブサイト、日本での ETS の代行をしているプロメトリック(株)のウェブサイト、ETS が提供する TOEFL テストの公式サイトより、PDF ファイル形式でダウンロードする。次に、TOEFL テスト公式サイトで個人のアカウントページを作成する。これはインターネットもしくは電話で TOEFL iBT 受験を申し込む際には必須となっている。

郵送で申し込む場合は、Bulletin に添付されている 4 ページからなる申込書（TOEFL Internet-based Test Registration Form）に記入する。記入済み申込書と受験料 225 ドル（国際郵便為替、送金小切手、クレジットカードの場合はカード番号を記入）を、最も近い希望テスト日の 4 週間前までに必着で、プロメトリック（株）宛に送付する。

【Bulletin の入手先（インターネット）】
国際教育交換協議会（CIEE）日本代表部
URL : http://www.cieej.or.jp/
プロメトリック(株)
URL : http://www.prometric-jp.com/
ETS　TOEFL 公式サイト
URL : :http://www.ets.org/toefl/

【テストの申込み先（郵送）】
プロメトリック（株）RRC 予約センター　TOEFL iBT 係
〒 104-0033 東京都中央区新川 1-21-2 茅場町タワー 15F

上記の情報は 2013 年 5 月現在のもので随時更新される場合があります。

だから「ゼッタイに覚えられる」！
本書の構成と特徴

全体の構成

Chapter 1【基本語彙】
: 200 語

TOEFLテストの過去問題をコンピューター分析し、その中から重要語を抽出、掲載しました。最も頻度の高い語は中学校で学習する程度の語で、それらはTOEFLテスト受験者には既知の常識語として本書では割愛してあります。【基本語彙】には、ハイスコアを目指す人が最低必要な語を取り上げました。定義部分には、日本語の意味 [訳語] だけでなく、英語による意味 [語義] や定義、同義語も掲載している場合もあります。訳語だけでなく、必ず語義を確認して、語の本来の意味を正しく覚えましょう。

Chapter 2【自然科学】
Chapter 3【社会・人文科学】
: 各 300 語

TOEFLテストでは専門知識は問われないとはいえ、高校の上級課程および大学の一般教養課程の知識は、TOEFLテスト受験において、英語力以前の前提知識とみなされています。そのため、これらの知識があるか、またこれらの分野に出てくる語彙に親しんでいるかが、TOEFLテストのスコアに大きく左右してきます。こうした語彙力を養成するため、アメリカの高校・大学の一般教養課程の教科書を総ざらいし、TOEFLテストの過去の問題分析結果に照らし合わせて必要な教養語としての重要語を選出しました。語によって日本語で解説を施しましたので、知識の確認、蓄積に役立ててください。

＊本書の見出し語の訳語は、TOEFLテストで出題されるものを中心に取り上げています。一般的な訳語は網羅されておりませんので、ご留意ください。
＊ Chapter 2、3 は分野ごとに見出し語が分類されています。本書は文脈での語彙理解に重点を置いているため、その分野の文章に頻出する、分野とは直接関係のない語が含まれている場合もあります。
たとえば＜動物＞セクションで紹介されている estuary（広い河口、河口域、入り江）は、＜動物＞とは直接関係のない語ですが、動物関連の文章によく登場する語であるため、このセクションに掲載されています。

復習テスト

Chapter 1【基本語彙】には〈動詞〉〈名詞〉〈形容詞〉〈副詞〉のあとにそれぞれ復習テストを、また最後に全体を通した総復習テストを掲載しました。Chapter 2、3 の【自然科学】【社会・人文科学】では、分野ごとに復習テストがあります。この復習テストで語の定義を英語で

本書は、TOEFLテストに欠かせない基本語彙および自然科学／社会・人文科学関連の教養語が無理なく身につくよう工夫され作成されています。

確認できるようになっています。できなかったものはテキストに印を付け、1回だけでなく繰り返し問題を解くようにしましょう。赤字になっている選択肢を付属のチェックシートで隠し、難易度を上げることもできます。

＊見出し語の派生語から出題される場合もあります。

本書の特徴

1. 最小にして最大の効果を得る精選800語

一般に市販されている語彙力増強のための本と比べると本書の800語という語彙数は少ないように思われるかもしれません。しかし、本書は中級、上級者向けに書かれたものであり、中学や高校で学ぶ初級程度の語は割愛されていることを考えれば、800語は決して少ない語彙数ではありません。見出し語の解説として載せた定義や同義語、例文中の語彙をしっかり勉強すれば、2000語近い語句が習得できるように配慮されています。

2. 読解力・語彙力アップに必須の例文

各見出し語の例文は、TOEFLテストのReading Sectionで扱われる内容の英文にならっています。また、例文には見出し語の派生語を使っているものもあります。内容的に難しいと思われるものも含まれていますが、これには以下の目的があります。

・TOEFLテストに出題される英文（特にReading Section）の内容に慣れる。
・文の読解、解釈に役立てる。
・見出し語の語彙とそれに関連した分野の語彙の増強、知識の蓄積に役立てる。

単に見出し語800語だけではなく、例文をしっかり勉強してこそ、効率よく語彙力がつくことをしっかり念頭において学習しましょう。

例文の学習例

1. 左ページの見出し語10語を英語から日本語へ、また日本語から英語へ、口頭であるいは実際に書けるようになるまで勉強する。
2. 次に左ページの見出し語を見ないで、赤シートで例文の語句を隠し、適語を入れて文を完成させてみる。
3. 正解を確認したら、英文の訳例を参考に文の意味をしっかりおさえる。完璧に文が理解できたら、英文を実際に声に出して何度も読む。

目と耳をフル活用
本書とCDの利用法

見出し語
1日の学習語彙は10語です。見開きの左側に学習語彙が掲載されています。「チャンツ音楽」は上から順に語が登場します。

定義・派生語
日本語の意味だけでなく、英語による語の定義や同義語も掲載しました。派生語については、発音の難しいものには発音記号またはアクセント記号を付けました。必ず語義を確認して、本来の意味を正しく覚えましょう。

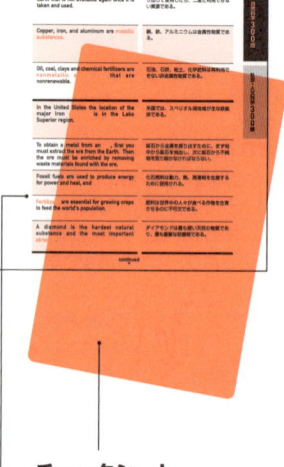

発音記号
見出し語の赤字の品詞について、すべて発音記号を付けました。見出し語が2語以上から成る場合は、各語の発音がそれぞれ参考として記載されています。

例文
見出し語、または見出し語の派生語を含む例文が掲載されています。TOEFLテストに出題される英文に慣れるだけでなく、見出し語に関連した分野の語彙の増強に役立ちます。

チェックシート
本書に付属のチェックシートは復習用に活用してください。見出し語の定義が身に付いているか、訳を参考にしながらチェックシートで隠されている語がすぐに浮かんでくるかを確認しましょう。

1日の学習量は2ページ、学習語彙数は10語となっています。1つの見出し語につき、定義と派生語、例文、例文の和訳が用意されています。まずは、該当のCDトラックを呼び出して、「チャンツ音楽」のリズムに乗りながら、見出し語と定義を「耳」と「目」で押さえましょう。

CD の使い方

付属のCDには、見出し語800語が「英語→日本語→英語」の順に収録されています。目で見て覚えるだけではなく耳で聞いて覚えることで、語彙の習得が一層確実になります。

パターン 1
CDを聞きながら、本を見て同時に発声してみましょう。実際に同時に読んでみると、思わぬところで語の読み違いをしていたことに気がつくこともあります。

パターン 2
今度はCDだけを聞いて、「英語→日本語→英語」のあとのポーズのところで、英語を繰り返してみましょう。
とにかく忙しくて時間がないときは、「チャンツ音楽」を聞き流すだけでもOKです。

CD の内容・構成
左ページの見出し語と日本語を収録しています。例文、復習テストの音声は収められていません。

CD-A
Day 1 - Day 40
Chapter 1【基本語彙】動詞・名詞・形容詞・副詞
Chapter 2【自然科学】
宇宙・気象・地学・環境・生物・動物・生理学

CD-B
Day 41 - Day 80
Chapter 2【自然科学】生理学・健康・化学・物理
Chapter 3【社会・人文科学】
政治・経済・社会・法律・教育・心理・文学語学・歴史・文化・芸術

例文の音声をインターネットでダウンロード購入できます！

詳しくは、音声ダウンロードコンテンツ
(http://www.alc.co.jp/elearning/onsei-dl/)
▶▶「キクタン TOEFL テスト頻出編：例文音声」にアクセス！

iTunes Store、amisoft、MORA、楽天など、お好きなダウンロードサイトよりお求めください。

※各ダウンロードサイトにより、音声の形式、再生可能なプレイヤーが異なりますので、事前にご確認ください。

Chapter 1
基本語彙 200 語

動詞　Day 1...Day 5
　　　▶ 16
　　　復習テスト　動詞
　　　▶ 26
名詞　Day 6...Day 10
　　　▶ 28
　　　復習テスト　名詞
　　　▶ 38
形容詞　Day 11...Day 15
　　　▶ 40
　　　復習テスト　形容詞
　　　▶ 50
副詞　Day 16...Day 20
　　　▶ 52
　　　復習テスト　副詞
　　　▶ 62

総復習テスト
▶ 64

基本語彙200語

自然科学300語

社会・人文科学300語

Day 1

CD-A1

基本語彙200語 動詞 1

001 absorb
/æbzɔ́ːrb, -sɔ́ːrb/

動 〈水分・熱・光などを〉**吸収する**、〈音・衝撃などを〉緩和する、吸収合併する（into）
= to suck in; to reduce the effect or intensity of; to gain control over
熟 be absorbed in ... ……に没頭して　**名** absorption 吸収

002 accomplish
/əkʌ́mpliʃ/

動 成し遂げる、完成する
= to achieve; to succeed in doing; to finish successfully
名 accomplishment 完成、成就、成果

003 accumulate
/əkjúːmjulèit/

動 貯める、蓄積する
= to make or become greater in quantity or size, esp. over a long period of time; to mount up; to collect
名 accumulation 蓄積

004 aggravate
/ǽgrəvèit/

動 さらに悪化させる、〈負債・罪などを〉一層重くする
= to make worse; to annoy; to vex
形 aggravating 腹の立つ、しゃくにさわる

005 apply
/əplái/

動 適用する [される]、申し込む
= to put into use; to make a request, as for a job
名 applicability 適用性　**形** applicable 適用できる、適切な　**名** ápplicant 志願者、応募者　**名** application 申し込み

006 bear
/béər/

動 〈人・物・事が〉**持っている**
= to have or show a sign, mark, or particular appearance

007 capture
/kǽptʃər/

動 とらえる、魅了する、獲得する
= to succeed in showing or describing; to take (a person) prisoner; to take captive; to gain
形名 cáptive 捕虜になった、監禁された。捕虜・監禁されている人（反 captor）

008 complete
/kəmplíːt/

動 完了する、完成する
= to finish; to bring to an end
副 completely 完全に　**名** completion 完成、完了　**熟** bring ... to completion ……を完成させる、仕上げる

009 confer
/kənfə́ːr/

動 〈贈物、名誉などを〉**授与する**、協議する
= to give (a title, honor, favor); to hold a conference
名 cónference 会議

010 confiscate
/kánfiskèit/

動 没収する、押収する、差し押さえる
= to seize by authority
名 confiscátion 没収、押収

continued ▼

When the plants do get water, they absorb it very quickly and conserve it carefully.	植物が水分を取り入れるときは、素早く吸収し、慎重に保存する。
She has accomplished a great deal in the last few weeks.	彼女はこの数週間で、相当な量を完成した。
She gradually accumulated an impressive collection of paintings.	彼女は絵画の見事なコレクションを、徐々に蓄えていった。
The lack of rain for crops aggravated the already serious shortage of food.	農作物への雨不足が、すでに深刻だった食料不足をさらに悪化させた。
Scientific discoveries are often applied to industrial processes.	科学上の発見は、しばしば生産工程に適用される。
Every United States coin bears a symbol of liberty.	すべての米国の硬貨には自由の象徴がついている。
He was an excellent photographer. He had an ability to capture human emotion in his photographs.	彼は優秀な写真家だった。彼は自分の写真の中に、人間の感情をとらえる能力をもっていた。
He finally completed the whole course.	彼はついに全課程を修了した。
She was invited to be in the Museum of Modern Art's (MOMA's) definitive "Art of Assemblage" exhibition, which conferred respectability on her technique.	彼女は、近代美術館（MOMA）の権威ある「アセンブラージュ芸術」展に出品するよう求められたが、このことは彼女の技能に高い評価を与えることになった。
Any illegally imported goods will be confiscated by the customs officer.	不法に輸入された品物はすべて、税関職員によって没収される。

基本語彙200語

自然科学300語

社会・人文科学300語

continued
▼

Day2 動詞 2 — 基本語彙200語

CD-A2

□ 011
construct
/kənstrʌ́kt/

動 **建設する**、組み立てる、作成する　名 cónstruct 構成物、構成概念
= to make or build; to pile up together
名 constrúction 建設

□ 012
consume
/kənsúːm/

動 **消費する**、使いつくす
= to eat up; to devour; to use up; to expend; to waste; to squander
名 consumption 消費　名 consumer 消費者

□ 013
contain
/kəntéin/

動 **含む**、抑える、自制する、阻止する
= to include; to enclose; to restrict
形 contained 自制した

□ 014
contribute
/kəntríbjuːt/

動 **貢献する**、寄付する、寄稿する、〈……の〉一助［一因］となる
= to help make something happen; to join with others in giving (money, help)
形 contributory 寄与する、貢献して

□ 015
convert
/kənvə́ːrt/

動 **変える**、転換する、改宗する
= to (cause to) change into another form; to transform; to accept a particular religion
名 convérter 変換器　名 conversion 転換、転向

□ 016
dedicate
/dédikèit/

動 **献呈する**、捧げる、奉納する
= to give to; to devote to
形 dedicated 献身的な　名 dedication 献身、献呈

□ 017
depict
/dipíkt/

動 **描く**、描写する、叙述する
= to show in [or as if in] a picture
名 depiction 描写、叙述

□ 018
describe
/diskráib/

動 **言葉で述べる**、描写する
= to say what something is like; to draw the figure of
名 description 記述、描写　形 descriptive 記述的な

□ 019
designate
/dézignèit/

動 **任命する**、示す、指示する
= to appoint; to indicate or specify
名 designation 任命、指名、指示

□ 020
distinguish
/distíŋgwiʃ/

動 **識別する**、〈……の〉特徴となる、著名になる
= to discern /disə́ːrn, -zə́ːrn/; to make éminent
形 distínct まったく別な、明瞭な　形 distinctive 特色のある　名 distinction 区別、特質、卓越　形 distinguished 著名な

---

continued
▼

If a flood control dam is constructed, everyone living in the area will benefit.	洪水調節ダムが建設されれば、その地域に住む人すべてが恩恵を受ける。
There is a growing gap between what the country produces and what it consumes.	国家が生産するものと消費するものとの間には、ギャップが増大しつつある。
This book contains all the information you need.	この本は、あなたが必要としているすべての情報を含んでいる。
Cave dwellers contributed a great deal to the formation of culture by discovering the means to control fire.	原始人は、火を管理する方法を発見することによって、文化の形成に大いに貢献した。
For many years scientists and engineers have been seeking ways to convert energy directly into electricity.	多年にわたり、科学者や技術者たちはエネルギーを直接電気に変える方法を探してきている。
I dedicate this volume to my wife in token of affection and gratitude.	本書を愛情と感謝の印として妻に献呈する。
In her classic work, *Gone With The Wind*, Margaret Mitchell depicts the South during the Civil War and Reconstruction period.	マーガレット・ミッチェルは彼女の傑作『風とともに去りぬ』で、南北戦争中および再編期の南部を描いている。
Harlem is often described as being a mostly black neighborhood in Manhattan.	ハーレムは、マンハッタンの中で主に黒人が居住する地域として語られることが多い。
The President has designated him as the next Secretary of State.	大統領は彼を次期国務長官に任命した。
It's not easy to distinguish between the two species, but there are some fairly obvious differences.	このふたつの種を識別するのは容易でないが、いくつかのかなり明白な違いがある。

基本語彙200語

自然科学300語

社会・人文科学300語

Day 3

動詞 基本語彙 200 語 3

CD-A3

□ 021 eradicate /irǽdəkèit/
動 根絶する、撲滅する、根こそぎにする
= to destroy; to uproot; to remove all traces of; to erase

□ 022 estimate /éstəmèit/
動 見積る、評価する
= to calculate approximately; to evaluate
形 estimated 推測の 名 estimation 判断、評価 熟 hold ... in (high) estimation ……を（大いに）評価する

□ 023 expand /ikspǽnd/
動 広がる、広げる、拡大する、発展する、さらに詳しく述べる
= to spread out; to increase in size, extent, etc.; to express more fully; to expatiate /ikspéiʃièit/
名 expansion 拡大、発展 名 expanse〈陸、海、空の〉広がり 形 expansive 膨張力のある、拡張的な

□ 024 exploit /iksplɔ́it/
動〈資源などを〉開発する、搾取する
= to utilize fully or advantageously
名 exploitation 開発、搾取

□ 025 extend /iksténd/
動〈土地、建物、領土などを〉広げる
= to stretch or enlarge to greater length, area, or scope
● expand は大きさ・量などが内部の力で大きくなることを意味する最も普通の語。extend は特に長さが大きくなる。
名 extension 拡張、延期、〈電話の〉内線 形 extensive 広範囲にわたる、大規模な 名 extent 広さ、範囲

□ 026 feed /fíːd/
動 食物［えさ］を食べる、えさを与える、養う
= to eat; to give food to or provide as food or nourishment

□ 027 grind /gráind/
動 細かく砕く、〈穀物などをうすで〉ひく、磨く
= to crush into fine particles; to shape, sharpen, or refine

□ 028 imply /implái/
動 暗示する、ほのめかす
= to express indirectly; to entail
名 implication 包含、言外の意味

□ 029 indicate /índikèit/
動 示す、表す
= to point out; to express briefly
名 indication 指摘、指示、徴候 形 indicative 暗示して

□ 030 influence /ínfluəns/
動 影響を及ぼす
= to have power over; to affect
形 influential 勢力のある、有力な 熟 under the influence of ... ……の影響を受けて

continued ▼

The Salk vaccine had virtually eradicated the threat of polio.	ソーク・ワクチンは、小児マヒの脅威を事実上根絶した。
The firm estimated the cost of the new house at £8,000.	その会社は、新しい家の費用を8,000ポンドと見積った。
Heat causes air to expand.	熱は空気を膨張させる。
By traveling west, they could find new resources to exploit.	西方に旅することによって、彼らは開発すべき新たな資源を見出した。
Fire extended humans' geographical boundaries by allowing them to travel into regions that were previously too cold to explore.	火は、それまで寒過ぎて探検できなかった地域への移動を可能にし、人間の（活動できる）地理的範囲を拡大した。
Warbler species peacefully coexist in the same trees by each feeding in a slightly different manner.	ウグイス科の仲間は、それぞれ少しずつ異なる方法でえさを食べることによって、同じ木に平和に共存している。
All pottery clay is first dried, and broken into small pieces by grinding.	すべての陶土はまず乾燥され、うすでひくことによって小片に砕かれる。
Answer all questions following a passage on the basis of what is stated or implied in that passage.	文中に書かれていること、暗に意味していることをもとに、パッセージに続くすべての質問に答えなさい。
Research indicates that men find it easier to give up smoking than women.	調査が示すところでは、男性のほうが女性より禁煙は簡単だと感じている。
Her writing has obviously been influenced by Pearl S. Buck.	彼女の文体は、明らかにパール・S. バックに影響されている。

基本語彙200語

自然科学300語

社会・人文科学300語

continued
▼

Day 4

動詞 基本語彙200語 4

□ 031 initiate
/iníʃièit/
動 始める、起こす、初歩を教える
=to begin or originate; to introduce (a person) to a new ...
名 initiative 率先　**熟** take the initiative (in doing) 率先して……する

□ 032 inspire
/inspáiər/
動 鼓舞する、〈人にある感情・思想を〉起こす
=to animate the mind or emotions of; to stimulate and influence
名 inspirátion 霊感、うまい思いつき、激励となる人［事］

□ 033 integrate
/íntəgrèit/
動 統合する、まとめる、人種的差別を廃止する
=to make into a whole; to unify; to join together; to unite; to open to all ethnic groups; to desegregate
名 integrátion 統合

□ 034 interact
/ìntərǽkt/
動 相互に作用する、互いに影響し合う
=to act on each other
名 interaction 相互作用

□ 035 modify
/mádəfài/
動 修正する、〈部分的に〉変更する、加減する
=to change; to alter; to make or become less extreme, or severe
名 modificátion（部分的）変更、修正、加減

□ 036 portray
/pɔːrtréi/
動 〈言葉で〉**描写する**、〈人物・風景などを〉描く
=to describe in words; to depict pictorially
名 pórtrait 肖像（画）　**名** portráyal 描写、記述

□ 037 precede
/prisíːd/
動 先に立つ、先に起こる
=to come before in time, place, or rank
形 preceding 先行する、すぐ前の　**形** precedent 先行して

□ 038 prevail
/privéil/
動 流行している、打ち勝つ、優勢である
=to be current; to triumph; to be predominant
形 prevailing 流行の、勢力のある　**形** prévalent 広く行われて　**名** prevalence /prévələns/ 流行、普及

□ 039 produce
/prədjúːs/
動 生産する、提示する、上演する
=to yield /jíːld/ ; to manufacture; to exhibit /igzíbit/
名 próduct 産出物、結果　**形** prodúctive 生産的な、豊富な　**名** prodúction 製造、製品、（映画）製作

□ 040 provoke
/prəvóuk/
動 〈人・動物を〉**怒らせる**、〈人を〉刺激して……させる、扇動する
=to incite to anger or resentment; to arouse /əráuz/
形 provócative 〈人を〉怒らせる、挑発的な

continued
▼

The government has initiated a massive new house-building program.	政府は大規模な新住宅建設計画に着手した。
Langston Hughes' first publication, *The Weary Blues* (1962) encouraged and inspired black creative artists.	ラングストン・ヒューズの最初の著書『ものういブルース』(1962)は、黒人の創作芸術家たちを勇気づけ、鼓舞した。
Different views must be integrated to give perspective to the whole picture.	全体像への展望を得るために、さまざまな見方を統合しなければならない。
Kids are free to act spontaneously and interact with one another.	子どもたちは、自発的に行動し、互いに影響し合うことができる。
The industrial revolution modified the whole structure of English society.	産業革命はイギリス社会の構造全体を変えた。
It is difficult to portray feelings in words.	感情を言葉で描写するのは難しい。
The flash of lightning preceded the sound of thunder by two seconds.	稲妻が光ってその2秒後に雷が鳴った。
A belief in magic still prevails among some tribes.	一部の部族の間では、呪術がいまだに流行している。
The pancreas is an organ in the body that produces insulin.	膵臓は、インシュリンを生産する体内の器官である。
His impudence provoked her into slapping his face.	彼が厚かましいので、彼女は怒って彼の顔をひっぱたいた。

基本語彙200語

自然科学300語

社会・人文科学300語

continued
▼

Day 5

基本語彙200語 動詞 5

CD-A5

□ 041
reconcile
/rékənsàil/

動 和解させる、〈人を〉仲直りさせる、和解させる、〈意見などを〉調和させる
=to settle; to re-establish friendship between
名 reconciliátion 和解、調和、一致

□ 042
reduce
/ridjúːs/

動 減らす、下げる
=to lessen in extent, amount; to diminish
名 reduction 縮小、割引

□ 043
remain
/riméin/

動 残る、〈……の〉ままである　**名**〈複数形で〉残物、遺物
=to continue without change of condition, quality, or place; to stay or be left over after the destruction of others

□ 044
reproach
/ripróutʃ/

動 とがめる、非難する、しかる
=to blame for something; to rebuke
形 reproachful とがめるような

□ 045
respond
/rispánd/

動 反応する、返答する、応じる
=to react; to reply; to answer
名 response 返答、反応　**熟** in response to ... ……に答えて

□ 046
restrain
/ristréin/

動 〈感情・欲望などを〉**抑える**
=to control; to check; to limit or restrict
熟 restrain from ... ……させないようにする　**名** restraint 抑制、拘束

□ 047
strive
/stráiv/

動 努力する
=to exert much effort or energy; to struggle; to contend
【活用】strive-strove-striven

□ 048
substitute
/sʌ́bstətjùːt/

動 代わりに用いる、代わりをする　**名** 代理人
=to use (a person or thing) in place of another; to take the place of another
名 substitútion 代理、代用

□ 049
survive
/sərváiv/

動 生き残る、生きながらえる
=to remain alive or in existence; to live longer than; to outlive
名 survival 生き残ること　**関** the survival of the fittest《生物》適者生存

□ 050
verify
/vérəfài/

動 立証する、確かめる、実証する
=to prove the truth or accuracy of; to substantiate
名 verificátion 立証、証明　**形** verifiable 立証できる、証明できる

continued
▼

The couple couldn't reconcile their differences, so they decided to get a divorce.	その夫婦は自分たちの意見の相違を一致させることができなかったので、離婚することに決めた。
The plague reduced the population to half its previous level.	その疫病は、人口をそれまでの水準の半分に減少させた。
The situation remains unchanged.	状況は変化しないままである。
It wasn't your fault -- you have nothing to reproach yourself with.	それはあなたの過ちだったのではない。自分をとがめることはない。
Nerves respond to a stimulus.	神経は刺激に反応する。
He was so angry that he couldn't restrain himself from punching him.	彼はあまりにも怒っていたので、彼を殴らずにはいられなかった。
He strove to overcome his fear of death.	彼は死への恐怖を克服しようと努力した。
Those who are on a diet should substitute sugar with saccharin.	食事制限をしている人は、砂糖の代わりにサッカリンを用いるべきである。
No crops survived the drought.	その干ばつを生き延びた農作物はなかった。
The prisoner's statement was verified by several witnesses.	その囚人の陳述は、数名の目撃者によって立証された。

基本語彙200語

自然科学300語

社会・人文科学300語

continued ▼

復習テスト 動詞

解答は P.234

1

1～10 の文で意味を成すものには YES に、
意味を成さないものには NO に○をつけなさい。

1. You became reconciled with your friend, so your relationship with him was aggravated. — YES / **NO**
2. If you strive, you can accomplish anything. — **YES** / NO
3. The advertisement captured the attention of everyone because it was so noticeable. — **YES** / NO
4. The police are trying to eradicate crime by expanding the drug industry. — YES / **NO**
5. You need not reproach yourself so much; it's not your fault. — **YES** / NO
6. It's difficult to distinguish the two because they are so different. — YES / **NO**
7. The cholera epidemic prevailed because the government couldn't contain its outbreak. — YES / **NO**
8. He was a very influential teacher. He could inspire self-confidence in his pupils. — **YES** / NO
9. The musical has produced a great sensation throughout the country. — **YES** / NO
10. You can reduce your expenses by consuming a lot. — YES / **NO**

2

1～10 の語の同義語を a～j から選びなさい。

1. influence — d
2. aggravate
3. provoke
4. survive
5. complete — c
6. modify — a
7. reproach
8. designate
9. produce
10. reduce

a. alter	b. outlive	c. finish	d. inspire	e. vex
f. yield	g. rebuke	h. arouse	i. diminish	j. appoint

3 1～10の語の定義に合う動詞を（　）の中に書きなさい。

1. to calculate approximately; to evaluate (　　　)
2. to express indirectly; to entail (　　　)
3. to point out; to express briefly (　　　)
4. to act on each other (　　　)
5. to be current; to triumph; to be predominant (　　　)
6. to react; to reply; to answer (　　　)
7. to remain alive or in existence; to live longer than; to outlive (　　　)
8. to prove the truth or accuracy of; to substantiate (　　　)
9. to suck in; to gain control over (　　　)
10. to put into use; to make a request, as for a job (　　　)

4 1～5の定義を表す正しい語をa～cの中から選びなさい。

1. to make or build; to pile up together
   a. convert   b. construct   c. absorb   b

2. to indicate or specify; to appoint
   a. designate   b. depict   c. describe   a

3. to seize by authority
   a. dedicate   b. aggravate   c. confiscate   c

4. to utilize fully or advantageously
   a. grind   b. exploit   c. consume   c

5. to control; to check; to limit or restrict
   a. reduce   b. reproach   c. restrain   c

Day 6

名詞 1 — 基本語彙200語

CD-A6

☐ 051 anguish /ǽŋgwiʃ/

名〈心身の〉**激しい苦痛**、苦悩
=an agonizing physical or mental pain
熟 in anguish 苦悩して 形 anguished 苦悩に満ちた

☐ 052 burden /bə́:rdn/

名 **重荷**、心配、苦しみ 動 負担させる、悩ませる
=a heavy duty or responsibility which is hard to bear
形 burdensome 負担となる、厄介な

☐ 053 chaos /kéiɑs/

名 **大混乱**、無秩序
=total disorder or confusion
● confusion は個々の区別がつかない混乱状態、chaos は手のつけられぬほどの混乱状態、disorder は順序が乱れていること
形 chaotic /keiɑ́tik/ 混沌とした、無秩序な（反 orderly）

☐ 054 complement /kɑ́mpləmənt/

名 **補足物**
=something that completes or makes up a whole

☐ 055 complexion /kəmplékʃən/

名 **様相**、顔色、外観
=a general character or nature; the natural color and appearance of the skin, esp. of the face

---

☐ 056 concord /kɑ́nkɔ:rd/

名〈人と人の〉**調和**、〈意見の〉一致、〈国際間の〉協定
=harmony; accord; concurrence
名 concórdance 一致、調和 形 concórdant (with) 合致して 反 discord 不調和

☐ 057 concurrence /kənkə́:rəns/

名 **一致**、同意、同時に発生すること
=an agreement of opinion; actions happening at the same time
動 concúr〈ふたつ以上の意見が〉一致する、同時に起こる 形 concúrrent 同時発生の、共同に作用する、同意見の

☐ 058 congestion /kəndʒéstʃən/

名 **過密**、渋滞
=a state which is overfilled
動 congést 渋滞させる 形 congested 混雑した

☐ 059 conjecture /kəndʒéktʃər/

名 **推量**、憶測 動 推測する
=ínference based on inconclúsive evidence; guesswork
形 conjéctural 推測的な、憶測好きな

☐ 060 core /kɔ́:r/

名〈物事の〉**核心**、〈リンゴなどの〉芯、眼目
=the most important part of anything; the hard central part of certain fruits, as an apple

continued
▼

She was in anguish over her missing child.	彼女は行方不明のわが子のことでひどく苦悩していた。
People on high incomes face a huge tax burden.	高額所得者は、莫大な税の負担に直面している。
Tornadoes left several Midwestern towns in a state of chaos.	大竜巻は、中西部のいくつかの町を大混乱に陥れた。
A fine wine is a complement to a good meal.	上質のワインがあってこそおいしい食事を味わえる。
This information puts a new complexion on the situation.	この情報は、状況に新たな様相を与える。
These neighboring states had lived in concord for centuries.	これらの隣接する諸国は、何世紀にもわたって仲よく暮らしてきた。
The President and the Congress are in concurrence concerning this decision.	大統領と議会は、この決定に関して一致している。
The concentration of all public facilities brought about congestion in the city.	あらゆる公共施設が集中したことが、その都市の過密を引き起こした。
The senator didn't know the facts; what he said was pure conjecture.	その上院議員は事実を知らなかった。彼が言ったことはまったくの臆測だった。
The belief in free enterprise is at the core of the country's political thinking.	自由企業制への信奉が、その国の政治的思惑の核心にある。

基本語彙200語

自然科学300語

社会・人文科学300語

continued
▼

Day 7

名詞 2 — 基本語彙200語

CD-A7

□ 061 **decade** /dékeid/
名 10年間
=a period of ten years

□ 062 **defect** /dí:fekt, difékt/
名 欠点、短所、弱点
=something missing or an imperfection; fault
形 deféctive 欠点のある、不完全な

□ 063 **defense** /diféns/
名 防衛、守備
=the act of defending
動 defend 守る、弁護する　形 defensive 防御的な、（すぐ）むきになる

□ 064 **deterioration** /ditìəriəréiʃən/
名 悪化、低下、退歩
=becoming or making worse
動 detériorate 悪くなる（反 ameliorate /əmíːljərèit/）
関 amelioration 改善、改良

□ 065 **device** /diváis/
名 装置、工夫、趣向
=something made for a particular purpose
動 devise /diváiz/ 工夫する、考案する

□ 066 **district** /dístrikt/
名 地区、地方、地域
=a territorial division created for governmental or other purposes
関 a Congressional district《米》下院議員選挙区

□ 067 **eloquence** /éləkwəns/
名 雄弁
=persuásive and fluent speech or díscourse
形 eloquent 雄弁な、感銘的な、表情豊かな

□ 068 **eulogy** /júːlədʒi/
名 弔辞、〈死者に対する〉頌（しょう）徳文、賞賛、賞辞
=great praise especially at a funeral
形 eulogístic 賛美の、ほめたたえる
動 eulogize /júːlədʒàiz/ 賛美する、ほめたたえる

□ 069 **extravagance** /ikstrǽvəgəns/
名 浪費、無節制
=spending too much and wastefully; being uncontrolled
形 extravagant 浪費する、〈人・行動などが〉とっぴな、〈要求・代価などが〉途方もない、法外な

□ 070 **famine** /fǽmin/
名 飢饉、食料不足
=a drastic and wide-reaching shortage of food
動 famish 飢えさせる、飢える

continued ▼

Prices have risen steadily during the past decade.	ここ10年の間に、物価はどんどん上昇した。
Before they leave the factory, all the electric appliances are carefully tested for defects.	すべての電気製品は、工場から出荷される前に、欠陥がないか丹念に試験される。
People built strong walls round their towns as a defense against enemies.	人々は敵から身を守るため、自分たちの町の周囲に頑丈な壁を築いた。
There is a marked deterioration in America's balance of trade.	米国の貿易収支には、著しい悪化が見られる。
The missile has a heat-seeking device which enables it to find its target.	そのミサイルは、標的を発見することを可能にする熱追跡装置を備えている。
The federal court system consists of a series of trial courts called district courts serving relatively small geographic regions.	連邦裁判制度は、比較的小さな地区を担当する、地方裁判所と呼ばれる一連の第一審裁判所から成る。
Love and business teach eloquence.	《諺》恋と商いは人を雄弁にする。
He was chosen to give the funeral eulogy for the boy.	彼は選ばれて、その少年への弔辞を述べた。
People started to complain about the government's extravagance.	人々は政府の浪費に対して不満を訴え始めた。
Many people die of starvation during famines every year.	毎年、飢饉の間に多くの人々が飢え死にする。

continued ▼

Day 8 — 名詞 基本語彙 200 語

CD-A8

□ 071
glossary
/ɡlɑ́səri/

名 〈難語・術語などの〉**用語集**、小辞典
= a list of specialized terms with accompanying definitions
名 gloss 〈ページの下や巻末についている簡潔な〉注釈、注解

□ 072
grievance
/ɡríːvəns/

名 〈特に不当な扱いに対する〉**不平（の原因）**、不満（の種）
= a complaint or cause for complaint, esp. when one feels one has been unfairly treated
動 grieve 深く悲しむ、悲嘆させる 名 grief 悲嘆、悲痛

□ 073
hypothesis
/haipɑ́θəsis/

名 **仮説**、前提
= an assumption subject to proof, as a conjecture that accounts for a set of facts and can be used as a basis for further investigation
形 hypothétical 仮説［仮定］の

□ 074
incidence
/ínsədəns/

名 **発生（率）**
= the extent or frequency of the occurrence of something
名 incident 出来事、〈特に重大事件に至る危険をもつ〉付随事件 形 incidéntal 付随的な 副 incidéntally 付随的に

□ 075
indictment
/indáitmənt/

名 **起訴**、告発
= accusation of a crime
動 indict /indáit/ 起訴［告発］する

□ 076
innovation
/ìnəvéiʃən/

名 **革新**、維新
= the introduction of new things

□ 077
jeopardy
/dʒépərdi/

名 **危険**（danger よりも形式ばった語）
= danger or risk of loss or injury
動 jeopardize /dʒépərdàiz/ 危険にさらす

□ 078
majority
/mədʒɔ́ːrəti/

名 **大多数**、大部分、過半数
= the greater number or part of something; most; a number more than half of a total
反 minority 少数

□ 079
mass
/mæs/

名 **多数**、大部分、大衆、大きなかたまり
= a large number; lots; a large solid lump or pile, usually without a clear shape
形 massive 大きくて重い、大きい、大規模な

□ 080
migration
/maiɡréiʃən/

名 **移住**、移動する動物の群
= moving from one country or region and settling in another
動 migrate /máiɡreit/ 移住する、〈鳥・魚が〉渡る

continued ▼

Technical terms and their explanations are found in the glossary at the back of the book.	専門用語とその説明は、巻末の用語集の中にある。
The trade union leader spoke about the grievances of the workers.	その労働組合指導者は、労働者たちの不満について話した。
He put forward the hypothesis that the bones belonged to an extinct type of reptile.	彼は、それらの骨が、爬虫類の絶滅した一種に属するものだという仮説を主張した。
There was a high incidence of disease there.	そこでは病気の高い発生率がみられた。
He brought in an indictment against the employer.	彼は雇用主を起訴した。
It brought about innovations in printing techniques.	それは印刷技術に革新をもたらした。
Many people put their lives in jeopardy by driving while intoxicated.	多くの人々が、酔ったまま運転して、自分たちの生命を危険にさらしている。
The majority party in parliament forms the government.	議会における多数党が、政府を組織する。
The mass of voters were in favor of these proposals.	多数の有権者が、これらの提案を支持した。
Scientists have studied the migration of fish over long distances.	科学者たちは魚の長距離に及ぶ移動を研究した。

基本語彙200語

自然科学300語

社会・人文科学300語

continued

Day 9

名詞 基本語彙200語 4

CD-A9

☐ 081
ordeal
/ɔːrdíːəl/

名 苦しい体験、きびしい試練
=a severely difficult or painful experience

☐ 082
precaution
/prikɔ́ːʃən/

名 用心、警戒
=an action taken in advance to protect against possible failure or danger

☐ 083
precept
/príːsept/

名 教訓、訓示、勧告
=a principle imposing a standard of action or conduct
名 preceptor /priséptər/ 教訓者、教師

☐ 084
prejudice
/prédʒudis/

名 偏見、先入観
=a preconceived préference; bias /báiəs/; irrational hatred of a particular group, race, or religion
• prejudice はしばしば誤った先入観として、bias はよい場合にも悪い場合にも用いられる

☐ 085
principle
/prínsəpl/

名 原理、法則、主義
=a basic truth, law, assumption
熟 in principle 原則として

☐ 086
progress
/prágres/

名 前進、進歩、発展
=movement toward a goal; development; steady improvement
熟 make progress 進歩する　名 progréssion 前進
形 progressive 進歩した

☐ 087
property
/prápərti/

名 土地、地所、不動産、資産、所有物、特性
=a building, a piece of land, or both together; a possession; a characteristic trait or quality

☐ 088
prospect
/práspekt/

名 将来性、眺望、見晴らし、予想、見通し、見込み、有望な人
=chances for success; a possibility; a scene; view; something expected
形 prospéctive 予期される、見込みの（ある）
副 prospéctively 予期して

☐ 089
range
/réindʒ/

名 〈活動・知識・経験などの及ぶ〉範囲
=the extent of perception, knowledge, experience, or ability

☐ 090
region
/ríːdʒən/

名 地方、地域
=any large, usually continuous segment of a surface or space; an area
• area はある地域を表す最も一般的な語、region はかなりの広さで文化・社会・地理的な面での特徴をもった地方、district は行政上の区画または他の地域と異なる特徴を持つ地方
形 regional 地方の、地域の

continued
▼

The parents went through a terrible ordeal when their child was kidnapped.	子どもが誘拐されたとき、その両親はひどい苦しみを経験した。
Equipment is always carefully sterilized as a precaution against infection.	感染に対する予防措置として、器具はつねに注意深く消毒される。
Example is better than precept.	《諺》実例は教訓にまさる。
Prejudice means literally prejudgment and is the result of powerful emotions and not of sound reasoning.	偏見（prejudice）とは、文字どおりあらかじめ（pre）判断する（judge）ことであり、健全な推論ではなく、強い感情の結果生じるものである。
These machines work on the same principle.	これらの機械は、同じ原理で動く。
He's not making much progress with his English.	彼の英語は、あまり進歩を遂げていない。
The city is growing and property is becoming more expensive.	その都市は発展途上にあり、土地が値上がりしつつある。
He finally found a job with excellent prospects.	彼はついに、すばらしい将来性のある仕事を見つけた。
America is a country with a wide range of temperature.	米国は、気温の幅が大きい国である。
Paris is one of the densely populated regions of Europe.	パリはヨーロッパにおける人口密集地域のひとつである。

基本語彙200語

自然科学300語

社会・人文科学300語

continued
▼

Day 10

名詞 基本語彙 200 語 5

CD-A10

□ 091 scrutiny
/skrúːtəni/

名 精密な調査［検査］、じろじろ見る［見られる］こと
= a close, careful examination or study
動 scrutinize 綿密に検査する、じっと見る

□ 092 settlement
/sétlmənt/

名 植民、植民地、開拓地、解決、和解、〈定住して〉身を落ち着けること
= establishment in a new region; a newly colonized region
動 settle 決める、定住させる［する］、身を固めさせる

□ 093 significance
/signífikəns/

名 重要（性）、意味、意義
= importance; consequence; meaning
形 significant 重要な、意味ありげな **副** significantly かなり **動** sígnify 意味する、示す

□ 094 site
/sáit/

名 敷地、用地、遺跡 **動** 用地を定める
= the place or plot of land where something was, is, or is to be located

□ 095 spontaneity
/spɑ̀ntəníːəti/

名 自発性
= happening voluntárily
形 spontaneous /spɑntéiniəs/ 自発的な、自然に起こる

□ 096 strain
/stréin/

名 緊張、張り
= the act of pulling or stretching tight; a great tension
形 strained 緊張した、緊迫した

□ 097 substance
/sʌ́bstəns/

名 物質、要旨、実質
= a material; gist /dʒíst/; truth; essence
熟 in substance 大体は、実際に **形** substántial 実体のある、相当な、本質的な **動** substántiate 実証する **副** substántially 大体は、十分に

□ 098 surface
/sə́ːrfis/

名 表面、外観 **動** 表面化する
= the outer or the topmost part of an object

□ 099 transaction
/trænsǽkʃən/

名 取引、処理
= the act of carrying out or conducting business
動 transáct 処理する、〈取引などを〉行う

□ 100 trial
/tráiəl/

名 試み、試練、裁判
= an attempt; hearing and judging a person, case, or point of law in a court

continued ▼

His actions came under continuous scrutiny in the press.	彼の行動は、報道界から絶えず詮索を受けた。
American history begins with the settlement of the Pilgrim Fathers in Plymouth.	米国の歴史は、ピルグリム・ファーザーズのプリマス植民とともに始まる。
The new discovery of oil was of great significance to the country.	新たな石油の発見は、その国にとって大きな意味を持つものだった。
George Washington was given the responsibility of selecting a site for the newly designated federal district.	ジョージ・ワシントンは、新たに構想された連邦地区（中央政府所在の特別行政区。ワシントン D.C. が選ばれた）の用地を選択する責任を与えられた。
His enthusiasm was somewhat lacking in spontaneity.	彼の熱心さには、どこかしら自発性が欠けている。
The additional work put a great strain on him.	仕事が増えたため彼に多大な負担がかかった。
Water, ice, and snow are not different substances: they are the same substance in different forms.	水、氷、そして雪は異なる物質ではなく、形態の異なる同じ物質である。
The Moon has no atmosphere, no surface water, and of course no life forms.	月には、大気も地表水も、もちろんいかなる形の生物も存在しない。
Price is the money value of a product or service as agreed upon in a market transaction.	価格とは、市場取引において合意された、製品ないしサービスの貨幣価値である。
We all learn by trial and error.	わたしたちは皆、試行錯誤によって学習する。

continued
▼

復習テスト 名詞

解答は P.234

1
1〜10 の文で意味を成すものには YES に、意味を成さないものには NO に○をつけなさい。

1. Eloquent speakers have defects in their speech. YES / NO
2. If you have good prospects, you are likely to succeed. YES / NO
3. If you have a heavy duty or responsibility, you may be put under strain. YES / NO
4. You are in concord with him, so you have many grievances against him. YES / NO
5. The black man suffered a terrible ordeal because of people's prejudice against him. YES / NO
6. Because he lacks concentration, he made no progress. YES / NO
7. He is a man of property; he owns a lot of buildings. YES / NO
8. She was in anguish because her son was kidnapped. YES / NO
9. Chaos means everything is in order. YES / NO
10. Her good complexion explains the deterioration in her health. YES / NO

2
1〜10 の語の同義語を a〜j から選びなさい。

1. significance
2. concord
3. majority
4. jeopardy
5. trial
6. conjecture
7. region
8. defect
9. grievance
10. anguish

---

a. an attempt
b. danger
c. concurrence
d. an area
e. importance
f. guesswork
g. pain
h. most
i. fault
j. a complaint

3 1〜10の語の定義に合う名詞を（　）の中に書きなさい。

1. inference based on inconclusive evidence; guesswork (　　　)
2. a period of ten years (　　　)
3. a list of specialized terms with accompanying definitions (　　　)
4. an action taken in advance to protect against possible failure or danger (　　　)
5. establishment in a new region; a newly colonized region (　　　)
6. a heavy duty or responsibility which is hard to bear (　　　)
7. a drastic and wide-reaching shortage of food (　　　)
8. a perceived preference; bias; irrational hatred of a particular group, race, or religion (　　　)
9. the hard central part of certain fruits, as an apple; the most important part of anything (　　　)
10. persuasive and fluent speech or discourse (　　　)

4 1〜5の定義を表す正しい語をa〜cの中から選びなさい。

1. an agreement of opinion; actions happening at the same time
   a. conjecture   b. concord   c. concurrence
2. a territorial division created for governmental or other purposes
   a. range   b. district   c. region
3. a principle imposing a standard of action or conduct
   a. precept   b. prospect   c. property
4. an agonizing physical or mental pain
   a. ordeal   b. burden   c. anguish
5. something made for a particular purpose
   a. defense   b. device   c. mass

Day 11

基本語彙200語 形容詞 1

CD-A11

□ 101 abstract
/ǽbstrækt/

形 抽象的な（反concrete）、観念的な（反practical）、《美》抽象派の（反representational 具象派の）
=existing as a quality or concept rather than as something real or solid
名 摘要、抜粋　動 abstráct 抜粋する

□ 102 abundant
/əbʌ́ndənt/

形 豊富な
=plentiful; more than enough
動 abound /əbáund/ たくさんいる、富む　名 abundance 豊富、裕福

□ 103 akin
/əkín/

形 同族で、同種で、類似して
=of the same kin; related; similar in quality or character
熟 akin to ... ……と同族で、同種で、類似して

□ 104 ample
/ǽmpl/

形 十分な、広い
=large; capacious /kəpéiʃəs/; sufficient; abundant
名 amplificátion 拡大　動 ámplify 拡大［増大］する、詳説する　名 ámplitude 広さ、十分なこと　副 amply 十分に、詳細に

□ 105 apparent
/əpǽrənt, əpéər-/

形 外見上、明白な［で］
=readily seen; visible; readily understood or perceived
副 apparently（実際はともかく）見たところでは（……らしい）

□ 106 appropriate
/əpróupriət/

形 適当な、適切な［で］　動〈金・物などを特定の目的に〉あてる
=suitable; proper
名 appropriation 充当（すること）

□ 107 autonomous
/ɔːtɑ́nəməs/

形 自治権のある、自主的な
=independent; self-contained; self-governing
名 autónomy 自治（権）、自主性

□ 108 compulsory
/kəmpʌ́lsəri/

形 強制的な、義務的な、必修の
=coercive /kouə́ːrsiv/; obligatory; required
名 compulsion /kəmpʌ́lʃən/ 強制、強い欲望

□ 109 congenial
/kəndʒíːnjəl/

形 気が合う、同性質の
=having the same tastes or temperament; sympathetic; suited to one's needs; agreeable
名 congeniality /kəndʒìːniǽləti/〈性質などの〉一致、適応性

□ 110 congenital
/kəndʒénətl/

形〈病気・欠陥などが〉生まれつきの、先天的な
=existing at birth but not hereditary; characteristic, as if by nature

continued
▼

Max Weber is known as a pioneer of American abstract painting.	マックス・ウェーバーは、米国の抽象絵画の先駆者として知られている。
In places like New England the abundant supply of timber made wooden bridges possible.	ニューイングランドのような場所では、豊富な木材の供給が、木造の橋をかけることを可能にした。
Jealousy is often akin to love.	嫉妬はしばしば愛と似ている。
She was given ample opportunity to express her views.	彼女は自分の意見を表現する十分な機会を与えられた。
The apparent improvement in this year's profits is due to the selling off of some of the company's property.	今年の利益の外見上の改善は、会社の資産の一部を売却した結果である。
You have to write in a style appropriate to your subject.	主題に適した文体で書かなければなりません。
Just before the outbreak of the Civil War, the South declared itself to be an autonomous nation.	南北戦争勃発の直前、南部諸州は自治国家となることを宣言した。
All young men are required to do two years of compulsory military service.	すべての男子は２年間の強制兵役に就かなくてはならない。
I find him very congenial. We get along very well.	彼とはとても気が合う。わたしたちはとても仲よくやっている。
Congenital birth defects can be reduced by regular pre-natal check-ups.	先天的な欠陥は、出生前の定期検診によって減らすことができる。

continued
▼

Day 12

形容詞 基本語彙200語 2

□ 111 conscientious
/kànʃiénʃəs/

形〈人・行為が〉**良心的な**、誠実な、注意深い
=scrupulous /skrúːpjuləs/; honest; careful
名 conscience 良心、善悪の観念

□ 112 conscious
/kánʃəs/

形〈人が〉**意識的な**、意識して、自意識の強い
=having an awareness of one's own existence and environment; awake; intentional; deliberate
副 consciously 意識的に 名 consciousness 意識

□ 113 constant
/kánstənt/

形 **一定の**、絶えず続く、不変の
=unchanging; continually recúrring; persístent; inváriable; stéadfast
関 continual〈しばしばよくないことなどが間隔をおいて繰り返して長期に連続していく意味で〉継続的な、頻繁な 関 continuous〈時間的・空間的に切れめなく続いていく意味で〉連続的な

□ 114 contemporary
/kəntémpərèri/

形 **同時代の**、現代の
=belonging to the same period of time; of about the same age; cúrrent; modern

□ 115 controversial
/kàntrəvə́ːrʃəl/

形 **論争の的になる**、議論好きの
=causing much argument or disagreement
名 controversy 論争 動 controvert 議論する、反駁する

□ 116 conventional
/kənvénʃənl/

形 **従来の**、伝統的な、因習的な
=cústomary; commonplace or ordinary
動 conventionalize 因習的にする 名 convention 慣習、しきたり、大会、協定

□ 117 credulous
/krédʒuləs/

形 **すぐ真に受ける**、信じやすい
=disposed to believe too readily; gullible /gʌ́ləbl/

□ 118 dubious
/djúːbiəs/

形 **疑わしく思って**、真意のはっきりしない
=arousing doubt; questionable; skeptical; doubtful

□ 119 durable
/djúərəbl/

形 **耐久性のある**、永続性のある、丈夫な
=able to last; long-lasting
名 durability 耐久性

□ 120 eccentric
/ikséntrik/

形 **一風変わった**、〈人・行動などが〉常軌を逸した
=deviating from a conventional or established pattern
名 eccentricity 風変わり、奇抜な点

continued ▼

Tom is a very conscientious student; he studies very hard until late at night.	トムはとてもまじめな学生である。彼は夜遅くまでよく勉強する。
A healthy man is not conscious of his breathing.	健康な人間は、自分の呼吸を意識しない。
A thermostat keeps the temperature constant.	温度自動調節器（サーモスタット）は、温度を一定に保つ。
Beethoven was contemporary with Napoleon.	ベートーベンはナポレオンと同時代の人だった。
Whether the skyscraper originated in New York City or in Chicago is a controversial matter.	摩天楼がニューヨークとシカゴのどちらで生まれたかは、議論の余地のある問題だ。
The electricity is produced by conventional energy converters that are based on mechanical, indirect conversion of energy.	電気は、エネルギーの機械的で間接的な変換に基づく旧来のエネルギー変換器によって生み出される。
She is so credulous that she believes everything she is told.	彼女はとても信じやすいので、言われたことは何でも信じてしまう。
He was so confident that he was never dubious of the plan.	彼は非常に自信があったので、その計画を疑ったことがなかった。
Leather is more durable than vinyl.	革はビニールよりも耐久性がある。
Everyone was dressed in eccentric clothes at the Halloween party.	ハロウィーン・パーティーでは、だれもが奇抜な服を身に着けていた。

continued
▼

Day 13

基本語彙200語 形容詞 3

□ 121 efficient
/ifíʃənt/

形 能率的な、有能な
=working well, quickly, and without waste
● efficient は時間・労力をむだにせずにてきぱきと仕事を果たす能力があるということで、人にも物にも用いる。effective は期待している効果があること。efficácious は薬・治療・手段・方法などの効力があること

□ 122 equivocal
/ikwívəkəl/

形 〈語句などが〉あいまいな、両意にとれる
=not clear; ambiguous; difficult to understand
名 equivocation あいまいな言葉（を使うこと）、〈言葉の〉ごまかし

□ 123 explicit
/iksplísit/

形 〈陳述などが〉明白な、明示的な
=precisely expressed; clear and specific
反 implícit 暗黙のうちの、含蓄的な

□ 124 extinct
/ikstíŋkt/

形 〈火・希望など〉消えた、〈生命・動物などが〉絶滅した
=no longer existing
名 extinction 消火、終息、絶滅　名 extinguisher 消火器　動 extinguish 〈火・光などを〉消す、〈情熱・希望などを〉失わせる

□ 125 futile
/fjúːtl/

形 むだな、役に立たない
=useless; having no useful result; ineffectual; unproductive; frívolous
名 futility 無用、無益

□ 126 imminent
/ímənənt/

形 〈危険など〉今にも起こりそうな、緊迫した
=about to occur; impénding
名 ímminence 切迫した危険［事情］

□ 127 impromptu
/imprámptjuː/

形 即興的な［に］、即座の［に］　名 即席演説
=not rehearsed; extémpore

□ 128 inquisitive
/inkwízətiv/

形 知り［聞き］たがる、探求的な
=unduly curious; eager to learn

□ 129 intensive
/inténsiv/

形 集中的な、強い、徹底的な
=concentrated and exhaustive
形 intense 〈光・温度などが〉激しい、熱烈な　名 intensity 強烈　動 intensify 強める　名 intension（精神的）緊張、強化

□ 130 intricate
/íntrikət/

形 入り組んだ、複雑な、難解な
=having many complexly arranged elements; difficult to solve or comprehend
名 íntricacy 複雑（さ）

continued
▼

The new machines are much more efficient and cheaper to run.	その新しい機械ははるかに効率が良く、稼働費も安い。
His speech was so equivocal that no one understood what he meant.	彼の話はとてもあいまいだったので、彼が何を言いたいのかだれも理解できなかった。
He was quite explicit about it, and left no doubt about what he meant.	彼はそのことについてはきわめて明快で、自分の言ったことに関して疑問の余地を残さなかった。
An extinct volcano is a volcano which is not currently erupting and which is not considered likely to erupt in the future.	死火山とは、現在は噴火しておらず、将来もしそうにないと考えられる火山である。
They made a futile attempt to rescue the survivors.	生存者たちを救い出そうとするのは、むだな試みだった。
The area was hit by a typhoon, and a flood seemed imminent.	その地域は台風に襲われ、今にも洪水が起こりそうだった。
He never prepared for the talk; it was always impromptu.	彼はスピーチの準備をしたことがなく、話はいつも即興だった。
Janet is very inquisitive about what happens around her.	ジャネットは、自分のまわりで起きていることを、とても知りたがる。
He was seriously ill and was transferred to the intensive care unit.	彼の病気は重く、集中治療室に移された。
An intricate system of interstate and state highways connects all of the major cities in the United States.	州間および州営高速道路の複雑な網の目が、米国のあらゆる主要都市をつないでいる。

continued
▼

Day 14 — 基本語彙200語 形容詞 4

□ 131 mutual
/mjúːtʃuəl/
形 相互の、相互に関係のある
=having or based on the same relationship one towards the other; equally shared by each one
名 mutuálity 相互関係、相関

□ 132 oblivious
/əblíviəs/
形 気づかない、忘れっぽい
=not noticing; forgetful; unaware or unmindful
名 oblívion 忘却

□ 133 obscure
/əbskjúər/
形 不明瞭な、あいまいな　動 覆い隠す、見えなくする、不明瞭にする
形 =difficult to understand; inconspícuous
動 =to prevent something from being seen or heard clearly
名 obscurity 暗さ、不明瞭、無名

□ 134 obsolete
/ὰbsəlíːt/
形 すたれた、時代遅れの
=no longer in use or fashion; no longer useful or functioning

□ 135 obvious
/ábviəs/
形 〈疑問の余地がないほど〉明らかな、明白な
=easily perceived or understood; clear
副 obviously 明らかに

□ 136 plausible
/plɔ́ːzəbl/
形 〈言葉・陳述などが〉もっともらしい、まことしやかな
=apparently valid or likely

□ 137 potential
/pəténʃəl/
形 〈十分に〉可能性のある　名 潜在（能）力
=possible but not yet realized; latent
名 potentiálity 可能性

□ 138 prolific
/prəlífik/
形 〈作家など〉多作の、多産の
=producing abundant works or results; producing offspring in abundance

□ 139 reluctant
/rilΛ́ktənt/
形 いやいやながらの、いやがって
=unwilling; avérse
名 reluctance 気が進まないこと　熟 with reluctance いやいやながら

□ 140 remarkable
/rimάːrkəbl/
形 優れた、注目すべき
=extraordinary; uncommon; worthy of notice
副 remarkably 著しく、非常に

continued ▼

They finally reached an agreement that will be to their mutual benefit.	彼らはついに、相互の利益のためになるであろう合意に達した。
He was quite oblivious of the danger.	彼は危険にまったく気づかなかった。
His explanation was somewhat obscure.	彼の説明はちょっと不明瞭だった。
The new technology made the conventional method of analysis obsolete.	その新技術は、従来の分析方法を時代遅れのものにした。
It was quite obvious that he was telling a lie.	彼がうそをついていたことは、きわめて明らかだった。
His explanation sounded plausible, but no one was convinced.	彼の説明はもっともらしく聞こえたが、だれも納得しなかった。
The new invention had enormous sales potential.	その新発明は、莫大な利益をもたらす可能性をもっていた。
Ernest Hemingway was a prolific writer. He wrote many novels.	アーネスト・ヘミングウェイは多作家であった。彼は多くの小説を書いた。
He was reluctant to join them because he still had a lot of work to do.	彼はまだしなければならない仕事がたくさんあったので、彼らに加わることをいやがった。
He had a remarkable memory.	彼は優れた記憶力を持っていた。

continued
▼

Day 15

形容詞 基本語彙200語 5

☐ 141 sophisticated
/səfístəkèitid/

形 洗練された、(高度の) 教養のある、精巧な
= experienced in and understanding the ways of society, esp. showing signs of this by good taste, clever conversation, etc.

☐ 142 subsequent
/sʌ́bsəkwənt/

形 次の、続いて起こる
= following in time or order; succeeding
副 súbsequently その後 名 súbsequence 続いて起こること

☐ 143 supreme
/sjuprí:m/

形 〈地位・権力などが〉最高位の、〈程度・品質などが〉最高の
= greatest in power, or rank; greatest in importance or degree
名 supremacy /suprémэsi/ 最高位、主権

☐ 144 sympathetic
/sìmpəθétik/

形 同情的な、思いやりのある、同感して
= feeling or showing sympathy; favorable; in agreement
動 sympathize 同情する、同感する 名 sympathy 同情

☐ 145 thrifty
/θrífti/

形 倹約な (反 extravagant)、繁盛する、元気に育つ
= wise in the management of money; frugal
名 thrift 倹約、節約

☐ 146 trivial
/tríviəl/

形 些細な、とるにたらない
= of little importance or significance; trifling; ordinary

☐ 147 unanimous
/ju:nǽnəməs/

形 満場 [全員] 一致の、合意して
= based on complete assent or agreement; sharing the same opinions or views
名 unanímity 全員異議のないこと、(満場) 一致 熟 with unanimity 満場一致で

☐ 148 versatile
/vэ́:rsətl/

形 多目的に使用できる、多才の
= having many different uses; having many different kinds of skills or abilities
名 versatílity 多才、多芸、多能

☐ 149 volatile
/vάlətl/

形 揮発性の、気まぐれな、変わりやすい
= evaporating readily at normal temperatures and pressures; changeable; lighthearted
名 volatílity 揮発性、移り気

☐ 150 vulnerable
/vʌ́lnərəbl/

形 〈非難などを〉受けやすい、傷つきやすい、弱い
= susceptible to attack; susceptible to injury; weak; easily harmed, or hurt; sensitive

continued ▼

The fashion magazines show what the sophisticated woman is wearing this year.	ファッション雑誌には、洗練された女性が今年何を着ているかが載っている。
The result of the statistical analysis and its interpretations are briefly stated in the subsequent section.	統計上の分析結果とその解釈は、この後に続くセクションで簡単に述べられている。
Soldiers who die for their country are said to make the supreme sacrifice.	祖国のために死んだ兵士は、最高の犠牲を捧げたといわれる。
He was very sympathetic to me when I was sick.	わたしが病気だったとき、彼は非常に同情的だった。
She is a thrifty housewife, but her husband is an extravagant man.	彼女は質素な主婦だが、彼女の夫は浪費家である。
They always fight over such trivial matters.	彼らは些細な事柄をめぐって、いつも争っている。
She was elected chairman by a unanimous vote.	彼女は満場一致で議長に選出された。
Nylon is a versatile material; it has many different uses.	ナイロンは多目的に使用できる素材であり、多くの異なる用途がある。
Flavor is determined by the sugars, organic acids, and volatile chemical compounds present in the fruit.	風味は、果物の中に存在する糖、有機酸、揮発性の化合物によって決まる。
His arguments were rather vulnerable to criticism.	彼の論点はかなり批判を受けやすかった。

continued
▼

復習テスト　形容詞

解答は P.235

1

1〜10の文で意味を成すものには YES に、
意味を成さないものには NO に○をつけなさい。

1. A thrifty person is an extravagant person. YES / NO
2. A controversial person causes much argument. YES / NO
3. A credulous person always feels doubtful. YES / NO
4. It's difficult to get along with someone you find congenial. YES / NO
5. You use equivocal words to state something explicitly. YES / NO
6. She is inquisitive because she is curious. YES / NO
7. Intricate problems are difficult to solve. YES / NO
8. Versatile materials are useless. YES / NO
9. If it's compulsory, you must do it. YES / NO
10. If you are conscious, you are aware. YES / NO

2

1〜10の語の同義語を a〜j から選びなさい。

1. imminent
2. remarkable
3. obvious
4. impromptu
5. potential
6. vulnerable
7. reluctant
8. oblivious
9. trivial
10. appropriate

---

a. unwilling　　b. extraordinary　c. extempore　　d. impending
e. forgetful　　f. clear　　　　　g. latent　　　　h. weak
i. suitable　　　j. trifling

3 1〜10の語の定義に合う形容詞を（　）の中に書きなさい。

1. deviating from a conventional or established pattern (　　　)
2. unchanging; continually recurring; persistent; invariable; steadfast (　　　)
3. no longer existing (　　　)
4. concentrated and exhaustive (　　　)
5. no longer in use or fashion; no longer useful or functioning (　　　)
6. apparently valid or likely (　　　)
7. producing abundant works or results; producing offspring in abundance (　　　)
8. showing good taste (　　　)
9. feeling or showing sympathy; in agreement; favorable (　　　)
10. based on complete assent or agreement; sharing the same opinions or views (　　　)

4 1〜5の定義を表す正しい語をa〜cの中から選びなさい。

1. existing at birth but not hereditary; characteristic, as if by nature
   a. congenial   b. congenital   c. eccentric

2. readily seen; visible; readily understood or perceived
   a. apparent   b. obsolete   c. obscure

3. scrupulous; honest; careful
   a. conscious   b. constant   c. conscientious

4. customary; commonplace or ordinary
   a. extraordinary   b. conventional   c. controversial

5. arousing doubt; questionable; skeptical; doubtful
   a. obvious   b. oblivious   c. dubious

Day 16

副詞 基本語彙200語 ①

□ 151 **accordingly** /əkɔ́ːrdiŋli/
副 **それに応じて**、適宜、よって、したがって、それゆえに
=in a way suitable to what has been said or what has happened; therefore; so

□ 152 **approximately** /əpráksəmətli/
副 **おおよそ**、ほぼ
=about

□ 153 **basically** /béisikəli/
副 **根本的に（は）**、元来、根本原理として
=with regard to what is most important and basic; in reality

□ 154 **briefly** /bríːfli/
副 **少しの間**、しばらく、簡単に、手短に（いえば）
=for a short time; quickly; concisely

□ 155 **characteristically** /kæ̀riktərístikəli/
副 **特質上**、特徴［特質］として、個性的に
=typically

□ 156 **commonly** /kámənli/
副 **一般に**、通例、よく
=usually; generally

□ 157 **comparatively** /kəmpǽrətivli/
副 **比較的に**、比較してみると、かなり
=when compared with others; relatively

□ 158 **consequently** /kánsəkwèntli/
副 **その結果**、したがって
=as a result; therefore

□ 159 **considerably** /kənsídərəbli/
副 **かなり**、相当に、ずいぶん
=much; a great deal

□ 160 **consistently** /kənsístəntli/
副 **一貫して**
=regularly; keeping the same pattern

continued
▼

Please inform us of your decision, and we will act accordingly.	あなたの決定をお知らせください。わたしたちはそれに応じて行動します。
A typical clay soil is composed of approximately 60 percent actual clay, 20 percent silt, and 20 percent sand.	典型的な粘土質土壌は、約60％の実際の粘土と、20％の沈殿、そして20％の砂から成り立っている。
Although elementary education is basically the same for all, high schools offer several different courses of study.	初等教育は根本的には万人に共通だが、高校ではいくつかの異なる課程がある。
The president stopped off briefly in London on his way to Geneva.	大統領はジュネーブに向かう途中、ロンドンにちょっと立ち寄った。
Many historians think that most of the beliefs and values which are characteristically American emerged in the context of the frontier experience.	多くの歴史家は、アメリカ的特徴をもった信念や価値観の大半は、フロンティア（辺境地帯）での経験という文脈の中で生まれたものだと考えている。
The drill is a technique commonly used in language teaching for practicing sounds or sentence patterns in a language.	ドリルは言語教育において、ある言語の音または文型を練習するためによく使われる。
Man is a comparatively new young species.	人類は、比較的新しく若い種である。
The economy is not doing well; manufacturing, especially, is suffering. Consequently, unemployment is rather high.	経済状態が良くない。製造業は特に損害を被っている。その結果、失業率がかなり高い。
The introduction of money as a medium of exchange facilitated transactions considerably.	交換の媒介としての貨幣の導入は、取引をかなり容易にした。
Public opinion polls consistently show that most Americans would rather live in small towns or rural areas if they could.	世論調査は一貫して、米国人の大半が、できればむしろ小さな町や田舎に住みたいと思っていることを示している。

continued

Day 17

副詞 基本語彙200語 2

CD-A17

□ 161 critically
/krítikəli/
副 批判的に、きわどく、危なく
=in a critical manner; dangerously

□ 162 definitely
/défənitli/
副 明確に、確かに
=without doubt; clearly; in a definite way

□ 163 directly
/diréktli, dai-/
副 直接に、まさに、すぐに
=in a direct manner; at once; very soon

□ 164 enormously
/inɔ́ːrməsli/
副 非常に、莫大に
=extremely

□ 165 entirely
/intáiərli/
副 まったく、完全に、もっぱら、ひたすら
=completely; in every way; only

□ 166 equally
/íːkwəli/
副 同様に、均等に、それと同時に、それにもかかわらず
=to an equal degree; in equal shares; at the same time; in spite of that

□ 167 essentially
/isénʃəli/
副 本質的に、本質上
=in reality, though perhaps not in appearance; basically

□ 168 eventually
/ivéntʃuəli/
副 結局は、ついに（は）、やがて（は）
=at last; in the end

□ 169 firmly
/fə́ːrmli/
副 確固として、しっかりと
=solidly; strongly

□ 170 formally
/fɔ́ːrməli/
副 形式的に、形式上
=in a formal manner

continued ▼

The teacher, though friendly, pleasant and informal in class, graded each student's work critically and carefully.	その教師は教室では親しげで、愉快で、打ちとけていたが、それぞれの生徒の勉強ぶりを批判的に、注意深く採点した。
The Harlem cabaret life of the period was definitely an important by-product of the new interest in black society.	当時のハーレムにおけるキャバレー生活は明らかに、黒人社会に向けられた新たな関心の重要な副産物だった。
The change which directly precipitated the emergence of suburbs was the popularization of the private car.	郊外の出現を直接的に促した変化とは、自家用車の大衆化だった。
The town has changed enormously in recent years.	その町は近年、非常に変化した。
She was not entirely happy about the result.	彼女はその結果に完全に満足しているわけではなかった。
We must help people find houses outside the city, but equally, we must remember that some city people want to remain where they are.	わたしたちは人々が都市の外に住居を見つける手助けをしなければならないが、同時に一部の都会の人々は自分たちのいる場所にとどまりたがっていることも忘れてはならない。
In many nations, patriotism is essentially the love of the land.	多くの国々において、愛国心は本質的に土地への愛情である。
After many attempts she eventually managed to get promoted.	何度も試みた後、彼女はついに、何とか昇進することができた。
The drive for success is firmly entrenched in American ideology.	成功への衝動は、米国のイデオロギーにしっかりと定着している。
Quite often an initial greeting is followed by the question, "How are you?" or, less formally, "How're you doing?"	最初の挨拶の後にはよく、"How are you?（ごきげんいかがですか？）"、あるいはよりくだけて "How're you doing?（調子はどう？）" という質問が続く。

基本語彙200語

自然科学300語

社会・人文科学300語

continued

Day 18

副詞 基本語彙200語 3

171 generally
/dʒénərəli/

一般に、多くの人に、通常、概して
=usually; by most people

172 gradually
/grǽdʒuəli/

徐々に、次第に、漸進［段階］的に
=slowly; by degrees

173 ideally
/aidíːəli/

理想的には［いえば］
=in an ideal way; in an ideal situation

174 immediately
/imíːdiətli/

直ちに、さっそく、直接に
=without delay; at once; directly

175 incidentally
/ìnsədéntəli/

ところで、ついでに、ついでながら
=by the way

176 inherently
/inhíərəntli/

本質的に、生得的に
=intrinsically; by its or one's nature

177 initially
/iníʃəli/

初め（のうち）は、最初（のうち）は
=at the beginning; at first

178 literally
/lítərəli/

文字どおりに、本当に、まったく
=in a literal sense; really

179 namely
/néimli/

すなわち
=that is (to say)

180 nearly
/níərli/

ほとんど、ほぼ、もう少しで、危うく
=almost; not quite or not yet completely

continued

The toothless, or baleen, whales belong to the suborder of Mysticeti. This is a group of generally large whales, formerly abundant in all the oceans of the world.	歯なしクジラ類、すなわちヒゲクジラ類は、ヒゲクジラ亜目に属する。これはかつて世界の大洋すべてに多数見られた、概して大型のクジラ群である。
The birth rate has been gradually increasing.	出生率は、徐々に増えている。
Americans think that, ideally, everyone should have a high school diploma.	米国人は、理想的には万人が高校の卒業証書を持つべきだと考えている。
The publication of Carson McCullers' book *The Heart Is a Lonely Hunter* (1940) immediately made her famous.	カーソン・マッカラーの著書『心はさびしい猟人』(1940) は、たちまち彼女を有名にした。
I must go now. Incidentally, if you want that book, I'll bring it next time.	もう行かなくちゃ。ところであの本が欲しいなら、今度持ってくるよ。
Schools in which students are segregated by race are considered to be "inherently unequal."	生徒が人種ごとに分離されている学校は、「本質的に不平等」とみなされる。
Ice expands when it initially forms, but as the air temperature falls, the ice contracts.	氷は最初に形成されるときに膨張するが、温度が下がるとその氷は収縮する。
The word "television," derived from its Greek (tele: distant) and Latin (visto: sight) roots, can literally be interpreted as sight from a distance.	ギリシャ語 (tele = 遠距離) およびラテン語 (visto = 見ること) の語根から派生した "television" という言葉は、文字どおり遠くから見ることと解釈できる。
There was one more topic to discuss, namely the global environment.	もうひとつ論題がある。すなわち地球環境の問題である。
Although no other game is exactly like baseball, perhaps the one most nearly like it is the English game of cricket.	野球とちょうど同じような競技はないが、最もそれに近いのは、恐らくイギリスの競技であるクリケットだろう。

continued

Day 19 — 副詞 基本語彙200語 4

□ 181 necessarily
/nèsəsérəli/
副 必ず、必然的に、〈否定文で〉必ずしも（……でない）
=in a way that must be so; unavoidably

□ 182 notably
/nóutəbli/
副 特に、とりわけ、著しく、目立つほどに、明白に
=especially; particularly; noticeably

□ 183 originally
/ərídʒənəli/
副 もとは、元来、初めは
=in the beginning; formerly; in a new and different way

□ 184 particularly
/pərtíkjulərli/
副 特に、とりわけ
=especially

□ 185 precisely
/prisáisli/
副 正確に、的確に
=exactly

□ 186 predominantly
/pridámənəntli/
副 圧倒的に、主に、主として
=mostly; mainly

□ 187 presumably
/prizú:məbli/
副 思うに、たぶん
=it may reasonably be supposed that; probably

□ 188 previously
/prí:viəsli/
副 前に、前もって
=before (that)

□ 189 primarily
/praimérəli/
副 主として、第一に
=mainly; chiefly

□ 190 rapidly
/ræpidli/
副 急に、素早く
=fast; quickly

continued

A republic is not necessarily a democracy, but the United States is a democratic republic.	共和制国家は必ずしも民主主義国家ではないが、米国は民主主義共和国である。
Many members were absent, notably the vice-chairman.	多くのメンバー、特に副議長が欠席だった。
"Jukebox" comes from Gullah, a dialect of English originally spoken by African slaves in the South Carolina area.	"ジュークボックス"は、もとはサウスカロライナー帯でアフリカ人の奴隷たちが話していた英語の一方言、ガラ方言からきている。
He particularly liked to read classic novels.	彼はとりわけ、名作小説を読むのが好きだった。
The plane arrived precisely on schedule.	飛行機はスケジュールどおり正確に到着した。
Historically, New York City policemen were predominantly Irish, and garbage collectors were mostly Italian.	歴史的にいって、ニューヨーク市の警察官は圧倒的にアイルランド系であり、ごみ収集人は大半がイタリア系だった。
If you've already eaten, you presumably won't want dinner.	もう食べたのなら、たぶん夕食は欲しくないでしょう。
The record was previously held by Sebastian Coe.	この記録は、前にセバスチアン・コーが保持していた。
A decade ago it was primarily a fishing village, but now it's a thriving tourist center.	10年前、そこは主として漁村だったが、現在では繁栄した観光地になっている。
The proportion of newcomers increased rapidly, so that by 1860 about 13 of every 100 persons in the U.S. were recent immigrants.	新来者の割合が急に増えたため、1860年になると米国における100人のうちおよそ13人が新しくやってきた移民だった。

continued
▼

Day 20

副詞 基本語彙200語 5

CD-A20

□ 191 **relatively** /rélətivli/
比較的、割合、相対的に
=when compared to others of the same kind; comparatively

□ 192 **remarkably** /rimá:rkəbli/
著しく、目立って、非常に
=unusually; noticeably

□ 193 **respectively** /rispéktivli/
それぞれ
=each separately in the order mentioned

□ 194 **slightly** /sláitli/
わずかに、少し
=to a small degree; a bit

□ 195 **solely** /sóulli/
〜だけに、単に、まったく、たったひとりで、単独で
=only

□ 196 **totally** /tóutəli/
まったく、すっかり
=completely; absolutely; in total

□ 197 **traditionally** /trədíʃənəli/
伝統的に
=in accordance with tradition

□ 198 **typically** /típikəli/
典型的に、例によって、一般に
=in a typical manner

□ 199 **undoubtedly** /ʌndáutidli/
確かに、疑う余地のないほどに
=unquestionably; without doubt

□ 200 **virtually** /vớ:rtʃuəli/
事実上、実質的には、ほとんど
=practically; almost; very nearly

continued ▼

Many millions of years ago the Colorado Plateau in the Grand Canyon area contained 10,000 more feet of rock than it does today and was relatively level.	何百万年も前、グランドキャニオン地域のコロラド高原には現在より1万フィートも高い岩があり、比較的平らだった。
Gibbons can move remarkably rapidly through the trees, swinging from branch to branch.	テナガザルは枝から枝へと飛び移り、非常に素早く木々の間を移動することができる。
The nurses and the miners got pay raises of 5% and 7% respectively.	看護師と坑夫は、それぞれ5%と7%の昇給を獲得した。
There are two flying squirrel species in North America, and their habitats overlap slightly.	北米には2種のムササビがおり、その生息地はわずかに重複する。
No longer is family property solely in the hands of the husband in the American family.	米国の家庭では、家族の財産はもはや夫の手だけに握られているのではない。
The cultural origins and musical sounds of country and western music are totally different from those of jazz.	カントリーウエスタンの起源と音楽的なサウンドは、ジャズのそれとはまったく異なる。
The Northeast has traditionally been at the helm of the nation's economic and social progress.	北東部は伝統的に、国の経済的および社会的進歩において指導的立場に立ってきた。
The first generation typically faced external and internal obstacles to assimilation: society's discrimination and their own reluctance to give up their language and culture.	第一世代は典型的に、社会からの差別を嫌い、自分たちの言語と文化を手放すことを渋るという、同化への外面および内面からの障害に直面した。
In recent years, many downtown areas undoubtedly have become more livable, more people-oriented, and more aesthetically interesting.	近年、町の中心街の多くは確かにより住みやすく、より人中心に、そして感覚的により興味深いものになった。
Virtually all the members were in agreement with the proposal.	事実上、すべてのメンバーがその提案に同意していた。

continued
▼

復習テスト 副詞

解答は P.236

1

1〜10 の文で意味を成すものには YES に、意味を成さないものには NO に○をつけなさい。

1. If X is slightly heavier than Y, the weights of X and Y are not very different. YES / NO
2. If a region is predominantly black, it is populated mostly by black people. YES / NO
3. I entirely agree with you, but I have some objections. YES / NO
4. We are nearly at the top of the hill; we are almost there. YES / NO
5. The population increased rapidly; that is, the population gradually increased. YES / NO
6. Initially she opposed the plan, but later she changed her mind. YES / NO
7. He is as clever as his brother; they are equally clever. YES / NO
8. That is undoubtedly true; it leaves a slight doubt. YES / NO
9. They asked him to leave the meeting; accordingly, he stayed there. YES / NO
10. It is considerably colder today than it was yesterday. The temperature lowered a bit. YES / NO

2

1〜10 の語の同義語を a〜j から選びなさい。

1. comparatively
2. rapidly
3. undoubtedly
4. particularly
5. solely
6. commonly
7. characteristically
8. presumably
9. approximately
10. firmly

---

a. typically
b. solidly
c. probably
d. quickly
e. generally
f. relatively
g. unquestionably
h. only
i. especially
j. about

3 1〜10の定義に合う副詞を（　）の中に書きなさい。

1. that is (to say) （　　　）
2. to a small degree; a bit （　　　）
3. at once; without delay; directly （　　　）
4. by its or one's nature; intrinsically （　　　）
5. at the beginning; at first （　　　）
6. without doubt （　　　）
7. in a literal sense; really （　　　）
8. mainly; chiefly （　　　）
9. usually; generally （　　　）
10. at last; in the end （　　　）

4 1〜5の定義を表す正しい語をa〜cの中から選びなさい。

1. with regard to what is most important and basic
   a. basically　b. inherently　c. solely

2. in a way that must be so; unavoidably
   a. precisely　b. ideally　c. necessarily

3. when compared to others of the same kind
   a. commonly　b. relatively　c. generally

4. each separately in the order mentioned
   a. typically　b. gradually　c. respectively

5. in reality, though perhaps not in appearance; basically
   a. inherently　b. essentially　c. characteristically

総復習テスト　基本語彙

解答は P.237

1 1～8の反対の意味をもつ語を a～h から選びなさい。

1. consume　　2. extend　　3. reproach　　4. eradicate
5. respond　　6. initiate　　7. integrate　　8. survive

| a. segregate | b. prevail | c. finish | d. produce | e. ask |
| f. diminish | g. praise | h. die | | |

2 1～15 と反対の意味をもつ語を下から選んで書きなさい。

1. implicit　(　　　　)　　2. concrete　(　　　　　　)
3. thrifty　(　　　　)　　4. willing　(　　　　　　)
5. old　(　　　　)　　6. productive　(　　　　　　)
7. variable　(　　　　)　　8. rehearsed　(　　　　　　)
9. clear　(　　　　)　　10. doubtful　(　　　　　　)
11. simple　(　　　　)　　12. conventional　(　　　　　　)
13. obscure　(　　　　)　　14. remarkable　(　　　　　　)
15. vulnerable　(　　　　)

ordinary	contemporary	impromptu	extravagant
abstract	intricate	explicit	constant
conspicuous	strong	eccentric	ambiguous
futile	reluctant	credulous	

3 1～5 と反対の意味をもつ語を a～e から選びなさい。

1. migration　　2. concord　　3. majority
4. deterioration　　5. chaos

a. order   b. amelioration   c. settlement
d. discord   e. minority

4 次の動詞の名詞形を書きなさい。

1. describe ( )   2. distinguish ( )
3. expand ( )   4. imply ( )
5. inspire ( )   6. consume ( )
7. apply ( )   8. absorb ( )
9. exploit ( )   10. extend ( )
11. confer ( )   12. portray ( )
13. prevail ( )   14. produce ( )
15. respond ( )   16. reconcile ( )
17. reduce ( )   18. restrain ( )
19. survive ( )   20. complete ( )

5 次の名詞の形容詞形を書きなさい。

1. chaos ( )   2. concord ( )
3. concurrence ( )   4. defect ( )
5. defense ( )   6. eloquence ( )
7. extravagance ( )   8. burden ( )
9. hypothesis ( )   10. progress ( )
11. prospect ( )   12. conjecture ( )
13. region ( )   14. spontaneity ( )
15. significance ( )

6   1〜10の副詞の意味を表すものをa〜jから選びなさい。

1. respectively
2. eventually
3. primarily
4. approximately
5. particularly
6. gradually
7. virtually
8. generally
9. relatively
10. literally

- a. at last; in the end
- b. almost; very nearly; practically
- c. mainly; chiefly
- d. each separately in the order mentioned
- e. about
- f. especially
- g. in a literal sense; really
- h. usually; by most people
- i. slowly; by degrees
- j. when compared to others of the same kind; comparatively

7   問題文の内容に最も適した単語をa〜cの中から選びなさい。

1. Because I was sick in the hospital, John came to teach the class instead of me. What did John do?
   - a. extended
   - b. influenced
   - c. substituted
2. I'm making much effort in order to succeed. What am I doing?
   - a. converting
   - b. striving
   - c. grinding
3. He was accused of cowardice. What happened to him?
   - a. reproached
   - b. preceded
   - c. captured
4. They used to quarrel all the time, but finally they made up. What did they do?
   - a. depicted
   - b. reconciled
   - c. inspired
5. The teacher took his radio away because he was playing it in the classroom. What did the teacher do?
   - a. described
   - b. accumulated
   - c. confiscated
6. His debt problem was made worse by the rise in interest rates. What happened to his debt problem?
   - a. dedicated
   - b. aggravated
   - c. integrated
7. He was taken prisoner. What happened to him?
   - a. captured
   - b. converted
   - c. influenced

8. He is writing an article for the magazine. What is he doing?
   a. distinguishing   b. interacting   c. contributing

9. The Town Hall was chosen as an emergency feeding center in the event of an enemy attack. In other words, it was _____.
   a. designated   b. modified   c. completed

10. The firm used its workers is gracefully for its own profit and advantage. What did the company do to its workers?
    a. absorbed   b. extended   c. exploited

11. He asked the construction firm to calculate the probable cost of the repairs to the roof. What did he ask the firm to do?
    a. accomplish   b. estimate   c. eradicate

12. She didn't say he was telling a lie, but she meant to say so indirectly. What did she do?
    a. applied   b. conferred   c. implied

13. My grandfather is responsible for giving food to the dog. What is he responsible for?
    a. feeding   b. bearing   c. prevailing

14. The writer described life in a refugee camp very vividly. What did the writer do?
    a. expanded   b. portrayed   c. produced

15. He refused to answer the question I asked, which made me very angry. What did his refusal to respond do to me?
    a. initiated   b. interacted   c. provoked

8 問題文の内容に最も適した単語を a～c の中から選びなさい。

1. He didn't have any evidence or proof; he just guessed. His statement was _____.
   a. core   b. conjecture   c. complexion

2. His speech is fluent and persuasive. How do you describe this kind of speech?
   a. decade   b. eulogy   c. eloquence

3. What do you call a list of specialized terms with accompanying definitions?
   a. glossary   b. grievance   c. device

4. What do you call a conjecture that accounts for a set of facts and can be used as a basis for further investigation?
   a. incidence
   b. glossary
   c. hypothesis

5. His foolish behavior may put his whole future in danger. His future may be in _____.
   a. mass
   b. jeopardy
   c. grievance

6. The police formally charged him with fraud and theft. What happened?
   a. defense
   b. grievance
   c. indictment

7. From the top of the hill there's a beautiful view over the valley. What do you see over the valley?
   a. prospect
   b. precept
   c. precaution

8. Several pieces of land on this street are for sale. What are for sale?
   a. districts
   b. properties
   c. regions

9. What do you call an unfair and often unfavorable feeling or opinion formed without thinking deeply and clearly or without enough knowledge, and sometimes resulting from fear or distrust of ideas different from one's own?
   a. eloquence
   b. assumption
   c. prejudice

10. He explained to me the importance of making the contract. What did he explain?
    a. significance
    b. major
    c. range

11. He's being tried in court for armed robbery. In other words he is on _____.
    a. site
    b. trial
    c. surface

12. He is greatly troubled by anxieties and difficulties. In other words, he is under _____.
    a. anguish
    b. ordeal
    c. strain

13. He wasn't forced to do it by anybody; he did it suddenly of his own will. What do you call this kind of quality?
    a. spontaneity
    b. innovation
    c. extravagance

14. My opinions are in agreement with yours. In other words, you and I are in _____.
    a. occurrence
    b. concurrence
    c. congestion

15. His health is becoming worse. His health is marked by _____.
    a. deterioration
    b. development
    c. famine

9 問題文の内容に最も適した単語を a 〜 c の中から選びなさい。

1. She is a capable worker. She works well, and quickly. She's very _____.
   a. futile   b. obscure   c. efficient
2. Some people are good at giving an extempore speech. What kind of speech are they good at giving?
   a. mutual   b. impromptu   c. frivolous
3. A complicated problem is difficult to solve. What kind of problem is difficult to solve?
   a. intensive   b. imminent   c. intricate
4. He has a good memory, but she does not. She is _____.
   a. obsolete   b. oblivious   c. obvious
5. Everyone supported and agreed to the proposal. In other words their opinion was _____.
   a. inconspicuous   b. supreme   c. unanimous
6. The details are discussed in the following chapter. In which chapter are the details discussed?
   a. impending   b. subsequent   c. continuous
7. She's frugal, so she never uses money wastefully. In other words she is _____.
   a. thrifty   b. sophisticated   c. trivial
8. She was deaf when she was born. Her deafness is characterized as _____.
   a. congenial   b. scrupulous   c. congenital
9. Wearing a seat belt while driving a car is required by law in this state. In other words, wearing a car seat belt is _____.
   a. compulsory   b. autonomous   c. conventional
10. She's gullible; she believes everything. In other words, she is _____.
    a. prolific   b. credulous   c. sympathetic
11. He is always dressed in funny-looking, strange clothes, so everyone says he is _____.
    a. eccentric   b. plausible   c. latent

12. Although he was seriously injured, he was aware of his own existence and environment. In other words he was _____.
    a. conscientious   b. uncommon   c. conscious
13. This decision caused much argument and disagreement. This decision was indeed _____.
    a. volatile   b. abstract   c. controversial
14. Dinosaurs died out a long time ago, and so they no longer exist. In other words dinosaurs are _____.
    a. extinct   b. explicit   c. abundant
15. His statement is so ambiguous that it can be interpreted in two different ways. His statement is _____.
    a. frugal   b. vulnerable   c. equivocal

10 次の語の中には１語だけ他と異なる意味の語が入っています。その語に○をつけなさい。

1. a. gradually   b. little by little   c. nearly
2. a. chiefly   b. plainly   c. primarily
3. a. extremely   b. particularly   c. especially
4. a. virtually   b. almost   c. rapidly
5. a. literally   b. namely   c. really
6. a. slightly   b. generally   c. usually
7. a. approximately   b. about   c. frequently
8. a. enormously   b. eventually   c. at last
9. a. fairly   b. relatively   c. comparatively
10. a. respectively   b. immediately
    c. each separately in the order mentioned

Chapter 2
自然科学300語

宇宙	Day 21...Day 23 ▶ 72 復習テスト　宇宙 ▶ 78	
気象	Day 24...Day 26 ▶ 80 復習テスト　気象 ▶ 86	
地学	Day 27...Day 29 ▶ 88 復習テスト　地学 ▶ 94	
環境	Day 30...Day 32 ▶ 96 復習テスト　環境 ▶ 102	
生物	Day 33...Day 35 ▶ 104 復習テスト　生物 ▶ 110	
動物	Day 36...Day 38 ▶ 112 復習テスト　動物 ▶ 118	
生理学	Day 39...Day 41 ▶ 120 復習テスト　生理学 ▶ 126	
健康	Day 42...Day 44 ▶ 128 復習テスト　健康 ▶ 134	
化学	Day 45...Day 47 ▶ 136 復習テスト　化学 ▶ 142	
物理	Day 48...Day 50 ▶ 144 復習テスト　物理 ▶ 150	

基本語彙200語

自然科学300語

社会・人文科学300語

Day 21

宇宙 自然科学300語 1

CD-A21

□ 201
astronomer
/əstrɑ́nəmər/
- 名 **天文学者**、天体観測者

□ 202
telescope
/téləskòup/
- 名 **望遠鏡**

□ 203
microscope
/máikrəskòup/
- 名 **顕微鏡**

□ 204
laboratory
/lǽbərətɔ̀ːri/
- 名 **実験室**、研究室［所］

□ 205
observatory
/əbzə́ːrvətɔ̀ːri/
- 名 **観測所**、天文台、気象台、展望台

□ 206
metric
/métrik/
- 形 **メートル（法）の**
- 関 metric system メートル法（度量衡法で単位を meter、liter、gram とする）

□ 207
analyze
/ǽnəlàiz/
- 動 **分析する**
- 名 analyzation 分析（すること） 名 analysis 分析、分解（反 synthesis 統合）

□ 208
prism
/prízm/
- 名 **プリズム**
- 分光・反射用：光の屈折や分散などを起こさせるもの。全反射を利用し、光線の方向を変える反射プリズム、光をスペクトルに分ける分光プリズム、各種の偏光を得る偏光プリズムがある

□ 209
spectrum
/spéktrəm/
- 名 **スペクトル**、〈プリズムなどによる白色光の〉分光
- 分光器を通して光を波長で分解した成分、またはその全体。光はプリズムを通すと7色の色帯を成す

□ 210
spectroscope
/spéktrəskòup/
- 名 **分光器**
- 光を波長によって分解しスペクトルを得る装置

continued
▼

Astronomers study the Earth as a body in space.	天文学者は地球を宇宙における天体として研究する。
Astronomers use telescopes to see and photograph objects in space.	天体観測者は宇宙の物体を見たり写真に撮ったりするために、望遠鏡を使う。
A microscope is an instrument for magnifying objects too small to be seen by the naked eye alone.	顕微鏡は裸眼では見えない微小な物体を、拡大して見せる器具である。
There are required safety procedures to be followed in laboratory work.	実験室での作業には、安全のための決められた進行手順がある。
A space observatory provides a clear view of space.	天文台では宇宙の姿をくっきりと見ることができる。
Distance, mass, and time are three basic measurements in the metric system.	長さ、質量、時間がメートル法の三大基本単位である。
The scientists' work is to observe, analyze, synthesize and test.	科学者の仕事は、観察、分析、統合、そして検査することである。
If light is passed through a prism, it will separate into different colors.	光はプリズムを通過するといくつかの色に分離する。
The pattern the light makes after passing through a prism is called a spectrum.	光がプリズムを通過した後にできる模様がスペクトルである。
You can get a spectrum of light from each star by using a spectroscope.	分光器を使って、星ひとつひとつから届く光のスペクトルを獲得できる。

continued
▼

Day 22

宇宙 自然科学300語 2

211	**planet** /plǽnit/	**名 惑星** ● 太陽系の惑星は太陽に近いものから順に、Mercury（水星）、Venus（金星）、Earth（地球）、Mars（火星）、Jupiter（木星）、Saturn（土星）、Uranus（天王星）、Neptune（海王星）
212	**constellation** /kànstəléiʃən/	**名 星座**
213	**celestial sphere** /səléstʃəl/ /sfíər/	**天球** 関連 celestial body 天体
214	**orbit** /ɔ́ːrbit/	**名 〈天体・人工衛星などの〉軌道**
215	**revolve** /riválv/	**動 公転する**、回転する、自転する
216	**axis** /ǽksis/	**名 地軸** ● 地球の中心を南北につらぬく軸
217	**solar system** /sóulər/ /sístəm/	**太陽系** ● 太陽の引力に支配されて運動する天体と、それらを包む空間。8個の惑星、各惑星の衛星の他、小惑星、彗星、惑星間物質などがある。質量の99.87%は太陽が占める
218	**light year** /láit/ /jíər/	**光年** ● 距離の単位で、1年間に光が真空中を走る距離。約9兆4,600億kmに相当する
219	**galaxy** /gǽləksi/	**名 銀河**、天の川（=the Milky Way） ● 天球を一周する帯状の天域に微光星集積して光る、川のように見える部分
220	**nebula** /nébjulə/	**名 星雲** ● 輪郭のぼんやりした雲状天体の総称。複数形は nebulae /nébjuliː/

continued ▼

Scientists listen for and send messages in the search for life outside the planet Earth.	科学者は地球という惑星の外に生命が存在するかどうかを探るため、メッセージを聞いたり、あるいは送ったりする。
Early people classified the stars by grouping the stars into imaginary patterns, or constellations.	古代の人々は星を分類して、想像上の図案、つまり星座を作成した。
Certain characters in Greek mythology were honored by assigning them a position on the celestial sphere.	ギリシャ神話の特定の登場人物は、天球に場所を割り当てられる栄誉を受けた。
Gravitational attraction between the Sun and planets holds the planets in orbit around the Sun.	太陽と惑星の間の引力によって、惑星は太陽の周囲を回る軌道に乗っている。
Earth revolves around the Sun.	地球は太陽の周囲を公転する。
The seasons result from the fact that the Earth remains tilted on its axis.	四季は地球の地軸が傾いていることから生じる。
The solar system is about 30,000 light years from the center of the galaxy.	太陽系は銀河の中心から約３万光年離れている。
A light year is a measurement of distances between stars.	光年は星と星の間の距離を測るのに使われる単位である。
Galaxies are large assemblies of stars containing millions to billions of stars.	銀河は数千兆もの恒星を含む巨大な恒星の集団である。
Objects found in outer space include nebulae, stars, open clusters, globular clusters, galaxies, and Cepheid variable stars.	宇宙で発見された物体には、星雲、恒星、散開星団、球状星団、銀河、ケフェイド変光星などがある。

continued
▼

Day 23

宇宙 自然科学300語 3

□ 221 **radiation** /rèidiéiʃən/
名〈光・熱などの〉**放射**、発光、放熱、発散
動 radiate〈熱・光などが〉放射する、〈太陽などが〉光を放つ

□ 222 **nova** /nóuvə/
名 **新星**
● 突然に現れて強く輝き、次第に光が暗くなっていく星。恒星が爆発して生じる現象で爆発を繰り返す星もある

□ 223 **spiral** /spáiərəl/
形 **らせん（形［状］）の**、らせん状の構造の

□ 224 **dust** /dʌ́st/
名 **塵**

□ 225 **comet** /kámit/
名 **彗星**、ほうき星
● 太陽引力のもとに運動する輪郭のぼんやりしたガス状に見える小天体。本体は汚れた氷。太陽に近づくと長い尾を引くものもある。昔は不吉のきざしとして恐れられた

□ 226 **asteroid** /ǽstərɔ̀id/
名 **小惑星**（=minor planet）
● 火星の軌道と木星の軌道との間およびその付近に散在する

□ 227 **eclipse** /iklíps/
名〈太陽・月の〉**食**
関 solar eclipse 日食　関 lunar eclipse 月食

□ 228 **meteorite** /míːtiərài t/
名 **隕石**

□ 229 **rotate** /róuteit/
動 **回転する［させる］**
名 rotation 自転

□ 230 **satellite** /sǽtəlàit/
名 **衛星**、人工衛星

continued

Electromagnetic radiation is energy in the form of waves from space. It includes radio waves, infrared, visible light, ultraviolet, gamma and X-rays.	電磁放射は宇宙からやってくる波形エネルギーである。それには電波、赤外線、可視光線、紫外線、γ線、X線がある。
A white dwarf may become a cold lump of matter, or it may flare up to become a nova.	白色矮星は冷たい物質のかたまりになったり、突然明るさを増して新星になる。
The Milky Way Galaxy is spiral in shape.	天の川は、らせん形をしている。
New stars develop in the gas and dust found in the spiral.	新しい恒星はらせん状にあるガスと塵の中で発達する。
A comet is an object in space that moves round the Sun in a long elliptical path and has a very bright head and a long tail.	彗星は長い楕円軌道で太陽の周囲を回る宇宙の物体であり、非常に明るい頭部と長い尾をもっている。
Asteroids and comets are members of the solar system.	小惑星と彗星は太陽系の構成員である。
Eclipses occur when the Earth blocks sunlight from the moon (lunar eclipse) or the moon blocks sunlight from the Earth (solar eclipse).	食は地球が月に向かう太陽光を遮る（月食）か、月が地球に向かう太陽光を遮る（日食）ときに起こる。
A meteor is a small piece of dust or rock that enters the Earth's atmosphere from space. Those that reach the Earth's surface are called meteorites.	流星は宇宙から地球の大気圏に突入する塵か岩石の小片である。地上に達するものを隕石という。
Jupiter rotates rapidly and has a turbulent atmosphere composed of hydrogen and helium.	木星は回転が速く、水素とヘリウムから成る大気が乱流している。
On October 4, 1957, the Russians launched the first artificial satellite, Sputnik I.	1957年10月4日に、ロシア人は最初の人工衛星スプートニク1号を打ち上げた。

continued
▼

復習テスト　宇宙

1 1〜10の語の定義を a〜j から選びなさい。

1. astronomer
2. laboratory
3. metric system
4. light year
5. spectrum
6. galaxy
7. telescope
8. spectroscope
9. prism
10. observatory

> a. an instrument which can be attached to telescopes and is used to examine light
> b. a transparent three-sided block, usually made of glass, that breaks up white light into different colors
> c. the distance that light travels in one year
> d. one who studies objects in space
> e. a place for scientific study and testing
> f. a tube-like scientific instrument that makes distant objects look nearer and larger
> g. a system of weights and measures based on the meter and gram and liter
> h. a set of bands of colored light in the order of their wavelengths, into which a beam of light may be separated
> i. large assemblies of stars
> j. a place from which scientists watch the moon, stars, etc.

2 選択肢 a、b のうち正しい語を選んで文を完成させなさい。

1. Imaginary groupings of stars are called (a. galaxies   b. constellations).

2. Force of attraction between objects is called (a. gravitation   b. radiation).

3. The curved path of the Earth going round the Sun, or the moon or a spacecraft going round the Earth is called an (a. asteroid   b. orbit).

4. Earth rotates on its (a. axis   b. planet).

5. A meteor that reaches the Earth's surface is called a (a. comet   b. meteorite).

6. A mass of gas and dust among the stars, appearing often as a bright cloud at night is called a (a. nebula   b. nova).

7. A place equipped for scientific study and testing is called a (a. lavatory   b. laboratory).

8. When the Earth is between the Sun and the moon, there is a (a. lunar eclipse   b. solar eclipse).

9. An instrument for magnifying objects too small to be seen by the naked eye is called an optical (a. telescope   b. microscope).

10. When the moon passes directly between the Sun and the Earth blocking the Sun's light, there is a (a. lunar eclipse   b. solar eclipse).

Day 24

気象 1 — 自然科学300語

□ 231 meteorologist
/miːtiərάlədʒist/

名 気象学者
名 meteorólogy 気象学

□ 232 atmosphere
/ǽtməsfìər/

名 大気、雰囲気

□ 233 greenhouse effect
/gríːnhàus/ /ifékt/

温室効果
● 大気中の二酸化炭素や水蒸気の蓄積による地表面気温の上昇

□ 234 dense
/déns/

形 密集した、濃厚な
関 a dense fog 濃霧　関 a dense forest 密林

□ 235 convection
/kənvékʃən/

名 対流
● 熱の伝わり方の一種。気体や液体の一部を熱したとき、その部分が熱膨張して軽くなり、浮力により上昇し、反対に他の冷たい部分が下方に向かって流れる循環の運動。流体の中の熱の伝導は、主に対流によって起こる
動 convect〈暖かい空気を〉対流で循環させる

□ 236 horizontal
/hɔ̀ːrəzάntl/

形 地平 [水平] 線上の、水平な
名 horizon /həráizn/ 地平（線）、水平線

□ 237 equator
/ikwéitər/

名 赤道
形 equatórial 赤道の、赤道付近の

□ 238 evaporation
/ivæ̀pəréiʃən/

名 蒸発（作用）、消散
動 evaporate 蒸発させる、消散させる

□ 239 dew
/djúː/

名 露
形 dewy 露の多い

□ 240 dew point
/djúː/ /pɔ́int/

露点（温度）
● 空気が冷え続けたとき、物体の表面に露ができ始める温度。このとき、水蒸気は飽和していて、湿度は100%となる。上昇した空気が冷えて露点に達すると雲ができる

continued
▼

Meteorologists study the atmosphere.	気象学者は大気を研究する。
Global warming has been said to be caused by a rise in the amount of carbon dioxide in the earth's atmosphere.	地球温暖化は、地球の大気中にある二酸化炭素量の増加によって引き起こされると言われている。
The lower atmosphere is warmed from below because of the greenhouse effect.	下層大気は温室効果により下から暖められる。
Cool denser air moves under and pushes warmer, less dense air upward.	冷たく密度の高い空気は下降し、暖かく密度の低い空気を上昇させる。
The process of warmer air being pushed upward by cooler air is called convection.	暖かい空気が冷たい空気により押し上げられる過程を対流という。
Horizontal movement of air is called wind.	水平な空気の流れを風という。
The equator receives more direct sunlight than the poles, so it is warmer.	赤道は両極よりも垂直に日光を受けるので、両極より気温が高い。
Water enters the atmosphere through evaporation and leaves by condensation.	水は蒸発作用により大気に入り、凝結により大気から出る。
Dew or frost forms on "C nights" — clear, calm, and cool nights.	露または霜は、晴れて（clear）風がなく（calm）冷えた（cool）夜、つまり C の夜に生じる。
If the dew point is above 0°C, water vapor will condense on surfaces as a liquid, called dew. If the temperature is at or below 0°C, water vapor will condense on surfaces as a solid, called frost.	もし露点が0℃より高くなると水蒸気は液体、つまり露となって表面に凝結する。もし気温が0℃以下なら水蒸気は固体、つまり霜となって表面に凝結する。

continued
▼

Day 25

気象 2 — 自然科学300語

CD-A25

□ 241
humidity
/hjuːmídəti/

名 **湿気**、湿度
形 humid 湿気のある、むしむしする

□ 242
hydrology
/haidrálədʒi/

名 **水文（すいもん）学**
● 地球上の水の生成・循環・性質・分布などを研究する

□ 243
precipitation
/prisipətéiʃən/

名 **降水（量）**
● 一定時間内に特定の地点で測定した、雨・雪・あられなどの水として降った量。水の深さは、ミリメートルで表す。雪・あられなどでは、溶かして水にした深さをいう。降雨量：降水量のうち雨として降った量

□ 244
hydrologic cycle
/hàidrəládʒik/ /sáikl/

水の循環 (=water cycle)
● 海から大気によって陸に運ばれ、また海に戻る一連の過程

□ 245
front
/fránt/

名 **前線**
● 寒・暖ふたつの気団が進行していく場合の境界面と地表とが交わる曲線。付近は一般に天気が悪い

□ 246
high atmospheric pressure
/hái/ /ætməsférik/ /préʃər/

高気圧

□ 247
low atmospheric pressure
/lóu/ /ætməsférik/ /préʃər/

低気圧

□ 248
weather forecast
/wéðər/ /fɔ́ːrkæst/

天気予報

□ 249
tornado
/tɔːrnéidou/

名 **トルネード**
● 北米大陸で、春から初夏にかけて発生する大竜巻。風速毎秒100mを超える大規模なものが多い

□ 250
hurricane
/hɔ́ːrəkèin/

名 **暴風**、ハリケーン
● 東経180度以東の太平洋・大西洋にある熱帯低気圧のうち、風速の激しいもの

---

continued
▼

Relative humidity is increased when more water vapor is added to the air or when the air is cooled.	相対湿度は空気中に含まれる水蒸気が増えるとき、または空気が冷たいときに上昇する。
Hydrology is the study of water.	水文学は水に関する研究である。
Precipitation that falls to the surface of the Earth is in a solid or liquid form, depending on the temperature in the different layers of air.	地上に降る降水は大気の各層の温度によって、固体または液体となる。
The Earth's hydrologic cycle is evaporation, condensation, and precipitation of water — a never-ending process.	地球の水の循環は蒸発、凝結、降水の過程を永遠に繰り返す。
A front is the leading edge of a moving cold- or warm-air mass. A cold front is at the front of a moving cold air mass. A warm front is at the front of a moving warm air mass.	前線は移動性寒気団または暖気団の先端部分である。寒冷前線は移動性寒気団の前方にあり、温暖前線は移動性暖気団の前方にある。
High atmospheric pressure is associated with dry air masses and fair weather.	高気圧は乾燥した気団および晴れの天気と関連がある。
Low atmospheric pressure is associated with fronts and cloudy weather with precipitation.	低気圧は前線と曇りや雨の天気と関連がある。
Weather forecasts are made from information about movement of air masses, fronts, and high- and low-pressure areas.	天気予報は気団、前線、低圧帯や高圧帯などの動きに関する情報をもとに作成される。
Thunderstorms and tornadoes are short-lived, small-area storms formed from cumulonimbus clouds.	雷雨やトルネードは積乱雲から生じる短命で局地的な嵐である。
A hurricane is a large circular storm that forms over tropical waters and moves to the northwest, then northeast after passing latitude 30°N.	ハリケーンは巨大な渦状の嵐であり、熱帯海上で発生し、まず北西に移動、北緯30度を通過後は北東に移動する。

continued
▼

Day 26

気象 自然科学300語 ③

CD-A26

□ 251 **hailstone** /héilstòun/
- 名 **ひょう**、あられ（1粒のことを言う）
- 名 hail ひょう（氷の粒状のかたまりで、雷雨とともに降る直径5mm以上のもの）

□ 252 **climate** /kláimit/
- 名〈一地方の〉**気候**

□ 253 **current** /kə́:rənt/
- 名 **海流**、気流
- 関 warm current 暖流　関 cold current 寒流

□ 254 **temperate** /témpərət/
- 形〈地域など〉**温帯性の**、〈気候・温度などが〉穏やかな、温和な
- 関 Temperate Zone 温帯　名 temperature 温度、気温　関 tropical 熱帯性の　関 tropical zone (=Torrid Zone) 熱帯

□ 255 **arid** /ǽrid/
- 形〈土地などが〉**乾燥した**、湿気のない、不毛の

□ 256 **anemometer** /ænəmɑ́mətər/
- 名 **風力計**、風速計

□ 257 **altitude** /ǽltətjùːd/
- 名 **海抜**、標高、水位

□ 258 **Coriolis effect** /kɔ̀:rióulis/ /ifékt/
- **コリオリ現象**
- 関 Coriolis force コリオリの力（回転座標系の中で運動している物体に、遠心力とは別に物体の進行方向に対して横向きに働くみかけの力。転向力。フランスの物理学者コリオリが発見）

□ 259 **barometer** /bərɑ́mitər/
- 名 **気圧計**、晴雨計
- 関 thermometer 温度計

□ 260 **drought** /dráut/
- 名 **干ばつ**

continued ▼

Hailstones fall only during thunderstorms.	ひょうは雷雨のときにしか降らない。
Climate is the average of the many kinds of weather that occur at a given place over a period of time.	気候は一定の期間にある場所で起こるさまざまな天気の平均状態である。
Ocean currents bring warmer or cooler water to a coastal area.	海流は暖かい海水または冷たい海水を沿岸地域にもたらす。
The major types of climate groups on the Earth are tropical, temperate, and polar.	地球の主な気候分類には熱帯、温帯、寒帯がある。
The driest climate is classified as arid.	最も降水量の少ない気候は乾燥気候と分類される。
An anemometer is used to measure the strength of winds.	風力計は風の強さを測るために使われる。
Climates are modified by mountains, large bodies of water, ocean currents, and altitudes.	気候は山、広く水の集まっているところ、海流、海抜に影響され変化する。
The atmosphere and things moving through it appear to turn because of the Coriolis effect.	大気とそこを通って動くものは、コリオリ現象のため、向きを変えるように見える。
Atmospheric pressure is measured by a barometer.	気圧は気圧計で測る。
Droughts may last a season, a year, or many years.	干ばつは1シーズン、1年、あるいは何年もの間続くことがある。

continued
▼

復習テスト　気象

1 1〜10の単語の定義を a〜j から選びなさい。

1. greenhouse effect
2. current
3. humidity
4. equator
5. dew
6. hail
7. anemometer
8. altitude
9. precipitation
10. temperate

> a. the smallest drops of water which form on cold surfaces during the night
> b. the amount of water vapor contained in the air
> c. the gradual slight warming of the air surrounding the Earth because heat cannot escape through its upper level
> d. climate that is neither hot nor cold
> e. rain, snow, etc. which has fallen onto the ground
> f. the height of an object or place above sea level
> g. an imaginary line drawn round the world halfway between its most northern and southern points (poles)
> h. a continuously-moving mass of liquid or gas, especially one flowing through a slower-moving liquid or gas
> i. frozen raindrops which fall as little hard balls of ice
> j. a machine for measuring the strength of winds

2 選択肢 a、b のうち正しい語を選んで文を完成させなさい。

1. The process of warmer air being pushed upward by cooler air is called (a. arid   b. convection).

2. The greenhouse effect causes increases in (a. winds   b. temperatures).

3. Warm air has less (a. density   b. dew) than cold air.

4. The temperature at which water vapor condenses on a surface is called the (a. dew point   b. current).

5. A (a. thunderstorm   b. hurricane) is an intense rainstorm with thunder, lightning, strong winds, and sometimes hail.

6. (a. Temperate   b. Polar) climates are neither very hot nor very cold.

7. (a. High   b. Low) atmospheric pressure is associated with fronts and cloudy weather with precipitation.

8. The leading edge of a moving air mass is a zone that is called a cold or warm (a. region   b. front).

9. A weather (a. forecast   b. mass) tells you about the coming weather.

10. A barometer is used to measure (a. temperature   b. atmospheric pressure).

Day 27

地学 1 — 自然科学300語

CD-A27

□ 261 **geologist** /dʒiálədʒist/	名 **地質学者** 名 geology 地質学
□ 262 **soil** /sɔ́il/	名 **土**、土壌 関 rich [poor] soil 肥えた［やせた］土
□ 263 **reservoir** /rézərvwɑ̀ːr/	名 **貯水池**
□ 264 **resource** /ríːsɔːrs/	名 **資源**、物資
□ 265 **oceanographer** /òuʃənágrəfər/	名 **海洋学者** 名 oceanógraphy 海洋学
□ 266 **coral** /kɔ́ːrəl/	名 **珊瑚** 関 reef 礁、暗礁、リーフ
□ 267 **salinity** /səlínəti/	名 **塩分**、塩分濃度、塩度
□ 268 **crust** /krʌ́st/	名 **地殻** ● 地球の最も外側の部分
□ 269 **magma** /mǽgmə/	名 **岩しょう**、マグマ ● 地中で、岩石が溶けた状態にあるもの。温度は650〜1,300℃。冷えると火成岩になる
□ 270 **layer** /léiər/	名 **層**

continued ▼

Geologists study the solid outer and liquid inner parts of the Earth.	地質学者は地球の外側の固体部分と内側の液体部分を研究する。
Soil with more pore space holds more water.	すきまの多い土壌ほど、水分を保持する。
A lake formed by a dam is called a reservoir.	ダムにより生じた湖を貯水池という。
Fresh water is a limited resource.	真水は限られた資源である。
Oceanographers study the oceans.	海洋学者は海を研究する。
Most beach sand is made up of quartz and grains of shell and coral.	海辺の砂はほとんど、石英と貝と珊瑚の細かなかけらでできている。
The salinity of seawater is affected by the rate of evaporation and precipitation.	海水の塩分は蒸発と降水の割合に影響される。
There are more than 2,500 different minerals found in the Earth's crust. Each mineral has its own unique set of physical properties.	地殻からは2,500種以上もの鉱物が発見されている。各鉱物は特有の物理的性質を有する。
Magma is an underground pocket of melted rock.	マグマは地中で溶融状態の岩石である。
The three main layers of the Earth are the crust, mantle, and core.	地球は地殻、マントル、核の3大層から成る。

continued ▼

Day 28

地学 2 — 自然科学300語

□ 271 mantle
/mǽntl/

名 マントル
- 地球の層状構造の中で地殻と核の間にある部分。地球の全体積の約82%を占める

□ 272 seismograph
/sáizməgræf/

名 地震［震動］計
名 seismography 地震学、地震観測（法）　関 seismólogy 地震学

□ 273 epicenter
/épisèntər/

名 震央
- 震源の真上の地表上の地点
関 hypocenter /háipəsèntər/ 震源：地震波が発生した場所

□ 274 lava
/lάːvə/

名 溶岩
- マグマが地表または水中に流れ出たもの。また固まったもの

□ 275 volcanic
/vɑlkǽnik/

形 火山の、火山性の
関 volcanic activity 火山活動　関 a volcanic eruption 火山（の）爆発　関 volcanic ash 火山灰　名 volcano 火山　関 an active [a dormant / an extinct] volcano 活［休／死］火山

□ 276 longitude
/lάndʒətjùːd/

名 経度、経線（略 lon(g).）
形 longitúdinal 経度［経線］の

□ 277 latitude
/lǽtətjùːd/

名 緯度（略 lat.）
関 the north [south] latitudes 北［南］緯　関 cold [warm] latitudes 寒帯［温帯］地方　関 high latitudes 高緯度（極）地方　関 low latitudes 低緯度地方、赤道付近

□ 278 International Date Line
/ìntərnǽʃənl/ /déit/ /láin/

国際日付変更線（=date line）（略 IDL）

□ 279 prime meridian
/práim/ /mərídiən/

本初子午線、グリニッジ子午線（=first meridian）
- 英国 Greenwich 天文台を通る子午線

□ 280 fault
/fɔ́ːlt/

名 断層

continued ▼

The mantle is a thick layer beneath the crust and extends down to the core at 2,900 km.	マントルは地殻の下の厚い層で、核まで下方 2,900km の幅がある。
A seismograph is an instrument that measures seismic waves.	地震計は地震波の計測器である。
News reports usually identify the epicenter of an earthquake.	ニュースの報道では通常、地震の震央を明らかにする。
Lava is rock in a very hot liquid state flowing from a volcano.	溶岩は火山から流れ出した非常に高温な液体状態の岩石である。
Mountains formed from lava and ash are called volcanic mountains.	溶岩と灰からできた山を火山という。
Time zones are roughly the width of 15° of longitude.	同一標準時間帯はおおむね、経度で 15 度の幅をもつ。
If you are at latitude 40°N, you are located 40° north of the equator.	もし北緯 40 度にいるなら、そこは赤道から北に 40 度の地点である。
On the opposite side of the Earth from the prime meridian is the international date line.	本初子午線の地球の裏側に国際日付変更線がある。
The prime meridian is a line that passes through Greenwich, England.	本初子午線は英国、グリニッジを通過する子午線である。
Most earthquakes are caused by rocks breaking and sliding past each other on a fault.	地震のほとんどは断層で岩石が破壊し、お互いにすべり込むことによって生じる。

continued ▼

Day 29 地学 3 自然科学300語

CD-A29

□ 281 **loess** /lóuəs/

名 **黄土**
- 中国北部・ヨーロッパ・アメリカ合衆国中部などの地表に広く厚く分布する黄灰色の土

□ 282 **glacier** /gléiʃər/

名 **氷河**
関 iceberg 氷山

□ 283 **fossil** /fásəl/

名 **化石**
関 fossil fuel 化石燃料　動 fossilize 化石化する

□ 284 **geyser** /gáizər/

名 **間欠泉**
- 熱湯や水蒸気を周期的に断続して噴出する温泉。地熱活動の激しい地域に多い。地下の空洞に流入した地下水が地熱で加熱され沸騰すると噴出する

□ 285 **dune** /djú:n/

名 **砂丘**（=sand dune）（海浜・砂漠など）

□ 286 **topographic** /tàpəgrǽfik/

形 **地形学の**
関 topographic map 地形図　名 topógraphy 地形学、地形測量［調査］

□ 287 **radioactive** /rèidiouǽktiv/

形 **放射性［能］のある**
関 radioactive rays 放射線

□ 288 **weathering** /wéðəriŋ/

名 **風化（作用）**
- 岩石が日射や空気・水などの作用で変質、分解し、くずれていく現象

□ 289 **erosion** /iróuʒən/

名 **浸食**
関 wind erosion 風食作用　形 erosive 浸食性の

□ 290 **geothermal energy** /dʒi:ouθə́:rməl/ /énərdʒi/

地熱力
名 géotherm 地熱　関 solar energy 太陽エネルギー（=sunlight）

continued
▼

Loess is a fine dust deposited by winds that creates fertile soils.	黄土は風に運ばれ堆積した微細な塵で、肥沃な土壌を生み出す。
Glaciers support evidence of continental drift. In the past, glaciers covered enormous amounts of land area.	氷河は大陸移動説の証拠となる。過去には、広大な土地が氷河に覆われていた。
Fossils are traces or the preserved remains of organisms that once lived on the Earth.	化石はかつて地球に生存した生物の痕跡、または残存物である。
Since the geyser in Yellowstone National Park erupts regularly about every hour, it was named Old Faithful.	イエローストーン国立公園の間欠泉は約1時間ごとに規則正しく噴出するので、「昔からの忠実者（オールドフェイスフル）」と名付けられた。
A dune is a sandhill, often long and low in shape, shaped by winds and found on seashores and in deserts.	砂丘は海岸または砂漠において、風によって堆積した砂地であり、長くなだらかなところが多い。
A topographic map shows the contour and elevation of the land.	地形図は土地の等高線と標高を示す。
Rocks that give off invisible radiation are said to be radioactive.	目に見えない放射線を放出する岩石を放射性があるという。
Weathering is the mechanical, chemical, or biological breakdown of rocks.	風化作用は岩石が機械的、化学的、生物学的に分解することである。
Two major processes that make up wind erosion are called deflation and abrasion.	風食作用を成り立たせる2大過程を風化、浸食という。
Geothermal energy results from the heating of rocks and water within the Earth's crust.	地熱力は地殻内部の岩石と水が熱せられて生じる。

基本語彙200語

自然科学300語

社会・人文科学300語

continued
▼

復習テスト 地学

解答は P.239

1 1〜7の単語の定義を a〜g から選びなさい。

1. coral
2. fossil
3. magma
4. lava
5. loess
6. geologist
7. oceanographer

---

a. hot, liquid rock inside the Earth
b. a type of soil like a yellowish powder, common in China and parts of Europe and North America
c. a white, pink, or reddish stonelike substance formed from bones of very small sea animals
d. one who studies the oceans
e. traces or the preserved remains of organisms that once lived on the Earth
f. magma that flows out onto the surface of the Earth
g. one who studies among other thing the solid outer and liquid inner parts of the Earth

2 選択肢 a、b のうち正しい語を選んで文を完成させなさい。

1. (a. Latitude   b. Longitude) describes a location on the Earth's surface east or west of the prime meridian.

2. (a. Latitude   b. Longitude) is described in degrees north or south of the equator.

3. A body of water stored in a natural or artificial lake is called (a. reservoir   b. resource).

4. A (a. geyser   b. fossil) is a fountainlike eruption of hot water and steam.

5. Farmer's crops grow in (a. dune   b. soil).

6. (a. Geothermal energy   b. Solar energy) is energy from the internal heat of the Earth.

7. A /An (a. hypocenter   b. epicenter) is the place on the Earth's surface which is just above the point underneath the Earth's surface where an earthquake begins.

8. A (a. seismograph   b. topograph) is an instrument used to measure seismic waves.

9. A /An (a. iceberg   b. glacier) is a large mass of ice that formed from an accumulation of snow above the snow line.

10. The (a. magma   b. mantle) is the layer below the Earth's crust.

Day 30

環境 ① — 自然科学300語

CD-A30

□ 291 **natural resources** /nǽtʃərəl/ /ríːsɔːrsiz/	**天然［自然］資源** ● 自然界に存在し、人間の生活や生産活動に利用できる物質の総称。特に石炭・石油・天然ガス・鉄鋼石などの各種鉱物などを指すことが多い
□ 292 **renewable resource** /rin(j)úːəbl/ /ríːsɔːrs/	**再利用資源**
□ 293 **nonrenewable resource** /nɑnrin(j)úːəbl/ /ríːsɔːrs/	**再利用のできない資源**
□ 294 **metallic substance** /mətǽlik/ /sʌ́bstəns/	**金属性物質**
□ 295 **nonmetallic substance** /nɑnmətǽlik/ /sʌ́bstəns/	**非金属性物質**
□ 296 **deposit** /dipɑ́zit/	名 **鉱床**（鉱石・石油・天然ガスなど）、埋蔵物 =a layer of a mineral, metal etc. that is left in soil or rocks through a natural process ● 鉱床：特定の有用鉱物が、採掘して採算がとれる程度に相対的に濃く集まったもの
□ 297 **ore** /ɔ́ːr/	名 **鉱石**（金属・非金属） ● 鉱物の集積のうち、有用鉱物を多量に含んでいて採掘対象となるもの
□ 298 **lubricant** /lúːbrikənt/	名 **潤滑油**、機械油、(潤)滑剤 動 lubricate 油［(潤)滑剤］を差す［塗る］
□ 299 **fertilizer** /fə́ːrtəlàizər/	名 **肥料**、〈特に〉化学肥料 動 fertilize 〈土地を〉肥沃にする、肥やす、土地に肥料を与える　名 fertilization 肥沃化
□ 300 **abrasive** /əbréisiv, -ziv/	名 **研磨剤**、研磨用具

continued ▼

The Earth's natural resources are being used up faster than they are being produced.	地球の天然資源は、生成されるよりも消費されるスピードのほうが速い。
Renewable resources will never run out: they will become available again sometime soon in the future.	再利用資源はけっしてなくならない。それは将来すぐに再び入手できるものだ。
A nonrenewable resource is one from the Earth that is not available again once it is taken and used.	再利用のできない資源は一度地球から採り出して使用したら、二度と利用できない資源である。
Copper, iron, and aluminum are metallic substances.	銅、鉄、アルミニウムは金属性物質である。
Oil, coal, clays and chemical fertilizers are nonmetallic substances that are nonrenewable.	石油、石炭、粘土、化学肥料は再利用できない非金属性物質である。
In the United States the location of the major iron deposits is in the Lake Superior region.	米国では、スペリオル湖地域が主な鉄鉱床である。
To obtain a metal from an ore, first you must extract the ore from the Earth. Then the ore must be enriched by removing waste materials found with the ore.	鉱石から金属を採り出すために、まず地中から鉱石を抽出し、次に鉱石から不純物を取り除かなければならない。
Fossil fuels are used to produce energy for power and heat, and lubricants.	化石燃料は動力、熱、潤滑剤を生産するために使用される。
Fertilizers are essential for growing crops to feed the world's population.	肥料は世界中の人々が食べる作物を生育させるのに不可欠である。
A diamond is the hardest natural substance and the most important abrasive.	ダイアモンドは最も硬い天然の物質であり、最も重要な研磨剤である。

continued
▼

Day 31

環境 2 — 自然科学300語

CD-A31

□ 301
petroleum
/pətróuliəm/

名**石油**、ガソリン

□ 302
mineral
/mínərəl/

名**鉱物**、鉱石（=ore）、無機物［質］

□ 303
conservation
/kànsərvéiʃən/

名〈資源・運動・文化財などの〉**保存**、保護、管理
名conservationist〈自然・資源の〉保護論者
動conserve 保存する、保護する

□ 304
harvest
/háːrvist/

名**収穫**、採収、収穫期、収穫高、収穫物、採収物

□ 305
oil well
/ɔ́il/ /wél/

油井（ゆせい）
● 石油を採るために掘った井戸

□ 306
oil field
/ɔ́il/ /fíːld/

油田

□ 307
crude oil
/krúːd/ /ɔ́il/

原油（=crude petroleum）
形crude 天然のままの、粗製の

□ 308
refinery
/rifáinəri/

名**精製所**、製油所
動refine 精製する

□ 309
coal
/kóul/

名**石炭**
関coal mine 炭鉱　関coal mining 採炭、石炭鉱業
関coal miner 炭鉱夫

□ 310
acid rain
/ǽsid/ /réin/

〈大気汚染による〉**酸性雨**
● 普通の雨に比べて酸性度が強い雨。石油や石炭などの化石燃料を燃やしたときに発生する硫黄酸化物が大気中で雨水に溶けてできる。環境破壊の大きな要因になっている
関acid 酸性の

continued
▼

For years people called petroleum, rock oil.	長い間、人々は石油を岩石の油と呼んだ。
Table salt, magnesium, and bromine are all minerals taken from seawater.	食塩、マグネシウム、臭素はすべて海水から採れる鉱物である。
In order to secure minerals for the future, we need efficiency, recycling, conservation of energy, and a reduction in consumption.	将来鉱物を確保するために、能率向上、再利用、エネルギー資源の保存、消費量軽減をする必要がある。
About 90% of the ocean harvest is fish; the rest consists primarily of whales and shellfish.	海からの収穫物の約90％は魚であり、残りは主に鯨や貝である。
The first oil well was drilled by the Pennsylvania Rock Oil Company in 1859.	1859年、ペンシルベニア・ロック・オイル・カンパニーが最初の油井を掘った。
Petroleum is pumped from wells drilled into oil fields.	石油は油田に掘った井戸からポンプでくみ上げる。
The petroleum pumped from the well is called crude oil.	油井からくみ上げた石油を原油という。
Crude oil is separated into its many useful products at a refinery.	原油は精製所で多くの有用な製品に分離される。
Coal is a fossil fuel made up in varying amounts of carbon, hydrocarbons, sulfur, and clay remains of former living things.	石炭は、炭素、炭化水素、硫黄、粘土状になった生物の遺体がさまざまな割合で混ざり合ってできた化石燃料である。
Some people are concerned that acid rain may kill fish in lakes and streams, stunt plant growth, and even damage buildings.	酸性雨のせいで湖や川の魚が死に、植物の成長が阻害され、建物すら損傷を受ける、と心配する人たちがいる。

continued
▼

Day 32 環境 自然科学300語 3

311 nuclear reactor
/njúːkliər/ /riǽktər/

原子炉
関 nuclear 核の、原子核の、原子力（利用）の　関 nuclear bomb 核爆弾

312 overgraze
/òuvərgréiz/

動〈牧草地などの〉**草を家畜に食い荒らさせる**、……に過放牧する

313 ultraviolet
/ʌ̀ltrəváiəlit/

形 **紫外線の**、紫外の、紫外線を生ずる［用いる］
関 ultraviolet rays 紫外線

314 ozone
/óuzoun/

名 **オゾン**
●酸素の同素体、微青色で、特異臭をもつ気体。酸化力が強く、殺菌・消毒、空気の浄化に利用される
関 ozone layer (=ozonosphere) オゾン層（大気圏中のオゾン濃度の高い層。生物に有害な太陽からの紫外線を吸収するなど、重要な役割を果たしている）

315 pollutants
/pəlúːtənts/

名 **汚染物**、汚染（物）質
動 pollute 汚す、汚染する　名 pollution 汚染、環境破壊、公害

316 irrigate
/írəgèit/

動〈土地に〉**水を注ぐ［引く］**、灌がいする

317 incineration
/insìnəréiʃən/

名〈ごみ・死体などの〉**焼却**
動 incinerate 焼却する　名 incinerator〈ごみなどの〉焼却炉

318 refill
/riːfíl/

動 **再び満たす**、補充する　名 詰め換え［補充］用の品物

319 toxic
/táksik/

形 **有毒な**、毒（性）の、中毒（性）の
名 tóxicant 毒物　名 toxicátion 中毒　名 tóxin 毒素、トキシン

320 sewage
/súːidʒ/

名 **下水汚物**、下水、汚水
関 sewage disposal 下水［汚水］処理　関 sewage works 下水処理場［施設］

continued
▼

A <u>nuclear reactor</u> is a container in which a controlled chain reaction releases energy. This energy can be used to produce electricity.	原子炉は核分裂連鎖反応を制御し、エネルギーを放出する装置である。このエネルギーは発電のために利用できる。
Animals are moved about to avoid <u>overgrazing</u>.	草を食い荒らさないように、動物の移動を行う。
<u>Ultraviolet</u> light can destroy simple life forms such as bacteria and harm other organisms.	紫外線は細菌などの単純な生命体を殺し、他の生物にも害を与える。
<u>Ozone</u> screens out harmful ultraviolet rays.	オゾンは有害な紫外線を締め出す。
<u>Pollutants</u> endanger the natural balance of life on Earth because they may be poisonous or cause disease.	汚染物質は有毒だったり病気を引き起こしたりするので、地球上の自然な生命のバランスを危うくする。
Water is used to <u>irrigate</u> fields of crops and maintain animals.	水は農耕地を灌がいし、動物を飼育するために使用される。
<u>Incineration</u> is the burning of waste at high temperatures in furnaces.	焼却とは高熱の炉の中で廃棄物を焼くことである。
Bottles are sometimes collected to be cleaned and <u>refilled</u>.	ビンは洗浄して再び補充するために時々収集される。
In some areas, factories dump industrial wastes into nearby bodies of water. These wastes include chemicals that are often poisonous or <u>toxic</u> to wildlife.	ある地域では、工場が廃棄物を付近の水域に流し込んでいる。これらの廃棄物には野生動物にとってしばしば有毒な化学物質が含まれている。
As the population increases, disposal of <u>sewage</u> is becoming more of a problem.	人口が増えるにつれ、下水汚物を処理することがますます大きな問題となっている。

continued
▼

復習テスト 環境

解答は P.239

1 1〜6の単語の定義を a〜f から選びなさい。

1. ore
2. nonrenewable resource
3. renewable resource
4. crude oil
5. refining
6. lubricant

---

a. one that will never again be available once used
b. petroleum pumped from wells that have been drilled in oil fields
c. a substance, especially a type of oil, used for making parts in a machine move easily and smoothly without rubbing or sticking
d. a process which separates crude oil into groups of hydrocarbons that can make gasoline, kerosene, and other petroleum products
e. a metal-bearing mineral that is mined at a profit
f. one that will never run out because it is continuously being replaced

2 選択肢 a、b のうち正しい語を選んで文を完成させなさい。

1. (a. Petroleum   b. Lubricant) is used as an energy source for transportation, heating, and electricity.

2. Air forms a shield against damaging (a. ozone   b. ultraviolet) rays from the sun.

3. (a. Ultraviolet rays   b. Pollutants) are chemical gases, dust and waste particles, and smoke.

4. Human waste, garbage, and drainage water are examples of (a. sewage   b. toxic).

5. Fish make up 90% of the ocean's (a. fossils   b. harvest).

6. (a. Carbon dioxide   b. Ozone) stops harmful ultraviolet rays from entering the atmosphere.

7. Air pollution is caused by (a. dust   b. pollutants).

8. The sulfur dioxide from burning coal can combine with water in the atmosphere to produce (a. nonrenewable resources   b. acid rain).

9. (a. Natural resources   b. Renewable resources) are things taken from the Earth such as water, food, timber and minerals.

10. Petroleum and (a. coal   b. metals) are called fossil fuels, since they were formed from plants and animals that died a long time ago.

Day 33

自然科学300語 生物 1

CD-A33

□ 321
cell
/sél/

名 細胞

□ 322
organ
/ɔ́:rgən/

名 器官、臓器
関 internal organs 内臓

□ 323
kingdom
/kíŋdəm/

名 〈分類上の〉界
●生物を分類する最上位の階級

□ 324
species
/spí:ʃi:z/

名 種（しゅ）
関 *The Origin of Species* 『種の起源』（C. Darwin の著書）

□ 325
virus
/váiərəs/

名 ウイルス、〈俗に〉病原体
関 viral disease ウイルス性疾患

□ 326
bacteria
/bæktíəriə/

名 細菌、バクテリア

□ 327
asexual
/eisékʃuəl/

形 無性の、無性生殖による、性別［性器］のない
関 asexual reproduction 無性生殖

□ 328
habitat
/hǽbitæt/

名 〈特に動植物の〉生息地、生育地、すみか、〈生物を取り巻く〉環境、居住環境
関 habitat group 生態類（生息環境を同じくする動物、植物）

□ 329
population
/pàpjuléiʃən/

名 〈ある地域内の〉個体群、個体数

□ 330
digestive
/daidʒéstiv, di-/

形 消化の、消化を助ける　**名 消化剤［薬］**
関 digestive organs [juice] 消化器［液］　**名 digestion 消化（作用［機能］）**

continued
▼

All living things are made of cells.	すべての生物は細胞からできている。
Your heart, your eyes, your lungs, and your stomach are all organs.	心臓、目、肺、胃はすべて器官である。
Scientists classify living things into five major groups or kingdoms. These are plants, animals, protists, monerans, and fungi.	科学者は生物を大きく5つのグループ、すなわち界に分類する。これは植物界、動物界、原生生物界、モネラ界、菌界である。
The shepherd, the wolf, and the coyote are in the same genus but are different species.	牧羊犬、狼、コヨーテは同じ属に含まれるが、種は異なる。
Viruses can remain inactive for years outside or inside a cell. They may become active only when the cell is under stress or in poor condition.	ウイルスは細胞の内外で何年も活動しないでいることがある。細胞が圧力を受けるかまたは細胞の状態が悪いときにだけ、ウイルスの動きが活発となる。
Since bacteria do not contain chlorophyll, most of them cannot make their own food.	細菌は葉緑素を含まないので、ほとんどが自ら養分を作ることができない。
Reproduction involving only one parent is called asexual reproduction.	片親のみから成る生殖を無性生殖という。
A habitat must meet all the needs of an organism. It must provide the organism with food and protection.	生息地は生物にとって必要なものすべてを満たしている必要がある。それは生物に食料と保護を与えるものでなければならない。
A group of the same kind of organisms living together in the same habitat is a population.	同じ生息地に一緒に住む同じ種族の生物のグループは個体群である。
Fungi feed by releasing digestive juices into their surroundings to break it down. Then they reabsorb it.	菌類は消化液を周囲にまき散らし、物質を分解し養分にする。そしてまたそれを吸収する。

continued
▼

Day 34

□ 331 invertebrate
/invə́ːrtəbrət/

名 無脊髄動物
形 脊髄のない、背骨のない、無脊髄動物（の）

□ 332 reptile
/réptil/

名 爬虫類の動物、〈広く〉両生類の動物
名 Reptilia 爬虫類（分類名）　形名 reptilian 爬虫類の（ような）。爬虫類の動物

□ 333 mammal
/mǽməl/

名 哺乳動物
名 Mammalia /məméiliə/ 哺乳類（分類名）
形名 mammalian /məméiliən/ 哺乳類の（動物）

□ 334 herbivore
/ə́ːrbəvɔ̀ːr/

名 草食動物
名 herbivora 草食動物（集合的）　形 herbivorous 草食性の

□ 335 carnivore
/káːrnəvɔ̀ːr/

名 肉食動物、食虫植物
名 carnivora 肉食動物（集合的）　形 carnivorous〈動物が〉肉食性の。食肉動物。〈植物が〉食虫の、食虫植物の

□ 336 omnivore
/ámnivɔ̀ːr/

名 雑食（性）動物
名 omnivora 雑食動物　形 omnivorous 雑食性の

□ 337 predator
/prédətər/

名 捕食者

□ 338 prey
/préi/

名 被食者、餌動物

□ 339 food chain
/fúːd/ /tʃéin/

食物連鎖
● A は B に、B は C にというように一般に小なるものはより大なるものに順次食われるという生物食性の関連
関 food cycle 食物環（=food web）

□ 340 camouflage
/kǽməflɑ̀ːʒ/

名 ごまかし

continued
▼

Invertebrates, fish, and plants were the dominant life forms during the Paleozoic Era.	無脊髄動物、魚類、植物は古生代に繁栄した生物だった。
Reptiles were the dominant life forms during the Mesozoic Era.	爬虫類は中生代に繁栄した生物だった。
Mammals have been the dominant life forms during the Cenozoic Era.	哺乳類は新生代に繁栄を続けている。
Rabbits are herbivores.	ウサギは草食動物である。
Lions are carnivores.	ライオンは肉食動物である。
An animal that eats both plants and animals is an omnivore.	植物と動物を両方食べる動物は雑食動物である。
Predator-prey relationships help to keep the size of populations in balance with their environment.	捕食者と被食者の関係は、個体数を環境と見合った規模に調整するのを助ける。
The frog is the predator of the grasshopper but the prey of the snake.	バッタの捕食者であるカエルは蛇の被食者である。
A food chain shows how energy is passed from one organism to another.	食物連鎖はある生物から別の生物へとエネルギーがどのように伝わるかを示す。
Organisms protect themselves by using devices such as camouflage, mimicry, and certain diversionary behavior.	生物はごまかし、擬態、特定の牽制のための行動をとって身を守る。

continued
▼

Day 35 生物 3 — 自然科学300語

□ 341 botanist
/bátənist/

名 植物学者
名 bótany 植物学　形 botánical 植物の、植物学(上)の、植物性の(薬品)　熟 botanical garden 植物園

□ 342 fertilization
/fə̀ːrtəlizéiʃən, -laiz-/

名 受精
動 fértilize 受精させる

□ 343 conifer
/kóunəfər/

名 針葉樹、球果植物
形 coníferous 針葉樹の

□ 344 annual
/ǽnjuəl/

名 一年生植物、一年草
● 春に種子から発芽して開花、結実し、その年に枯れる植物

□ 345 biennial
/baiéniəl/

名 二年生植物、二年草
● 秋に発芽し、冬を越して成長、開花、結実して1年未満で枯死する草本。越年草

□ 346 perennial
/pəréniəl/

名 多年生植物、多年草
● 地上部が枯れても地下部が残り、毎年新しく芽を出して成長する草本。葉が残るものもある

□ 347 phototropism
/foutátrəpìzm/

名 光屈性、屈光性
● 植物の屈性のひとつ。茎・葉・根などが、光の刺激に対して一定の方向に曲がる性質。一般に、葉・茎は光に向かい(向日性)、根はその逆(背日性)を示す

□ 348 photosynthesis
/fòutəsínθisis/

名 光合成
● 緑色植物が光エネルギーを吸収して、二酸化炭素と水から有機物を合成する反応。光を吸収する明反応と炭水化物を作る暗反応から成る。酸素を放出し、地球の環境を支える。炭酸同化

□ 349 chlorophyll
/klɔ́ːrəfil/

名 葉緑素、クロロフィル
● 植物色素の一種。光合成を行う中心的な物質。多くの植物細胞では、葉緑体の中に含まれる

□ 350 ecology
/ikálədʒi/

名 生態学
● 生物と環境との関係を研究する学問

continued
▼

Botanists look at plant structure to find out what plants have in common.	植物学者は植物の構造を観察し、植物が共有するものを発見する。
When a sperm cell joins with an egg cell, fertilization occurs.	精細胞が卵細胞と結合するとき、受精が起こる。
Although conifers usually grow in areas where it is cold, some can be found in warm regions.	一般に針葉樹は寒い地方で育つが、暖かな地域で見受けられるものもある。
Annuals grow from seed, bloom, produce seeds, and die all in one growing season.	一年生植物は一度の栽培期に、種子から発芽して開花し、結実し、枯死する。
Biennials grow for two seasons. In the first season, they grow roots, stems, and leaves. In the second season, they flower and produce seeds.	二年生植物は2期にわたって成長する。1期めには根、茎、葉が生える。2期めには開花し、結実する。
Perennials grow year after year.	多年生植物は毎年、成長する。
The leaves and stems of a plant grow toward sunlight. This response is called phototropism.	植物の葉と茎は日光に向かって成長する。この反応を光屈性という。
Plants use carbon dioxide during photosynthesis.	植物は光合成を行うとき、二酸化炭素を使う。
Chlorophyll inside the chloroplasts uses the Sun's energy to make food.	葉緑体内部の葉緑素は、太陽エネルギーを利用して養分を生成する。
The word ecology comes from two Greek words meaning "the study of homes."	生態学という言葉は、「住居研究」を意味する2語のギリシャ語に由来する。

continued
▼

復習テスト　生物

1　1〜10の単語の定義を a〜j の中から選びなさい。

1. habitat
2. herbivores
3. botanists
4. omnivores
5. prey
6. carnivores
7. perennials
8. camouflage
9. predators
10. population

---

a. animals that feed on other animals
b. place where an organism lives
c. the method of blending into the surroundings to protect oneself from enemy
d. animals that eat other animals; meat eaters
e. scientists who study plants
f. a group of organisms living together in the same habitat
g. an animal that is hunted for food
h. plants that grow year after year
i. animals that feed on plants
j. animals that eat both plants and animals

2 選択肢 a、b のうち正しい語を選んで文を完成させなさい。

1. Many diseases of animals and plants are caused by (a. species b. viruses).

2. Cheese and yogurt are partly composed of (a. bacterial b. asexual) cells.

3. Since (a. carnivores b. conifers) have narrow leaves that lose little water, they are also able to grow in dry areas.

4. Some flowers and vegetables have to be planted each year. These plants are called (a. biennials b. annuals).

5. The process by which green plants use the energy from sunlight to make food is called (a. photosynthesis b. phototropism).

6. The study of how living things interact with each other and with their non-living environment is called (a. biology b. ecology).

7. A (a. virus b. prey) has no cell parts and does not grow or move like a living thing.

8. Members of the same (a. predators b. species) have many more structural characteristics in common than members of the same kingdom.

9. Reproduction involving only one parent is called (a. sexual b. asexual) reproduction.

10. All the consumers in a (a. kingdom b. food chain) depend on the other organisms for their food.

Day 36

動物 1 — 自然科学 300 語

□ 351 metamorphosis
/mètəmɔ́ːrfəsis/

名 変態
- 動物が卵からかえって成体になるまでにいろいろな形態をとること。カエルの場合のオタマジャクシ（tadpole）など

□ 352 larva
/láːrvə/

名 幼虫
- 複数形は larvae /láːrviː/
- 関 pupa さなぎ

□ 353 caterpillar
/kǽtərpìlər/

名 イモムシ、毛虫（チョウ・ガの幼虫）

□ 354 cocoon
/kəkúːn/

名 繭（まゆ）

□ 355 pollinator
/pálənèitər/

名 受粉媒介者、授粉者（昆虫など）
名 pollination 授粉［受粉］（作用）　（注）pollin-, pollini-「花粉（pollen）」の意

□ 356 nutrient
/njúːtriənt/

名 栄養素、栄養分、栄養になるもの
名 nutrition 栄養物

□ 357 estuary
/éstʃuèri/

名 広い河口、河口域、入り江
形 estuarine 河口（域）の

□ 358 bioluminescent
/bàioulumənésənt/

形 生物が発光する
名 bioluminescence〈ホタル・菌類・深海魚などの〉生物発光［ルミネセンス］

□ 359 cold-blooded
/kóuldbládid/

形 冷血の

□ 360 amphibian
/æmfíbiən/

名 両生類、両生動［植］物
形 両生類の、水陸両生の

continued

All insects undergo incomplete or complete metamorphosis in their development from eggs to adults.	すべての昆虫は卵から成体へと成長する中で、不完全または完全変態を経験する。
Ninety percent of all insects go through complete metamorphosis. They develop in four stages: (1) the egg, (2) the larva, (3) the pupa, and (4) the adult.	全昆虫の90％は完全変態を経験する。これらの成長は、(1) 卵、(2) 幼虫、(3) さなぎ、(4) 成体と4期に分かれる。
The larvae of butterflies and moths are called caterpillars. The larvae of flies are called maggots. Beetle larvae are called grubs.	チョウやガの幼虫をイモ虫という。蝿の幼虫をウジ虫という。カブト虫の幼虫を地虫という。
Larvae prepare for the pupa stage by spinning a cocoon or other covering.	幼虫は繭やその他の覆いを作ってさなぎ期に備える。
Insects are important pollinators of plants and are food sources for other animals.	昆虫は植物の重要な受粉媒介者であり、他の動物の食料源である。
Inanimate factors that affect living things in lakes and ponds are temperature, amount of oxygen, sunlight, minerals, and nutrients.	湖や池の生物に影響を与える非生物的要因に、温度、酸素の量、日光、無機物、栄養素がある。
Marshes, mudflats, bays, and swamps are estuaries. Many animals, such as oysters, clams, lobsters, shrimps, and crabs spend all or part of their lives in estuaries.	河口域には沼地、干潟、湾、湿地がある。カキ、二枚貝、ロブスター、エビ、カニなど多くの動物が死ぬまで、または一時期を河口域で過ごす。
The deep-ocean ecosystem includes fish that glow in the dark. Animals that glow, or produce their own light, are bioluminescent.	深海の生態系には、闇の中で発光する魚も含まれる。動物が発光、つまり自ら光を発するのは生物発光という現象である。
If you've had a cold-blooded pet like a fish, a frog, or a turtle, you might know that sudden temperature changes can be deadly to them.	魚やカエルやカメのような冷血動物のペットを飼ったことがあるなら、突然の温度変化が彼らにとって命取りとなることを知っているだろう。
Frogs and toads are amphibians. Amphibians have one life with two stages. During the first stage of their life, they live in water. During the second stage, they live on land.	カエル、ヒキガエルは両生類である。両生類の生存期間は2期に分けられる。第1期は水中で、第2期は陸上で過ごす。

continued

Day 37 動物 2 — 自然科学300語

CD-A37

□ 361 **hibernation** /hàibənéiʃən/
名 **冬眠**
動 hibernate 冬眠する（反 estivate /éstəvèit/ 夏眠する）

□ 362 **lizard** /lízərd/
名 **トカゲ**

□ 363 **molting** /móultiŋ/
名 **脱皮**
動 molt 脱皮する、抜け［生え］変わる

□ 364 **warm-blooded** /wɔ́:rmblʌ́did/
形 **温血の**、定温の（36℃〜42℃）

□ 365 **incubation** /ìnkjubéiʃən/
名 **孵化**
動 incubate 卵を抱く、かえす、卵がかえる　関 artificial incubation 人工孵化

□ 366 **circulatory system** /sə́:rkjulətɔ̀:ri/ /sístəm/
循環系
・血液やリンパ液を流す動物体内の管系

□ 367 **digestive system** /daidʒéstiv, di-/ /sístəm/
消化（器）系（口・胃・腸など）

□ 368 **respiratory system** /réspərətɔ̀:ri/ /sístəm/
呼吸（器）系
関 respiration 呼吸　関 respire 呼吸する、息をつく

□ 369 **skeletal system** /skélətl/ /sístəm/
骨格組織
関 skeleton 骨格

□ 370 **nervous system** /nə́:rvəs/ /sístəm/
神経系
関 nervous 神経の、神経組織から成る

continued

Amphibians go through the process called hibernation during cold weather.	両生類は寒い間、冬眠という過程を経験する。
Snakes, lizards, turtles, crocodiles, and alligators are reptiles and are all cold-blooded vertebrates.	ヘビ、トカゲ、亀、クロコダイルやアリゲータなどのワニは爬虫類で、すべて冷血脊椎動物である。
Molting is part of the maturation process of snakes. When snakes molt, their thin outer skins loosen. Then the snakes hook a piece of the loose skin to a sharp object and crawl out of it.	脱皮はヘビの成長過程の一部である。ヘビが脱皮するとき、まず薄い外皮が緩くなる。次にヘビは緩くなった皮の一部を鋭い物に引っ掛け、そこから抜け出る。
Unlike cold-blooded animals, the bodies of warm-blooded animals stay at about the same temperature no matter what the temperature is in their environment.	冷血動物と違って、温血動物は周囲の温度が何度であれ、ほぼ一定の体温を維持する。
When the incubation period is over, baby birds crack open the shells of their eggs and hatch.	卵をかえす時期が過ぎると、雛は卵の殻を破って孵化する。
The circulatory system of mammals includes the heart and the blood vessels.	哺乳類の循環系には心臓と血管がある。
Mammals have different digestive systems depending on the food they eat. Mammals that eat meat have simple stomachs and short intestines. Mammals that eat plants have complex stomachs and long intestines.	哺乳類の消化系は何を食べるかによって異なる。肉を食べる哺乳類の胃は単純で、腸は短い。植物を食べる哺乳類の胃は複雑で、腸は長い。
The organs of the respiratory system enable mammals to breathe.	呼吸系の器官によって、哺乳類は呼吸することができる。
The skeletal system of mammals is a framework for the entire body. The bones of the skeleton support the body and protect the soft organs inside.	哺乳類の骨格組織は体全体の枠組みである。骨は体を支え、軟らかな内部器官を保護する。
Of all the body systems of mammals, the nervous system is the most complex. Mammals have large brains and very sharp senses.	哺乳類の体の全組織のうち、最も複雑なのは神経系である。哺乳類は大きな脳と非常に鋭い感覚を有する。

continued
▼

Day 38 自然科学300語 動物 3

□ 371 pouched
/páutʃt/

形 **袋のある**、袋状の
関 pouched animal 有袋動物 [類]　名 pouch 〈有袋類などの〉嚢、袋

□ 372 primates
/práimeits/

名 **霊長類**
名 primatólogy 霊長類学　名 primate 霊長類の動物

□ 373 stimulus
/stímjuləs/

名 **刺激**、刺激（物）
• 複数形は stimuli /stímjulài/
動 stimulate 刺激する、刺激となる　名 stimulátion 刺激　形 stímulative 刺激的な

□ 374 response
/rispáns/

名 〈刺激に対する〉**反応**

□ 375 color-blind
/kʌ́lərblàind/

形 **色覚異常の**

□ 376 reflex
/ríːfleks/

名 **反射作用**、反射運動
名 refléction 反射（作用）　形 refléctive 反射的な、反射する

□ 377 instinct
/ínstiŋkt/

名 **本能**、生来の傾向
形 instínctive 本能的な

□ 378 conditioning
/kəndíʃəniŋ/

名 **条件づけ**
• 条件反応・条件反射を形成すること。また、その形成過程

□ 379 extinct
/ikstíŋkt/

形 **絶滅した**
名 extínction 死滅、絶滅　反 extant 現存の、実在の

□ 380 endangered
/indéindʒərd/

形 〈種などが〉**絶滅の危機にひんした**

continued

Mammals are classified by the way in which their young develop before birth: egg-laying, pouched, or placental.	哺乳類は子の発育の仕方により、卵生、有袋、胎生に分類される。
Of all the many orders of mammals, the primates are the most highly developed.	哺乳類にはたくさんの種類があるが、霊長類が最も高度に発達している。
Animals receive stimuli from their environment through their senses. Stimuli can be changes in temperature, the smell of food, darkness, or brightness.	動物は感覚器官を通して、環境から刺激を受ける。温度、食物の匂い、暗さまたは明るさなどの変化は刺激になる。
Examples of animal responses to danger are curling up in a ball, and changing colors to blend into the surroundings. Some animals respond to danger by playing dead.	危険に対する動物の反応には、体を丸めたり色を変えて周囲に溶け込むなどの例がある。死んだふりをする動物もいる。
Bulls are color-blind. They see the world in shades of black, gray, and white.	雄牛は色覚異常である。雄牛は黒と灰色と白の色合いで世界を見ている。
All animals have reflexes. The fur on a cat's back stands on end when the cat is frightened. An octopus changes color when it senses danger.	動物はすべて反射作用をもっている。ネコは驚くと背中の毛を逆立たせる。タコは危険を感じると色を変える。
Spiders spin webs, but they do not have to learn to make webs. Spinning a web is an innate behavior pattern — an instinct.	クモは巣をはる。しかしクモは巣をはることを学習する必要はない。巣をはることは先天的な行動であって、本能である。
Animals learn new behavior through conditioning and through trial and error.	動物は条件付けと試行錯誤により、新しい行動を学習する。
Extinct animals that once lived in North America include the California grizzly bear, the Carolina parakeet, and the Labrador duck.	かつて北アメリカに住んでいたが絶滅した動物に、カリフォルニア灰色グマ、カロライナインコ、カササギガモがいる。
The California condor, the Bengal tiger, and the mountain gorilla are examples of endangered species. Without special protection, an endangered species will become extinct.	カリフォルニアコンドル、ベンガルトラ、マウンテンゴリラは絶滅の危機にひんした種の例である。絶滅の危機にひんした種は、特別の保護がなければ、いずれ絶滅してしまうだろう。

continued
▼

復習テスト　動物

1　1～10の単語の定義を a～j から選びなさい。

1. digestive system
2. estuary
3. circulatory system
4. response
5. respiratory system
6. skeletal system
7. color-blind
8. nervous system
9. stimulus
10. extinct

---

a. the system that enables mammals to breathe
b. the system that supports and protects the body's organs
c. unable to see the differences between colors
d. something that causes an animal to react
e. the word that describes a species of animal or plant that no longer exists
f. the system that controls body activities
g. an area in which fresh water and saltwater mix
h. the system that moves blood through the body
i. an animal's reaction to a stimulus
j. the system that breaks down food

2 選択肢 a、b のうち正しい語を選んで文を完成させなさい。

1. Most insects go through a series of changes in body size and shape as they develop from egg to adult. This series of changes, or growth stages, is called (a. metamorphosis   b. hibernation).

2. Two forms of innate behavior are reflexes and instincts. (a. Reflexes   b. Instincts) are simple, automatic actions. (a. Reflexes   b. Instincts) are complex patterns of behavior that involve a series of steps.

3. Areas near shorelines where fresh water and saltwater mix are called (a. rivers   b. estuaries).

4. Fish, amphibians, and reptiles are (a. warm-blooded   b. cold-blooded). This means that their body temperatures change with the temperatures of their surroundings.

5. In (a. conditioning   b. trial and error), an animal connects a stimulus with a response. (a. Conditioning   b. Trial and error) involves practicing a behavior over and over again.

6. Amphibians protect themselves from extreme cold or heat by resting. In cold weather, they bury themselves in muddy soil or in pond bottoms. This winter rest is called (a. fertilization   b. hibernation).

7. Several times a year, snakes shed their worn outer skin. This is called (a. molting   b. instinct).

8. Vertebrates that keep a high and fairly consistent body temperature are (a. cold-blooded   b. warm-blooded).

9. Because birds are warm-blooded, a baby bird developing in an egg must be kept warm. The nesting mother bird warms or (a. incubates   b. molts) the eggs with her body heat.

10. Monkeys, apes, and humans are (a. reptiles   b. primates). All have large brains, fingers capable of grasping, and eyes that can focus on one spot.

Day 39 生理学 自然科学300語 ①

CD-A39

□ 381
umbilical cord
/ʌmbílikəl/ /kɔ́:rd/

へその緒

□ 382
fetus
/fí:təs/

名 胎児（哺乳動物、特にヒトの妊娠3カ月以後）
関 embryo /émbriòu/ 〈妊娠8週末までの〉胎児、胎芽、胚

□ 383
labor
/léibər/

名 分娩、出産、陣痛、陣痛時間

□ 384
uterus
/jú:tərəs/

名 子宮
形 uterine /jú:tərin/ 子宮の

□ 385
navel
/néivəl/

名 へそ
関 navel string=umbilical cord へその緒　関【口語】belly button へそ

□ 386
infancy
/ínfənsi/

名 幼年期、幼少、幼時、幼児（=ínfants）
名 infant 幼児（通例歩行前の乳児を指すが、7歳未満の小児を指すことも多い）

□ 387
ultrasound
/ʌ́ltrəsàund/

名 超音波、超可聴音
● 周波数が可聴周波領域を超える約2万 hertz 以上の音波
名形 ultrasónic 超音波（の）

□ 388
baby tooth
/béibi/ /tú:θ/

乳歯 (=milk tooth)
関 permanent tooth 永久歯

□ 389
eyesight
/áisàit/

名 視力、視覚

□ 390
diet
/dáiət/

名 日常の飲食物、〈治療・体重調節のための〉規定食、食事療法　形 食事の、規定食［治療食］の
関 dietary fiber 食物繊維

continued
▼

The umbilical cord contains blood vessels that carry food and oxygen from the placenta to the embryo.	へその緒には胎盤から胎芽へ養分と酸素を運ぶ血管が含まれる。
By the end of its third month, an embryo looks human and is called a fetus. The fetus is 9cm long and weighs about 15g (the weight of a post card).	３カ月後には胎芽は人間らしく見え、この時期から胎児という。胎児は身長９cm、体重 15g（葉書の重さ）である。
Labor widens the opening of the uterus. This opening expands to about 10cm so the baby can pass out of the uterus.	分娩は子宮口を広げる。子宮口は赤ん坊が子宮から出てこられるように、10cm程度に広がる。
During labor, the baby is pushed out of the uterus and through the birth canal.	分娩中、赤ん坊は子宮から産道を通って外に押し出される。
The small piece of the umbilical cord remaining on the baby will heal and leave a scar — the belly button, or navel.	赤ん坊の小さく残ったへその緒は傷が癒え、跡を残す。それがへそである。
After birth, the stages of life include infancy, childhood, adolescence, adulthood, and older adulthood.	誕生後の人生は幼年期、少年期、青年期、成人期、壮年期と続く。
When ultrasound images show abnormal development, it is sometimes possible to perform surgery while the fetus is still growing in the uterus.	超音波画像が異常な発達を示す場合は、胎児が子宮内で成長している間に手術をすることも時には可能である。
All of the baby teeth are lost and replaced by permanent teeth.	乳歯はすべて抜けて、永久歯にはえ代わる。
As people get older, their hearing and eyesight worsen somewhat.	年をとると、聴力と視力はある程度落ちる。
A healthy diet is especially important during the first three months of embryo/fetus development.	胎芽または胎児が成長する最初の３カ月間は、健康な食事をとることが特に大切である。

continued
▼

Day 40

生理学 2 — 自然科学300語

□ 391 trait
/tréit/
名 特性、特色、特徴

□ 392 heredity
/hərédəti/
名 遺伝
形 hereditary /herédətèri/ 遺伝（性）の、遺伝的な

□ 393 genetics
/dʒənétiks/
名 遺伝学
形 genetic 遺伝学的な、遺伝子の［による］

□ 394 reproductive organs
/rìːprədʌ́ktiv/ /ɔ́ːrɡənz/
生殖器
関 reprodúce 生殖する、繁殖する［させる］

□ 395 stamen
/stéimən/
名 おしべ
反 pistil /pístl/ めしべ

□ 396 hybrid
/háibrid/
形 雑種の 名 雑種

□ 397 gene
/dʒíːn/
名 遺伝子

□ 398 phenotype
/fíːnətàip/
名 表現型
● 遺伝子（群）によって発現された形質の型（生物が示す外面的な形態または内面的な生理的形態）
関 genotype /dʒénətaip/ 遺伝子型（生物個体の特性を決める遺伝子構成のこと。表に現れない劣性（recéssive）遺伝子を含めて指すため個体に現れる形質とまったく一致するとは限らない）

□ 399 hemophilia
/hìːməfíliə/
名 血友病
● 血液凝固因子の一部が欠落して起こる遺伝性の出血性疾患。小さな傷でも止血が困難で、多くは伴性劣性遺伝のため男性だけに現れる
名形 hemophiliac 血友病（患）者（=bleeder）。血友病の

□ 400 genetic engineering
/dʒənétik/ /èndʒiníəriŋ/
遺伝子工学
● 特定の遺伝子の合成・切断・活性化などの操作を行い、細胞に新しい働きをさせるための実験方法およびその応用などを研究する学問

continued

Traits are characteristics, such as leaf shape, eye color, and stripes, that are passed from parent to offspring.	特性とは葉の形、目の色、縞など親から子へと受け継がれる特徴である。
Some traits, such as height and weight, are controlled by both heredity and environment.	身長や体重といった特性は遺伝と環境に左右される。
The father of genetics, Gregor Mendel, was a monk and a farmer's son. He discovered heredity by testing large numbers of plants.	遺伝学の父、グレゴール・メンデルは修道士であり、農家の息子だった。彼は数多くの植物を調査し遺伝を発見した。
The reproductive organs of a pea plant are arranged so that the plant can pollinate itself.	エンドウの生殖器は自家受精できるようにできている。
When pollen from the male stamen is transferred to the female pistil, a long pollen tube carrying the male cell forms. When the pollen tube extends through the pistil, a male cell fertilizes an egg cell to make a seed.	花粉がおしべからめしべに移ると、精細胞を運ぶ長い花粉管が形成される。花粉管がめしべに届くと、精細胞は卵細胞と受精し種子をつくる。
Mendel crossed thousands of pure and hybrid plants and kept careful records of his findings.	メンデルは純粋種と雑種を何千回となく交配し、丹念にその結果を記録した。
Genes contain all the information about the traits that an organism inherits from its parents.	遺伝子は生物が両親から受け継ぐ特性に関するあらゆる情報を含む。
An organism's appearance due to inherited traits is its phenotype.	生物の表現型とは、遺伝的な特性の発現である。
Hemophilia, color blindness, and white-eye in fruit flies are all results of sex-linked genes.	血友病、色覚異常、白色の眼をしたミバエはすべて、伴性遺伝子の結果である。
One of the most exciting uses of genetic engineering is the production of lifesaving proteins. In 1979 the protein insulin was produced by combining bacterial DNA with the DNA (gene) for insulin.	遺伝子工学の最も素晴らしい活用法のひとつに、人命を救うタンパク質の生成がある。1979年、細菌のDNAにインシュリンのDNA（遺伝子）を組み込んでタンパク質のインシュリンを生産した。

continued
▼

Day 41

CD-B1

生理学 — 自然科学300語 ③

□ 401 theory of natural selection
/θíːəri/ /əv/ /nǽtʃərəl/ /silékʃən/

自然選択[淘汰]
- Darwinism の用語で適者生存の過程。自然界における生存競争の結果、適者は生存繁栄し、不適者は滅びること
- 関 the survival of the fittest 適者生存

□ 402 mutation
/mjuːtéiʃən/

名 突然変異、突然変異体
- オランダの植物学者、de Vries が初めてこの義で用いた
- 形名 mutant 突然変異の[による]。突然変異体、変種 関 gene mutation 遺伝子突然変異

□ 403 marsupial
/mɑːrsúːpiəl/

名 有袋類、有袋動物（カンガルーなど）
- 形 有袋類の

□ 404 paleontologist
/pèiliəntάlədʒst/

名 古生物学者
- 名 paleontólogy 古生物学

□ 405 esophagus
/isάfəgəs/

名 食道

□ 406 pancreas
/pǽnkriəs/

名 膵臓（すいぞう）
- 関 pancreátic juice 膵液　名 pancreatitis 膵炎

□ 407 intestine
/intéstin/

名 腸
- 関 the large [small] intestine 大[小]腸

□ 408 antibody
/ǽntibὰdi/

名 〈血清中の〉抗体（=immune body：免疫体）

□ 409 metabolism
/mətǽbəlìzm/

名 新陳代謝
- 生物体が常に新しい栄養物質を取り入れ、消化した古い物質を排泄すること

□ 410 white blood cell
/hwáit/ /blʌ́d/ /sél/

白血球（=leukocyte /lúːkəsàit/）
- 血球成分の一種。体外から侵入した細菌を殺して感染防御にあたるなど、生体内でさまざまな機能を果たす
- 関 red blood cell 赤血球（血球の有形成分のひとつ。脊椎動物などにみられる。赤色色素のヘモグロビンを含み、酸素や二酸化炭素を連搬する）

continued

Darwin's **theory of natural selection** states that those organisms with traits that enable them to adapt to their environment survive and reproduce.	ダーウィンの自然淘汰の原理によれば、環境に適応できる特性を持った生物が生き残り、繁殖する。
Some **mutations** make organisms better adapted to their environment.	突然変異により、生物は環境によりよく適応するようになる。
There are 117 different species of **marsupials** in Australia.	オーストラリアには117種の有袋動物がいる。
The clues that **paleontologists** look for are bits of evidence left by plants and animals of long ago.	古生物学者が探究する手がかりは、大昔の植物や動物が残したわずかな証拠である。
Once food is well chewed and mixed with saliva, the tongue moves the food back into the throat. When one swallows, the food enters the **esophagus**.	食物がよくかみ砕かれて唾液と混ざり合うと、舌は食物を咽喉の奥へと運ぶ。食物は飲み込まれると、食道に入る。
The **pancreas** releases a "juice" containing several enzymes into the small intestine.	膵臓はさまざまな酵素を含む「液」を小腸に放出する。
Foods such as lettuce, celery, fruits, and grains contain a complex carbohydrate called fiber. This carbohydrate cannot be digested. Fiber passes into the large **intestine**.	レタス、セロリ、果物、穀類などの食物は繊維という複合体の炭水化物を含む。この炭水化物は消化されない。繊維は大腸へと入る。
Antibodies help fight disease-causing bacteria and viruses.	抗体は病気の原因となる細菌やウィルスと戦うことを助けるものである。
Through **metabolism**, the body produces many useful products, as well as waste products.	新陳代謝を通して、体は排泄物と同様、多くの有用物を生産する。
White blood cells are large, colorless cells that attack and destroy disease-causing organisms. Red blood cells are tiny, disk-shaped cells that carry oxygen to all the cells of the body.	白血球は大きく無色の細胞で、病気の原因となる生物を襲い破壊する。赤血球は小さく平らな細胞で、体のすべての細胞に酸素を運ぶ。

continued
▼

復習テスト　生理学

1 1〜10の単語の定義をa〜jから選びなさい。

1. umbilical cord
2. genetics
3. fetus
4. esophagus
5. heredity
6. genotype
7. phenotype
8. hemophilia
9. genetic engineering
10. paleontologist

> a. a ropelike structure that connects the embryo with the placenta
> b. a scientist who studies plants and animals of long ago
> c. an embryo in the later stages of development
> d. a sex-linked disease whose victims bleed excessively
> e. the science of changing an organism's organs, cells, etc., by artificially changing its genes
> f. the genetic make-up of an organism
> g. a tube 25cm long that connects the mouth and the stomach; a passageway for food
> h. the science of heredity
> i. the passing of traits from one generation to the next
> j. the appearance of an animal due to inherited traits

2 選択肢 a、b のうち正しい語を選んで、文を完成させなさい。

1. The muscles of the mother's uterus begin to tighten, or contract, and then relax. The contractions of the uterus are called (a. fetus   b. labor).

2. Doctors have a new tool called (a. metabolism   b. ultrasound) that uses echoes to help them see the baby while it is in the uterus.

3. (a. Antibodies   b. Traits) are characteristics passed from parent to offspring.

4. (a. Heredity   b. Genetics) is the passing of traits from parent to offspring.

5. (a. Traits   b. Genes) are made of DNA and are arranged on chromosomes.

6. For people with (a. esophagus   b. hemophilia), even a small cut can be serious, because it takes a long time for their blood to clot.

7. (a. Mutations   b. Selections) are sudden, random changes in genes that are passed from one generation to the next.

8. The process by which organisms that are well adapted to their environment survive and reproduce is (a. evolution   b. natural selection).

9. The (a. esophagus   b. pancreas) is a large gland which produces digestive juices.

10. (a. Metabolism   b. Antibody) includes all the chemical processes that take place in the body. The waste products of (a. metabolism   b. antibodies) include carbon dioxide, water, salts, heat, and urea.

Day 42

CD-B2

自然科学300語 健康 1

□ 411
ulcer
/ʌ́lsər/

名**潰瘍**（かいよう）
● 皮膚・粘膜などの表層が有害な刺激によって損傷を受け、下部組織にまで及ぶ欠損を生じた状態。欠損の浅いものを「びらん」という

□ 412
indigestion
/ìndidʒéstʃən, -dai-/

名**消化不良**、〈不消化による〉胃痛

□ 413
appendicitis
/əpèndəsáitis/

名**虫垂炎**
● 虫垂に起こる炎症。右下腹部の痛みが症状の特徴。俗に盲腸・盲腸炎といわれる
名 appendix 虫垂

□ 414
constipation
/kànstəpéiʃən/

名**便秘（症）**
動 cónstipate 便秘させる

□ 415
diarrhea
/dàiərí:ə/

名**下痢**

□ 416
anemia
/əní:miə/

名**貧血（症）**
● 血液中の赤血球数または血色素量が減少した状態。血液の酸素運搬が円滑に行われず、高度になると皮膚粘膜が蒼白になり、倦怠感・めまい・頭痛・耳鳴りなどをきたす

□ 417
leukemia
/lu:kí:miə/

名**白血病**
● 造血臓器で、白血球系に属する細胞が無制限・無秩序に増殖する悪性腫瘍性疾患
形名 leukemic /lù:kí:mik/ 白血病の（患者）

□ 418
bronchitis
/brɑŋkáitis/

名**気管支炎**
名 bronchium 気管支　形 bronchial /brɑ́ŋkiəl/ 気管支の　関 bronchial asthma /ǽzmə/ 気管支喘息
形 bronchitic 気管支炎の

□ 419
pneumonia
/njumóunjə/

名**肺炎**
関 acute pneumonia 急性肺炎　形 pneumonic 肺炎の

□ 420
emphysema
/èmfəsí:mə/

名**気腫**、〈特に〉肺気腫
● 肺組織が弾力性を失って呼気が十分にできず、肺が異常にふくらんでいる状態。中年以上の男性に多い。主症状は息切れで、喫煙による気管支の炎症などが原因とされる

continued

An ulcer is an open sore on the wall of the stomach or small intestine, caused by overproduction of hydrochloric acid.	潰瘍は塩酸の出過ぎから胃または小腸の壁がただれ、穴が開いて起こる。
Indigestion causes stomach pain. Indigestion can occur when one eats greasy or spicy foods, or when one eats too quickly.	消化不良は胃痛を引き起こす。消化不良は、脂っこいものや辛いものを食べたり、急いで食べたりすると起こる。
Appendicitis is a painful disease that occurs when the appendix becomes swollen from bacteria and wastes trapped inside it.	虫垂炎は、虫垂が細菌や中にたまった老廃物のせいで膨れる痛みを伴う病気である。
Constipation is a condition in which the feces are hard because too much water is absorbed by the large intestine.	便秘は大腸が水を吸収しすぎて、糞便が硬くなり過ぎた状態である。
When the feces are watery because too little water is absorbed by the large intestine, one suffers from diarrhea.	大腸が水をほとんど吸収せず糞便が水っぽいときは下痢である。
Anemia is a disease in which the body produces too few red blood cells.	貧血は体内の赤血球の生産が極端に減少する病気である。
Leukemia is a disease in which the body produces too many white blood cells.	白血病は体内の白血球の生産が極端に多くなる病気である。
Bronchitis is caused by the infection of the bronchial tubes.	気管支炎は気管支の炎症によって起こる。
A bacterial or viral infection of the lining of the lungs causes pneumonia.	肺の裏側に細菌やウィルスが感染して、肺炎が起こる。
Emphysema is a disease in which the walls of the alveoli become less elastic, so the lungs are not able to exchange normal amounts of oxygen and carbon dioxide with each breath.	肺気腫は肺胞の壁の伸縮性が低下し、肺が呼吸のたびに、正常量の酸素と二酸化炭素を交換できない病気である。

continued
▼

Day 43

CD-B3

421 heart attack
/hɑ́ːrt/ /ətǽk/

心臓発作
関 heart failure 心臓病、心臓まひ、心不全　関 heart disease 心臓病、心疾患

422 stroke
/stróuk/

名 (脳) 卒中
● 脳の循環障害によって、急激に精神・神経症状が出現する状態

423 hypertension
/hàipərténʃən/

名 高血圧 (症) (=high blood pressure)
形 hypertensive 高血圧 (性の)、高血圧患者
名 hypotension (=low blood pressure) 低血圧

424 nephritis
/nəfráitis/

名 腎炎
● 腎臓の糸球体に炎症性の病変を生じる疾患。小児期、次いで青少年期に多い。尿の異常・むくみ・高血圧が主症状
形 nephritic /nifrítik/ 腎炎の、腎臓の

425 kidney stone
/kídni/ /stóun/

腎石、腎結石
● 腎臓内に結石のできる疾患

426 kidney failure
/kídni/ /féiljər/

腎臓病

427 diabetes
/dàiəbíːtiːz, -tis/

名 糖尿病
● インシュリンの不足によって起こる代謝障害。血液中の糖濃度が高くなり、尿中に糖が含まれるようになる。口の渇き・多飲・多尿・体重減少が主症状
形名 diabetic /dàiəbétik/ 糖尿病 (性の)、糖尿病患者

428 microbe
/máikroub/

名 微生物、細菌
名 microbíology 微生物学

429 immunity
/imjúːnəti/

名 免疫 (性)
形 immune /imjúːn/ 免疫 (性) の　動 immunize 免疫にする　名 immunólogy 免疫学

430 vaccine
/væksíːn/

名 〈広く〉ワクチン
=a substance which contains a weak form of the bacteria or virus that causes a disease and is used to protect people from that disease
名 vaccinátion ワクチン接種、(特に) 種痘　動 váccinate ワクチン注射 [接種] をする

continued
▼

A heart attack is a disease that occurs when an artery carrying blood to the heart becomes blocked and the heart muscle does not get enough blood.

心臓発作は心臓に血液を送る動脈がふさがってしまい、血液が心筋に十分行き渡らなくなるときに起こる病気である。

A stroke is a disease that occurs when an artery carrying blood to the brain becomes blocked by a clot and the brain cells do not get enough oxygen.

脳卒中は脳に血液を送る動脈が血液のかたまりでふさがれてしまい、酸素が脳細胞に十分行き渡らなくなるときに起こる病気である。

Hypertension is a disease in which one's blood pressure rises dangerously because of the narrowing of arteries.

高血圧は、動脈が細くなるせいで危険なほどに血圧が上がる病気である。

Nephritis is a disease in which the kidneys become swollen and damaged, so the blood is not properly filtered.

腎炎は腎臓がはれあがって炎症を起こし、血液が適切にろ過されない病気である。

Kidney stones are a disease in which minerals accumulate and form tiny crystals that block the collecting tubes of the kidneys.

腎結石は無機物が蓄積して小さな結晶となり、腎臓に集まる管をふさいでしまう病気である。

Kidney failure is a disease in which the kidneys do not work properly, which causes poisonous wastes to build up.

腎臓病は腎臓の働きが悪く、有毒な老廃物がたまってしまう病気である。

Diabetics, people with diabetes, give themselves injections of insulin because insulin is a protein: if it were taken orally it would be digested.

糖尿病の患者はタンパク質であるインシュリンを注射する。口から飲むとインシュリンは消化されてしまう。

Microbes include viruses, bacteria, protozoans, and fungi. Most microbes are harmless. However, some cause disease because they interfere with the body's systems.

微生物にはウィルス、細菌、原生動物、菌類が含まれる。ほとんどの微生物は無害である。しかし、中には体の働きを妨げて病気の原因となるものもある。

If you have had chicken pox, your body has acquired immunity to chicken pox because it has the antibodies to the chicken pox virus.

水痘にかかったことがあるなら、水痘ウイルスの抗体を得て水痘への免疫ができている。

Before you began school, you probably were given vaccines for polio, whooping cough, mumps, and measles.

学校に入る前に、たぶん小児マヒ、百日ぜき、おたふくかぜ、麻疹のワクチンを受けたであろう。

continued
▼

Day 44 CD-B4

□ 431	**calorie** /kǽləri/	名 **カロリー** ● 熱量の単位（略 cal.）
□ 432	**food additive** /fúːd ǽdətiv/	**食品添加物** 関 presérvative 防腐剤　関 food coloring 着色剤
□ 433	**ingredient** /ingríːdiənt/	名 **材料**、成分、構成要素
□ 434	**in shape** /in ʃéip/	**体調が良い**、好調で、本来の状態で 熟 in good [poor] shape〈体の〉調子が良い [良くない]
□ 435	**sense organ** /séns ɔ́ːrgən/	**感覚器官**、受容器
□ 436	**central nervous system** /séntrəl nə́ːrvəs sístəm/	**中枢神経系**
□ 437	**cerebrum** /səríːbrəm, sérə-/	名 **大脳**
□ 438	**cerebellum** /sèrəbéləm/	名 **小脳**
□ 439	**medulla** /mədʌ́lə/	名 **延髄** (=medulla oblongata /ɑ̀blɔːŋɡɑ́ːtə/)、脊髄 ● 脳の最下端に位置し、上方は橋（きょう）、下方は脊髄に続く部分。呼吸や心臓の働きなど生命の維持に重要な中枢が数多く存在する
□ 440	**spinal cord** /spáinl kɔ́ːrd/	**脊髄** ● 脳と抹消器官の連絡・反射機能をつかさどる神経中枢。脊柱管内にあり、小指ほどの太さで延髄の下方に細長く続く

continued
▼

Some foods, such as butter, meat, and cheese, are high in calories. These foods produce large amounts of energy.	バター、肉、チーズなどの食物はカロリーが高い。これらの食物は多量のエネルギーを生産する。
Some people question the safety of certain food additives and prefer not to buy foods that contain them.	食品添加物の安全性を問題にし、それが含まれる食料品を買わないようにする人もいる。
When you buy a new food product, it is wise to look carefully at the label. The ingredients in the product are listed in order by weight.	新製品を買うときは、ラベルを注意して見るといい。製品の成分が質量順に記載してある。
When your body is healthy, fit, and in shape, you not only look good but you feel good.	身体が健康で調子が良く、体調が良ければ、見栄えがいいし、気分もいい。
Information received through sense organ receptors is carried to the brain. Receptors are in the retina of the eye, the cochlea of the ear, the mucus layer of the nose, the taste buds of the tongue, and in the skin.	感覚受容器を通して受け取る情報は脳に運ばれる。受容器は目の網膜、耳の蝸牛殻、鼻の嗅粘膜、舌の味覚球、皮膚にある。
The brain is part of the central nervous system. Without a brain, your body could not function.	脳は中枢神経系の一部である。脳なしには、体は機能できない。
Recent studies have shown that the right half of the cerebrum specializes in artistic and musical abilities, as well as imagination. The left half of the cerebrum specializes in the abilities to read, write, speak, think logically, and do mathematics.	最近の研究によれば、大脳の右半分は想像力に加えて芸術と音楽の能力をつかさどる。大脳の左半分は読む、書く、話す、論理的に考える、計算をするといった能力をつかさどる。
Neurons from the cerebrum carry commands in the form of impulses to the cerebellum.	大脳からのニューロンは、インパルスを形成して指令を小脳へ伝える。
The medulla controls the heart rate and the breathing rate. It also regulates swallowing and the muscular actions of the digestive system.	延髄は心拍数と呼吸数を調節する。また嚥下や、消化系の筋肉運動を管理する。
The spinal cord has two main jobs. First, it relays information between the brain and the rest of the body. Second, the spinal cord controls simple innate behaviors called reflexes.	脊髄には大きくふたつの機能がある。ひとつは、脳と体の残りの部分との情報のやりとりを中継する。もうひとつは、反射作用という先天的な単純行動を制御する。

continued
▼

復習テスト　健康

1 1〜10の単語の定義を a〜j から選びなさい。

1. microbe
2. immunity
3. vaccine
4. calorie
5. central nervous system
6. anemia
7. diabetes
8. stroke
9. pneumonia
10. sense organ

---

a. the unit in which food energy is measured

b. a substance that can give one immunity against a disease

c. a serious disease of the lungs that causes inflammation and difficulty in breathing

d. a microscopic organism that may cause disease

e. the body system made up of the brain and spinal cord

f. a part of the body, such as the eye, nose, tongue, ear, or skin, through which the brain receives messages from the outside world

g. the bursting or blockage of an artery in the brain, damaging the brain and sometimes causing a loss of the ability to move a part of the body

h. resistance to a disease

i. condition in which there are too few red cells in the blood

j. a disease in which there is too much sugar in the blood

2 選択肢 a、b のうち正しい語を選んで文を完成させなさい。

1. (a. Diabetes   b. Bronchitis) is the number three killer in the United States, right behind heart disease and cancer. It is caused by the failure of the pancreas to make insulin.

2. You can acquire (a. immunity   b. anemia) to certain diseases in two ways. One way is by getting the disease. Another way is by receiving a vaccine.

3. A (a. nephritis   b. vaccine) contains dead or weakened disease-causing microbes. The microbes in the vaccine will not cause the disease. However, they will cause your body to produce antibodies.

4. If you take in more (a. minerals   b. calories) than your body needs, you will put on weight.

5. (a. Food additives   b. Ingredients) are chemicals added to food to prevent spoiling, improve how the food looks or tastes, or increase the amount of nutrients in the food.

6. The (a. cerebrum   b. cerebellum) is the largest section of the brain. It receives messages from the sense organs and interprets them. It also controls body movements, thinking, memory, and speech.

7. The (a. cerebrum   b. cerebellum) helps you maintain your balance and coordinate the movement of your muscles.

8. Many neurons from the cerebrum and cerebellum pass through the brain stem. The lower part of the brain stem is called the (a. ulcer   b. medulla).

9. The (a. spinal cord   b. cerebrum) extends from the medulla all the way down the back.

10. When feces are watery because too little water is absorbed by large intestine, this is called (a. constipation   b. diarrhea).

Day 45 化学 ①

自然科学300語

CD-B5

□ 441
element
/élərmənt/

名 **元素**、成分、要素

□ 442
molecule
/máləkjù:l/

名 **分子**
・物質を構成するもので、その化学的性質を失わない最小の単位。いくつかの原子が化学結合で結びついたもの

□ 443
atom
/ǽtəm/

名 **原子**
・物質構成の基本的要素。すべての物質は原子から生じたイオン、または原子の組み合わせによる分子でできている

□ 444
chemical formula
/kémikəl/ /fɔ́:rmjulə/

化学式

□ 445
carbon dioxide
/ká:rbən/ /daiáksaid/

二酸化炭素、炭酸ガス
関 carbon 炭素 関 dioxide 二酸化物

□ 446
carbohydrate
/kà:rbouháidreit/

名 **炭水化物**

□ 447
fat
/fǽt/

名 **脂肪**

□ 448
protein
/próuti:n/

名 **タンパク質**

□ 449
enzyme
/énzaim/

名 **酵素**
関 enzyme detérgent 酵素洗剤

□ 450
nitrogen
/náitrədʒən/

名 **窒素**

continued
▼

Water is a compound of two elements: hydrogen and oxygen.	水は水素と酸素のふたつの元素から成る化合物である。
A molecule of water is the smallest amount of water possible.	水の分子は水としての最小単位である。
If you looked at a single molecule of water, you would find that it is two atoms of hydrogen joined with one atom of oxygen.	水の分子をひとつだけ見たら、水素原子2個が酸素原子1個と結合しているのがわかるだろう。
From the chemical formula of a compound, you can tell what elements are present in a molecule of that compound. You can also tell how many atoms of each element are in the molecule. For example, the chemical formula of water is H2O.	化学式からは、化合物の分子にどんな元素が存在するかがわかる。また、その分子に各元素の原子がいくつあるのかもわかる。たとえば、水の化学式は H2O である。
Green plants use carbon dioxide and water to make food. Most animals give off carbon dioxide as a waste product.	緑色植物は二酸化炭素と水を使って養分を作り出す。ほとんどの動物は二酸化炭素を排泄物として放出する。
Sugars and starches, or carbohydrates, are compounds made up of carbon, hydrogen, and oxygen. Carbohydrates give your body energy.	糖とでんぷん、つまり炭水化物は炭素、水素、酸素から成る化合物である。炭水化物は体内にエネルギーをもたらす。
If you eat too many carbohydrates and proteins, your body will change them to fat. This fat is stored under the skin and around internal organs.	炭水化物とタンパク質を取り過ぎると、それらは体内で脂肪に変わる。この脂肪は皮下、および内蔵のまわりに蓄積される。
Proteins are the raw materials that your body needs for building new cells. They are necessary for growth and repair.	タンパク質は体が新たな細胞を生成するのに必要な原料である。タンパク質は体の成長と回復に必要とされる。
Enzymes help start, stop, and regulate all chemical activities in living things.	酵素は生物におけるあらゆる化学反応の開始、停止、調節に関与する。
Animals get nitrogen to make proteins by eating plants or plant-eating animals.	動物は植物または草食動物を食べて窒素を得て、タンパク質を作る。

continued
▼

Day 46 化学 2 自然科学300語

CD-B6

□ 451 **solution** /səlúːʃən/
名 **溶解**、分解
形 soluble /sάljəbl/ 溶ける、溶解できる、溶性の

□ 452 **diffuse** /difjúːz/
動 〈気体・液体を〉**拡散する**、〈光熱・臭気などを〉発散［放散］する
名 diffusion 拡散、放散　形 diffusible 拡散性の

□ 453 **sulfur** /sʌ́lfər/
名 **硫黄**
関 sulfuric acid 硫酸

□ 454 **sulfur dioxide** /sʌ́lfər/ /daiάksaid/
二酸化硫黄、亜硫酸ガス

□ 455 **sodium chloride** /sóudiəm/ /klɔ́ːraid/
塩化ナトリウム、食塩
関 sodium ナトリウム　関 chloride 塩化物

□ 456 **hydrocarbon** /hàidroukάːrbən, -drə-/
名 **炭化水素**
（注）hydro-「水の、水素の」の意

□ 457 **mineral** /mínərəl/
名 **無機物**、〈複数形で〉炭酸水、炭酸飲料（= mineral water）

□ 458 **vitamin** /váitəmin/
名 **ビタミン**
● 動物の発育と栄養を保つのに微量ながら不可欠の有機物の総称。エネルギー源にはならず代謝に関与する

□ 459 **hormone** /hɔ́ːrmoun/
名 **ホルモン**
● 動物の内分泌器官または組織から分泌される生理活性物質。他の特定の器官または組織に影響を与え、神経とともに生体内の情報伝達を行う

□ 460 **insulin** /ínsəlin/
名 **インシュリン**
● 膵臓でできるタンパク質ホルモン。糖尿病の特効薬

continued
▼

When a solid-like sugar dissolves in water or in any other liquid, a solution is formed.	砂糖のような固形物が水または他の液体に溶けるとき、溶解が起こる。
When you pass a bakery, you smell molecules from cake and bread diffusing in the air.	パン屋の前を通ると、空気中に拡散したケーキとパンの分子の匂いがする。
Sulfur is used in making insect and weed killers.	硫黄は殺虫剤や除草剤の製造に利用される。
Industries that burn coal must use the best available devices to remove sulfur dioxide and fly ash from factory exhaust.	石炭燃焼を伴う産業では、可能な限り最善の設備を使って、工場の排ガスに含まれる二酸化硫黄と飛散灰を除去しなければならない。
Sodium chloride, or salt, is used as a food, in medicines, and as a food preservative.	塩化ナトリウム、つまり塩は食物として、また薬に、さらに食物の防腐剤として使用される。
Hydrocarbons are made of just two elements: hydrogen and carbon.	炭化水素は水素と炭素のふたつの元素だけから成る。
Minerals are elements that the body needs to carry on vital functions. Calcium, iron, and sodium are examples of minerals.	無機物は体内の機能を活性化するのに必要な成分である。カルシウム、鉄、ナトリウムは無機物の例である。
Vitamins are carbon compounds that the body needs to grow and function properly. Each vitamin is identified by a letter — A, B, C, D, E, or K.	ビタミンは体の成長と機能を維持するのに必要な炭素化合物である。各ビタミンはA、B、C、D、E、Kのアルファベットで分類される。
Hormones help regulate body activities such as growth, development, and reproduction.	ホルモンは成長、発育、生殖といった体内の働きの調節に関与する。
Insulin stimulates the liver to remove sugar from the blood and store it. It also regulates the use of sugar by the cells of the body.	インシュリンは肝臓を刺激し、血液から糖を取り除いて蓄える。また、体内の細胞で使われる糖を調節する。

continued
▼

Day 47 化学 3 自然科学300語

CD-B7

461 drug
/drʌ́g/
名 薬、薬物、麻薬（=narcotic）
関 drug addict 麻薬常用者　関 drug abuse 麻薬の乱用

462 stimulant
/stímjulənt/
名 興奮薬、興奮剤　形 興奮性の

463 depressant
/diprésnt/
名〈特に筋肉・神経などの〉抑制薬　形 抑制作用のある

464 narcotic
/nɑːrkátik/
名 鎮静剤、麻酔薬、麻薬、睡眠薬、麻薬中毒患者
形 麻薬中毒者の、麻薬性の、睡眠性の、麻薬の
名 narcotism 麻薬中毒

465 amphetamine
/æmfétəmìːn/
名 アンフェタミン（中枢神経刺激剤）

466 cocaine
/koukéin/
名 コカイン
・コカの葉から採った有機塩基

467 hallucinogen
/həlúːsənədʒen/
名 幻覚薬［剤］
動 hallucinate /həlúːsənèit/ 幻覚に陥らせる、幻覚を起こす　名 hallucinátion 幻覚、妄想、錯覚　形 hallucinogénic〈薬剤などが〉幻覚を起こさせる

468 marijuana
/mæ̀rəhwɑ́ːnə/
名 大麻（=hemp）、マリファナ

469 alcohol-related
/ǽlkəhɔ̀ːlriléitid/
形 飲酒に関連した
関 alcoholic アルコール中毒の。アルコール中毒者

470 nicotine
/níkətìːn, ⁻ ⁻/
名 ニコチン
名 nícotinism 慢性ニコチン中毒

continued

When a drug is used according to directions, it can help your body recover from an illness.	薬は指示に従って使用されたときに、病気からの回復を助ける。
Caffeine is a stimulant that is found in coffee, tea, and cocoa. Drinking large amounts of these beverages can make people lose their appetite and become nervous.	カフェインはコーヒー、茶、ココアに含まれる興奮薬である。これらを飲み過ぎると食欲が減退し、いらいらするようになる。
Narcotics, such as heroin and codeine, are strong habit-forming depressants that are made from the drug opium.	ヘロインやコデインといった鎮痛剤は習慣性のある強力な抑制薬で、アヘンから作られる。
Doctors prescribe narcotics to relieve pain and tension and relax the muscles.	医者は痛みと緊張を抑え、筋肉の張りを和らげるために鎮静剤を処方する。
Some people abuse amphetamines by taking them just for excitement. This is very dangerous, because it can lead to physical dependence.	刺激を得るためだけにアンフェタミンを乱用する者がいる。アンフェタミンは身体依存を引き起こすので非常に危険である。
Drugs like marijuana, alcohol, and cocaine are often referred to as stepping-stone drugs, because their abuse often leads users to other drugs.	マリファナ、アルコール、コカインのような麻薬は乱用すると他の麻薬に手をつけることが多いので、よく踏み石の麻薬といわれる。
Hallucinogens are drugs that cause the mind to perceive things that are not real. LSD is a dangerous hallucinogen.	幻覚薬は現実にないものを知覚させる麻薬である。LSDは危険な幻覚薬である。
Marijuana is another hallucinogen. This drug comes from the leaves and flowers of the hemp plant.	マリファナも幻覚薬である。この麻薬は大麻の葉と花から作る。
Almost 50 percent of the United States highway deaths that occur each year are alcohol-related.	米国のハイウェイにおける毎年の死亡事故の約50%には、アルコールが関係している。
Tobacco contains a habit-forming drug called nicotine. Nicotine is a stimulant that increases the heart rate, raises the blood pressure, and narrows small blood vessels.	煙草はニコチンという習慣性のある薬物を含む。ニコチンは心拍数を速め、血圧を上げ、小さな血管を細くする興奮薬である。

continued
▼

復習テスト 化学

解答は P.242

1 1〜10の単語の定義を a〜j から選びなさい。

1. molecule
2. element
3. atom
4. protein
5. drug
6. chemical formula
7. alcohol-related
8. nicotine
9. sodium chloride
10. drug abuse

---

a. the smallest part of a compound that still has the chemical properties of the compound
b. a substance other than food that produces a change in the body
c. any matter that is made up of only one kind of atom
d. having something to do with alcohol
e. the written symbol for the elements of a compound
f. a stimulant contained in tobacco
g. the improper use of a drug
h. one of the tiny particles that make up all matter
i. salt
j. a substance that the body uses for the growth and repair of tissues

2 選択肢 a、b のうち正しい語を選んで文を完成させなさい。

1. Most matter is made up of two or more elements chemically joined together to form a/an (a. atom b. compound).

2. Matter is made of (a. atoms b. compounds). Atoms of the same kind are (a. elements b. compounds). The smallest unit of a compound (two or more elements chemically combined) is a molecule.

3. (a. Solution b. Diffusion) is the random movement of molecules from one place to another. Odors are caused by (a. solution b. diffusion).

4. (a. Stimulants b. Depressants), or "uppers," speed up the nervous system and increase the heart and breathing rates.

5. (a. Stimulants b. Depressants), or "downers," are drugs that slow down the central nervous system. These drugs decrease the heart and breathing rates and make a person feel sleepy.

6. (a. Fibers b. Fats), like carbohydrates, are nutrients that provide energy.

7. (a. Cocaine b. Marijuana) is a stimulant that comes from the coca plant. It produces feelings of excitement. However, once the excitement wears off, the user is left feeling nervous, confused, and depressed.

8. In addition to (a. nitrogen b. nicotine), cigarette smoke contains poisonous gases and tars · chemical substances that are known to cause some forms of cancer.

9. People who abuse drugs often start to depend on them. This need for a drug is called drug (a. depressant b. dependence).

10. LSD and marijuana are (a. depressants b. hallucinogens) that cause loss of coordination, changed or erratic behavior, hallucinations, and often panic or depression.

Day 48 物理 ① 自然科学300語

CD-B8

□ 471 **physical science** /fízikəl/ /sáiəns/
自然科学
- 生命科学を除く物理、科学・天文学などの分野

□ 472 **technology** /teknálədʒi/
名 **科学技術**、生産［工業］技術、テクノロジー

□ 473 **potential energy** /pəténʃəl/ /énərdʒi/
位置エネルギー
- 物体の位置する場所によって決まるエネルギー

□ 474 **kinetic energy** /kinétik/ /énərdʒi/
運動エネルギー
- 運動している物体が持っているエネルギー

□ 475 **velocity** /vəlásəti/
名 **速度**

□ 476 **accelerate** /æksélərèit/
動 **加速する**
名 acceleration 加速度、加速

□ 477 **air resistance** /ɛər/ /rizístəns/
空気抵抗
- 空気中を運動する物体が空気から受ける抵抗。大きさは相対速度に比例する

□ 478 **momentum** /mouméntəm/
名 **運動量**、勢い、はずみ

□ 479 **gravitational force** /grævətéiʃənl/ /fɔːrs/
重力（作用）、引力（=gravitátion）
=force of grávity

□ 480 **electric force** /iléktrik/ /fɔːrs/
電気力

continued ▼

Physical science is important to understanding how things work and why things happen as they do.	自然科学は物体がどのように作用し、なぜそれが起こるのかを理解するのに重要である。
Tractors, X-ray machines, computers, and medicines are all examples of technology.	トラクター、X線写真撮影機、コンピューター、薬はすべて、科学技術の例である。
Potential energy is stored energy which can be released when matter moves. For example, lifting a book takes energy stored in the muscles of your body.	位置エネルギーは物が動くときに放出される、蓄えられたエネルギーである。たとえば、本を持ち上げると、体の筋肉に蓄えられたエネルギーが消費される。
When you let go of the book, it begins to move. The book's potential energy is changed into kinetic energy, or the energy of motion.	本を放すと、本は動き始める。位置エネルギーは運動エネルギーに変わる。
Velocity includes both speed and direction. If an automobile travels 80 kilometers north in an hour's time along a highway, then the velocity of the automobile is 80 kilometers per hour due north.	速度には速さと方向が含まれる。自動車がハイウェイを1時間に80km北に進むとき、自動車の速度は北に時速80kmである。
If you dropped a marble and a bowling ball at exactly the same instant from the top of a building, both would fall through the air at the same velocity and strike the ground together. This is because falling objects all accelerate at the same speed.	建物の屋上からビー玉とボーリング球を同時に落とすと、空中を同じ速度で落下し同時に地上に達する。これは落下する物体はすべて、同じスピードで加速するからである。
An open parachute encounters a large amount of air resistance. Therefore, the skydiver's fall is slowed.	開いたパラシュートは空気抵抗を多く受ける。そのため、スカイダイバーの落下は遅くなる。
Even if a bowling ball and a ping-pong ball are traveling at exactly the same velocity, the bowling ball will have much more momentum. It will exert greater force because it has more mass.	たとえボーリング球とピンポン球が同じ速度で動いているとしても、ボーリング球のほうがはるかに運動量が大きい。ボーリング球のほうが質量が大きいので、より大きな力が生じる。
Isaac Newton, an English mathematician, set forth the universal law of gravitation. It states that a gravitational force is present between any two objects in the universe.	英国の数学者、アイザック・ニュートンは万有引力の法則を発表した。それによると、重力はすべての物体間に存在する。
Lightning results from the action of electric forces.	稲妻は電気力作用から生じる。

continued
▼

Day 49

物理 2 — 自然科学300語 — CD-B9

□ 481 **friction** /fríkʃən/
名 (物理的) **摩擦**

□ 482 **inertia** /ináːrʃə/
名 **慣性**
・静止、あるいは等速運動をしている物体が、外力が作用しないかぎりそのまま静止状態あるいは等速度運動を続けようとする性質。惰性

□ 483 **centripetal force** /sentrípətl/ /fɔ́ːrs/
求心力、向心力
関 centripetal 中心に近づこうとする、求心性の

□ 484 **magnetic pole** /mæɡnétik/ /póul/
磁極
関 mágnet 磁石

□ 485 **static electricity** /stǽtik/ /ilektrísəti/
静電気
関 static 静止の、静的な

□ 486 **electric discharge** /iléktrik/ /dístʃɑːrdʒ, distʃɑ́ːrdʒ/
放電

□ 487 **conductor** /kəndʌ́ktər/
名 **伝導体**、導体、導線、避雷針 (=lightning rod)

□ 488 **integrated circuit** /íntəɡrèitid/ /sɔ́ːrkit/
集積回路 (=chip) (略 IC)

□ 489 **reflection** /riflékʃən/
名 **反射**、反射光、反射熱、反響音
動 refléctive 反射する

□ 490 **refraction** /rifrǽkʃən/
名 **屈折 (作用)**、屈折
形 refráctive 屈折する、屈折による

continued ▼

A hockey puck travels fast and far on smooth ice because friction is reduced.	アイスホッケーのパックがなめらかな氷の上を速く遠くへと動くのは、摩擦が少ないからである。
The law of inertia explains why you keep moving forward when the car you are riding in stops suddenly.	慣性の法則は、なぜ乗っている車が突然止まっても体が前方へ動き続けるのかを説明する。
The moon orbits the earth in a circular path, with the Earth at the center of the orbit. The force that causes circular motion is centripetal force. Without this force, the moon would simply move off into space.	月は地球を軌道の中心として、地球のまわりを回る。円形運動を引き起こす力は求心力である。この力がなければ、月は宇宙の彼方へと離れていく一方だろう。
The magnetic needle of a compass always points to the north and south magnetic poles.	羅針盤の磁針は常に、北磁極と南磁極を指している。
You can produce static electricity with a plastic comb. When you comb your hair, your hair loses electrons to the plastic, and your hair becomes positively charged. Since opposite electric charges attract, they stick to each other.	プラスチック製のくしで静電気を作ることができる。くしで髪をとかすと、髪の電子はプラスチックへ移動し、髪は正に帯電する。プラスチックの負電荷と引きつけ合うので、髪とくしがくっつく。
The movement of particles in the air by wind and rain can cause a buildup of electric charges in a cloud. An electric discharge occurs when the electric charge becomes too great. That is, it will discharge to the ground or to another cloud, in the form of a bolt of lightning.	風や雨による空気中の粒子の運動は、雲に電荷の蓄積を起こす。この電荷が非常に強くなると、放電が起こる。すなわちその電荷は地上に、または別の雲に稲妻となって放電する。
Electrons can move from a lightning bolt to a metal lightning rod, down the conductor attached to the rod, and into the Earth.	電子は稲妻から金属の避雷針へ、そして避雷針に取りつけられた伝導体を下がって地中へと移動できる。
Integrated circuits have made possible the amazing pocket calculators, electronic watches, computers, and other electronic machines that are in general use today.	集積回路は超小型計算機、電子時計、コンピューターやその他、今日では一般的になった電子機器の使用を可能にした。
A mirror's reflection of light waves allows you to see yourself in the mirror. The reflection of sound waves causes echoes.	光の反射によって、鏡に映った自分の姿を見ることができる。音波の反射は反響を引き起こす。
A rainbow is the result of the refraction of light waves.	虹は光の波の屈折から生じる。

continued
▼

Day 50

自然科学300語 / 物理 3

CD-B10

491 Doppler effect
/dɑ́plər/ /ifékt/

ドップラー効果
- 音波や光波などの波動で、波源と観測者が互いに遠ざかる［近づく］とき観測される、波長が長く［短く］なる現象
- 関 Doppler radar ドップラーレーダー（ドップラー効果を利用して目標の速度を測定する）

492 vibrate
/váibreit/

動 **振動する［させる］**、共振する
名 vibration 振動

493 intensity
/inténsəti/

名 **強さ**、強度

494 decibel
/désəbèl/

名 **デシベル**
- 電力・音などの比強度を対数目盛りで表す単位（記号 dB, db）

495 frequency
/frí:kwənsi/

名 **周波数**、振動数

496 pitch
/pítʃ/

名 **音の高低**、調子

497 resonance
/rézənəns/

名 **共鳴**、共振
形 resonant 鳴り響く、共鳴を起こす

498 fluorescent light
/fluərésnt/ /láit/

蛍光
関 fluorescence 蛍光発光、蛍光性、蛍光

499 infrared light
/ìnfrəréd/ /láit/

赤外線 (=infrared、infrared radiation)

500 mirage
/mirɑ́:ʒ/

名 **蜃気楼**（しんきろう）

continued
▼

Many drivers have been caught speeding by radar equipment that uses the Doppler effect.

ドップラー効果を利用したレーダー装置から、多くの運転者がスピード違反で捕まっている。

When you shout, your vocal cords vibrate with more energy than they do when you whisper. A vibration with more energy produces sound waves with more energy.

ささやくときよりも叫ぶときのほうが、声帯は強いエネルギーで振動する。エネルギーの強い振動のほうが、エネルギーの強い音波を生じる。

The more energy a sound wave has, the greater its amplitude. The loudness, or intensity, of a sound depends on the amplitude of the sound waves involved.

音波のエネルギーが強いほど、振幅は大きくなる。音の大きさ、つまり強さはその音波の振幅で決定する。

Intensity is measured in decibels. The decibel (dB) is named after Alexander Graham Bell, the inventor of the telephone.

(音の)強さはデシベルで表示される。デシベル(dB)は電話の発明者、アレクサンダー・グレアム・ベルにちなんでつけられた。

The frequency of a sound wave depends on how rapidly the source of the sound is vibrating. The faster the vibration, the higher the frequency.

音波の周波数は音源が振動する速さで決まる。振動が速いほど周波数は高くなる。

Pitch describes the highness or lowness of a sound that the ear hears. High-frequency sound waves produce high-pitched sounds.

ピッチ(調子)は耳に入る音の高低を表す。周波数の高い音波は調子の高い音を生じる。

Musical instruments produce musical sounds using a property called resonance. For example, if you pluck a guitar string, it vibrates. The vibrating string causes the body of the guitar to vibrate, or resonate.

楽器は共鳴という特性を利用して音楽的な音を出す。たとえば、ギターの弦を引くと振動する。振動する弦はギターの胴体を振動させる、つまり共鳴させる。

Paintings are kept away from the light of fluorescent lamps because, like sunlight, unfiltered fluorescent light contains a large amount of ultraviolet light, which causes the colors of the paint to fade.

絵画は蛍光灯の光で照らさないようにしている。日光と同じで、フィルターを通さない蛍光灯にはかなりの紫外線が含まれており、色あせを引き起こすからである。

Female mosquitoes have antennae that detect the infrared light given off by warm-blooded animals. They can see the infrared light given off by warm bodies.

メスの蚊は温血動物が発する赤外線を感じ取るアンテナを持っている。こうして、温かい体が発する赤外線を認識できる。

A mirage is an illusion caused by the refraction of light waves, making objects that are far away appear to be nearby, floating in the air, or upside down.

蜃気楼は光の波の屈折によって起こる幻影である。はるか彼方にある物体が、空中に浮かんだり逆さまになったりして、あたかも近くにあるかのように見える。

continued
▼

復習テスト　物理

1　1〜10の単語の定義をa〜jの中から選びなさい。

1. physical science
2. technology
3. potential energy
4. kinetic energy
5. velocity
6. acceleration
7. gravitational force
8. friction
9. centripetal force
10. static electricity

a. the energy of position
b. the energy of motion
c. the force that slows and stops objects
d. the force of attraction between all objects in the universe
e. an increase in the rate of speed of a moving object
f. the branch of science that investigates matter and energy
g. the force that causes circular motion
h. the electric charge that builds up on an object
i. the use of science in real-life situations
j. a measurement of both the speed of an object and the direction of its motion

2 選択肢 a、b のうち正しい語を選んで文を完成させなさい。

1. Falling objects all accelerate at the same speed. Any object falling near the surface of the earth will accelerate 9.8m/s/s. This means the (a. velocity   b. momentum) of an object increases by 9.8 meters per second every second it falls.

2. There can be no (a. velocity   b. air resistance) when there is no air.

3. In general, if two objects are moving with the same velocity, the one with more mass will have greater (a. momentum   b. acceleration).

4. The amount of (a. gravitational   b. electric) force decreases as the distance between the objects involved increases.

5. Run a comb through your hair and then hold the comb just above some tiny pieces of torn newspaper. The paper will be attracted to the comb and possibly stick to it. This attraction is caused by (a. gravitational force   b. electric force).

6. If the driver of a moving car suddenly applies the brakes, because of (a. friction   b. inertia) the passengers will keep moving at a constant velocity until some outside force acts to slow them down. Seat belts protect people from the effects of the law of inertia.

7. The word (a. gravitational   b. centripetal) means enter-seeking. (a. Centripetal   b. Gravitational) forces are always directed toward the center of a circle.

8. If you bring the north poles of two magnets together, they repel each other. If, however, the north pole of one magnet is brought near the south pole of another magnet, the magnets attract each other. This rule is called the law of (a. magnetic poles   b. static electricity).

9. Materials in which the electrons can move easily are called (a. conductors   b. magnetics). Materials in which electrons cannot move easily are called insulators.

10. The change in pitch of the sound you hear when a car moves toward you, passes, and then moves away is an example of (a. the Doppler effect   b. resonance).

Chapter 3
社会・人文科学 300 語

政治	Day 51...Day 53 ▶ 154 復習テスト 政治 ▶ 160	
経済	Day 54...Day 56 ▶ 162 復習テスト 経済 ▶ 168	
社会	Day 57...Day 59 ▶ 170 復習テスト 社会 ▶ 176	
法律	Day 60...Day 62 ▶ 178 復習テスト 法律 ▶ 184	
教育	Day 63...Day 65 ▶ 186 復習テスト 教育 ▶ 192	
心理	Day 66...Day 68 ▶ 194 復習テスト 心理 ▶ 200	
文学語学	Day 69...Day 71 ▶ 202 復習テスト 文学語学 ▶ 208	
歴史	Day 72...Day 74 ▶ 210 復習テスト 歴史 ▶ 216	
文化	Day 75...Day 77 ▶ 218 復習テスト 文化 ▶ 224	
芸術	Day 78...Day 80 ▶ 226 復習テスト 芸術 ▶ 232	

基本語彙２００語

自然科学３００語

社会・人文科学３００語

Day 51 政治 1 — 社会・人文科学 300 語

CD-B11

□ 501 absolute monarch
/ǽbsəlùːt, ˌ－－ˈ－/ /mάnərk/

絶対[専制]君主
関 absolute mónarchy 絶対君主制[国]　関 monarch 君主、帝王、主権者、最高支配者

□ 502 totalitarian government
/toutǽlitéəriən/ /gʌ́vərnmənt/

全体主義政府
関 totalitarian 全体主義の、一国一党の。全体主義者
関 totalitarianism 全体主義

□ 503 democracy
/dimάkrəsi/

名 民主主義、民主制、民主政治、民主主義の国、民主国
名 démocrat 民主主義者　形 democrátic 民主的な

□ 504 representative democracy
/rèprizéntətiv/ /dimάkrəsi/

代表民主制 (=republic)
● 国民が選んだ代表によって政治を運営する共和政体

□ 505 constitution
/kὰnstətjúːʃən/

名 憲法
● 国家の基本的条件を定めた根本法(米国、日本などのものを成文憲法という。米国の憲法は成文憲法としては最古のもので、1787年に起草、1789年に発効、1790年に全州により批准された。英国のものは成文化されたものがなく、慣習法による不文法でそれを不文憲法という)

□ 506 federal system
/fédərəl/ /sístəm/

連邦制
関 federal 連邦の、連邦政府の、合衆国の　関 federalism 連邦主義[制度]　関 the Federal Government (of the U.S.) 〈各州の state government に対して〉米国連邦政府[中央政府]

□ 507 separation of powers
/sèpəréiʃən/ /əv/ /páuərz/

三権分立 (行政・立法・司法)

□ 508 legislative
/lédʒislèitiv, -lət-/

形 法律を制定する、立法部の　名 立法府[部] (=legislative branch)
動 legislate 法律を制定する　名 legislation 法律制定、立法、法律　名 legislature 立法部[府]

□ 509 executive
/igzékjutiv/

形 行政上の　名 行政府[部] (=executive branch)
関 Executive Mansion 《米》大統領官邸 (=the White House)

□ 510 judicial
/dʒuːdíʃəl/

形 司法の、裁判の
関 judicial branch 司法府[部]

continued
▼

In times past, kings or queens often held all the power in their nation's governments. They were called absolute monarchs.	過去には、王や女王がしばしば自分たちの国の統治におけるすべての権力を握っていた。彼らは絶対君主と呼ばれた。
In some nations, one person or a small group of people holds all the power. This type of government is called a dictatorship or a totalitarian government.	一部の国々では、ひとりの人間ないし小人数の集団がすべての権力を握っている。このタイプの政府は独裁政権、ないしは全体主義政府と呼ばれる。
In a democracy, the people rule directly or they elect officials who will act for them.	民主制においては、国民が直接支配するか、自分たちのために行動する役人を選挙する。
In a representative democracy, the people elect representatives to carry on the work of government for them.	代表民主制においては、国民は自分たちのために政治の仕事を遂行する代表を選挙する。
In the United States the people are governed according to the provisions of their constitution.	米国の人々は、彼らの憲法の規定に従って統治されている。
In a federal system, the powers of government are divided between a national government and state governments.	連邦制においては、政治の権限は国の政府と州政府とに分割されている。
The three-way division of power is known as the separation of powers.	権力の三方向への分割は、三権分立の名で知られている。
Article 1 of the Constitution established Congress as the legislative branch, or lawmaking branch, of the government.	憲法第1条は議会を立法府、つまり法律を定める部門として制定した。
The executive branch is responsible for seeing that the nation's laws are carried out. It is headed by the president.	行政府は、国法が実行されているかを監視する責任を負う。行政府は大統領に指揮される。
The judicial branch was established to judge the laws and punish lawbreakers. The Supreme Court is the head of the judicial branch.	司法府は、法律を審査し法律違反者を罰するために制定された。最高裁判所は司法府の最高機関である。

continued
▼

Day 52 政治 2 社会・人文科学300語

511 checks and balances
/tʃéks/ /ənd/ /bǽlənsiz/

均衡と抑制
- 政府各部門において、自部門の権限に抵触する他部門の決定・施策を修正または無効にできる権限を付与することにより、各部門の力に制限を加え均衡を保つ。米国政治の基本原理

512 veto
/víːtou/

動〈法案・議案を〉**拒否する**
名（大統領・知事・上院などが法案に対して有する）拒否権

513 amendment
/əméndmənt/

名**修正**、改正
関 the Amendments〈米国憲法の〉修正個条

514 the Bill of Rights
/ðə/ /bíl/ /əv/ /ráits/

権利章典（米；憲法修正第1-10条）

515 civil rights
/sívəl/ /ráits/

市民権、公民権、〈特に黒人など少数民族グループの〉平等権

516 suffrage
/sʌ́fridʒ/

名**選挙権**、投票、参政権
名 suffragist 参政権拡張論者 関 universal [women's] suffrage 普通選挙権［婦人参政権］

517 ratification
/rætəfikéiʃən/

名**批准**、裁可
動 rátify 批准する、裁可する

518 the House of Representatives
/ðə/ /háus/ /əv/ /rèprizéntətivz/

〈米国議会・州議会の〉**下院**（=the House）
関 representative (=congressman) 下院議員

519 congressional district
/kəŋgréʃənl/ /dístrikt/

下院議員選挙区
関 congress〈米国または南米、中米共和国の〉議会

520 the Senate
/ðə/ /sénət/

上院
関 senator 上院議員

continued
▼

To make sure that no branch of the federal government becomes too powerful, a system of checks and balances was included in the Constitution.	連邦政府のいずれの部門も強力になり過ぎないことを確実にするため、均衡と抑制の制度が憲法に取り入れられた。
The president has the power to veto, or turn down, a law proposed by Congress, the legislative branch of the federal government.	大統領は、連邦政府の立法府である議会から提出された法案に拒否する権限、すなわち拒否権をもっている。
Since the Constitution went into effect in 1789, only 26 amendments have been added to it.	憲法が1789年に発効されて以来、わずか26の修正個条がこれにつけ加えられたのみである。
The first right, or freedom, guaranteed in the Bill of Rights is freedom of religion.	権利章典によって保障されている最初の権利、つまり自由は、宗教の自由である。
Until after the Civil War, the protection of civil rights was left largely to the individual states.	南北戦争後まで、公民権の保護は主として各州にゆだねられていた。
One of the most important civil rights in the U.S. was the right to vote, or suffrage.	米国の公民権の中で最も重要なもののひとつは、投票する権利、つまり選挙権であった。
Women held marches and demonstrations for years before finally gaining the right to vote with the ratification of the Nineteenth Amendment in 1920.	女性たちは1920年の修正19条批准によってついに選挙権を獲得するまで、何年にもわたって行進やデモを続けた。
The number of representatives that each state may elect to the House of Representatives is based on the size of the state's population.	各州が下院議員として選べる議員の数は、その州の人口規模に基づいている。
Each representative is elected from a congressional district. Each state legislature is responsible for dividing the state into as many congressional districts as it has members in the House.	下院議員はいずれも、ひとつの下院議員選挙区から選挙される。各州の立法府はその州を、下院における議員数と同じだけの下院議員選挙区に分割する責任を負う。
The Constitution provides that each state, regardless of size, be represented in the Senate by two members. These members are known as senators.	憲法は各州の人口の大小に関係なく、上院を2名の議員で代表することと規定している。これらの議員たちは上院議員として知られている。

continued
▼

Day 53

CD-B13

社会・人文科学300語 / 政治 3

□ 521 bill
/bíl/

名議案、法案

□ 522 lobbyist
/lάbiist/

名ロビイスト
・院外活動をする人
名lobbyism（院外からの）議案通過[否決]運動、院外活動　**名動**lobby 院外団。議案通過[政策決定]に圧力をかける

□ 523 cabinet
/kǽbənit/

名内閣
・国家の行政権を担当する最高機関。大統領・元首などに対する助言機関（米国では国務省以下の各省の長官によって組織される）

□ 524 county
/káunti/

名〈米〉郡
・Louisiana と Alaska を除く各州の最大行政区画（Louisiana では parish、Alaska では borough がこれに相当する）

□ 525 the Republican Party
/ðə/ /ripʌ́blikən/ /pάːrti/

共和党
関Republican 共和党員（米国では象〈elephant〉を漫画化して共和党の象徴とする）

□ 526 the Democratic Party
/ðə/ /dèməkrǽtik/ /pάːrti/

民主党
関Democrat 民主党員（米国ではロバ〈donkey〉を漫画化して民主党の象徴とする）

□ 527 naturalization
/nætʃərəlizéiʃən, -laiz-/

名帰化
関naturalize 帰化する、〈外国人に〉市民権を与える

□ 528 quota
/kwóutə/

名移民割り合て制度、定員（受け入れる移民・会員・学生など）

□ 529 inalienable right
/inéiljənəbl/ /ráit/

奪うことができない権利（=unalienable）

□ 530 majority rule
/mədʒɔ́ːrəti/ /rúːl/

多数決原理
関majority 大多数、過半数

continued ▼

Before any bill is considered by Congress, it is carefully studied by a standing committee. The committee holds hearings to consider the bill.	いかなる議案も、議会で検討される前に、常任委員会によって慎重に調査される。この委員会は議案を検討するため、聴聞会を催す。
Lobbyists work for interest groups by keeping them informed about proposed legislation and by talking to decision-makers about their group's concerns.	ロビイストは利益団体に法案に関する情報を提供し、その団体の関心事について政策決定者たちと話し合うことによって、利益団体に奉仕する。
The present cabinet consists of the heads of the 13 executive departments, plus the United States representative to the United Nations. The title of most cabinet members is Secretary.	現在の（米国の）内閣は、13省の長の他に、国連への代表から成っている。大部分の内閣構成員の肩書は長官である。
Most of the states are divided into parts called counties.	州の大半は、郡と呼ばれる地域に分割されている。
In 1860 Abraham Lincoln became the first candidate nominated by the Republican Party to be elected president.	1860年、アブラハム・リンカーンは共和党から指名されて大統領に選ばれた最初の候補者となった。
For more than 125 years, the Democratic Party and the Republican Party have been the nation's two major political parties.	125年以上にわたって、民主党と共和党はこの国（米国）の二大政党である。
The legal process by which non-U.S. citizens may become a citizen is called naturalization.	外国人が市民となるための法的手続きは、帰化と呼ばれる。
The quota system is not used for refugees, or people fleeing their nations.	移民割り当て制度は難民、つまり母国を逃れてきた人々には適応されない。
We hold these truths to be self-evident: That all men are created equal; that they are endowed by their Creator with certain inalienable rights; that among these are life, liberty, and the pursuit of happiness. (Statement of Basic Human Rights in the Declaration of Independence)	われわれは以下の事実を自明のことと考える。すなわち、あらゆる人間は平等につくられていること、彼らは彼らの創造主から、いくつかの奪うことができない権利を与えられていること、それらの権利の中には生存、自由、幸福の追求が含まれていること。（米国独立宣言における基本的人権の声明）
The republic works because Americans believe in majority rule. When disagreements occur, the decision of the majority is accepted by all.	アメリカ人が多数決原理を信奉しているから、共和国はうまく機能している。不一致が生じたときは、多数の決定が全員によって受け入れられる。

continued
▼

復習テスト　政治

1　1〜10の単語の定義を表すものをa〜jから選びなさい。

1. amendment
2. Bill of Rights
3. suffrage
4. civil rights
5. Congress
6. the House of Representatives
7. bill
8. quota
9. absolute monarch
10. constitution

> a. the political, social, and economic rights guaranteed to all American citizens
> b. a limit on the number of immigrants who may come to the U.S. each year
> c. the lawmaking body of the national government
> d. a written change made in the constitution
> e. an all-powerful king or queen
> f. a written plan of government describing how a government is organized, listing the government's purpose, some of the nation's basic laws, and the rights of the nation's people
> g. the larger of the two houses of Congress
> h. a proposed law being considered by a lawmaking body
> i. the first ten amendments to the constitution
> j. the right to vote

2 選択肢 a、b のうち正しい語を選んで文を完成させなさい。

1. (a. The Supreme Court   b. The system of checks and balances) gives each branch of the government powers to check, or limit, the powers of the other two branches.

2. (a. The House of Representatives   b. The Senate), or the House, as it is sometimes called, has 435 members. All representatives are elected for two-year terms.

3. (a. Congressional districts   b. The separation of powers) is the divisions of a state, each of whose voters elect one member of the House of Representatives.

4. (a. Ratification   b. Veto) is the refusal of the president or a governor to sign a bill, which is then sent back to Congress or the state legislature with a message giving the reasons for its rejection.

5. Today (a. the House   b. the Senate) has 100 members — two senators elected from each of the 50 states.

6. A (a. senator   b. lobbyist) is a person who is paid to represent a certain group point of view, or interests, at congressional committee hearings.

7. The heads of executive departments in the federal government, who also act as advisors to the president, are called (a. cabinet members b. lobbyists).

8. The (a. majority rule   b. quota) system is the system in which the decision of more than half of the people is accepted by all.

9. A (a. federal system   b. county) is a state subdivision established to carry out state laws, collect taxes, and supervise elections.

10. (a. Totalitarian government   b. Representative democracy) is a system of government in which the people elect representatives to carry on the work of government for them.

Day 54

社会・人文科学300語 — 経済 ①

CD-B14

□ 531 standard of living
/stǽndərd/ /əv/ /líviŋ/

生活水準（=living standard）

□ 532 free enterprise system
/fríː/ /éntərpràiz/ /sístəm/

〈資本主義経済下の〉**自由企業制**
関 free economy 自由経済　関 free market 〈自由競争によって価値が決まる〉自由市場

□ 533 property
/prápərti/

名 **財産**、資産、地所

□ 534 financial
/finǽnʃəl, fai-/

形 **財政上の**、金融上の
関 financial crisis 金融危機　名 financier 財政家
名 financing 資金調達、融資、金融

□ 535 copyright
/kápiràit/

名 **著作権**、版権　形 著作権のある、版権で保護された（=copyrighted）　動 〈本・音楽・演劇などの〉著作権［版権］を取る
関 copyright reserved 版権所有　関 hold the copyright on a book その本の版権を持っている

□ 536 capital
/kǽpətl/

名 **資本（金）**、元金、蓄え
関 capital investment 資本投資　名形 capitalist 資本家。資本主義の、資本の　関 capitalist country 資本主義国

□ 537 capitalism
/kǽpətəlizm/

名 **資本主義**

□ 538 monopoly
/mənápəli/

名 **市場独占**、専売（権）、独占（権）、専売［独占］企業
動 monopolize ……の独占［専売］権を得る、独占する　名 monopolist 独占［専売］者

□ 539 merger
/mə́ːrdʒər/

名 〈会社などの〉**合併**、合同（=amalgamation）、吸収合併
動 merge 〈会社などを〉併合［合併］させる［する］

□ 540 conglomerate
/kənglámərət/

名 **(巨大) 複合企業**、コングロマリット
名 conglomerator（巨大）複合企業経営者

continued ▼

Many Americans enjoy a high standard of living.	多くのアメリカ人が、高い生活水準を享受している。
The American economy is described as a free enterprise system, which allows private business the freedom to operate for profit with minimum government interference and regulation.	米国経済は自由企業制といわれる。この体制は、政府による最小限の介入や規制の中で、私企業に利益追求のための営業活動の自由を与えるものだ。
The government protects the rights of individuals to own property and make a profit.	政府は、個人が財産を所有し利益を上げる権利を保護している。
The United States has developed an economic system in which most of its people can find work and achieve financial success.	米国は、国民の大半が仕事を見つけ、財政上の成功を収めることができるような経済体制を発展させてきた。
Americans have the right to profit from their ideas and inventions and from what they write. This right is protected by copyright.	アメリカ人は、自分たちの発想と発明、そして自分たちが書いたものからの利益を享受する権利をもっている。この権利は著作権によって守られている。
Capital is money that people save to invest in buildings, machines, and other forms of property used to produce goods and services.	資本とは、財とサービスを生み出す建造物、機械、その他の財産形態に投資するために蓄える金銭のことである。
The theoretical foundation of the American economic system was provided by Adam Smith, whose economic theory of "laissez faire" had a strong influence on the development of capitalism.	米国の経済体制の理論的な基礎はアダム・スミスによってもたらされた。彼の「レッセ・フェール（自由放任主義）」の経済理論は、資本主義の発展に強い影響を与えた。
An unfair practice of big business owners in the late 1800s and early 1900s was the forming of monopolies.	19世紀末と20世紀初頭に大企業経営者が採用した不公正な手段は、市場独占の形成だった。
The merger is one method of trying to form a monopoly.	合併は、市場独占を形成するひとつの方法である。
A single conglomerate may control communication systems, insurance companies, hotel and restaurant chains, and other types of businesses.	ひとつのコングロマリット（複合企業）が通信網、保険会社、ホテル・レストランチェーン、その他のビジネスを支配することもある。

continued
▼

Day 55 経済 2 社会・人文科学300語

CD-B15

□ 541 **public utilities** /pʌ́blik/ /juːtíləti:z/
公共事業 [企業]

□ 542 **proprietorship** /prəpráiətərʃìp/
名 自営業、所有権
関 proprietor 持ち主、所有者、経営者、事業主（商店・ホテル・土地など）

□ 543 **stock** /stɑ́k/
名 株（式）、株式資本
関 stock company 株式会社　関 stock exchange 株式取引
関 Stock Exchange 株式[証券]取引所　関 stockholder 株主

□ 544 **dividend** /dívədènd/
名 配当金（株式・保険）

□ 545 **Gross National Product** /gróus/ /nǽʃənl/ /prɑ́dəkt/
国民総生産（関 GNP）
● 国民が一定期間に生産した財・サービスの総生産額から原材料費などを引いたもの。各企業が生産した付加価値の総額

□ 546 **mass production** /mǽs/ /prədʌ́kʃən/
大量生産、量産、マスプロ

□ 547 **wholesaler** /hóulsèilər/
名 卸売業者、問屋
形 wholesale 卸[卸売]の　関 wholesale prices 卸値　関 at [by] wholesale 卸売で　関 retailer 小売商人　関 retail 小売、小売店。小売の、小売で

□ 548 **installment plan** /instɔ́ːlmənt/ /plǽn/
分割払い
関 installment 分割払い込み金　関 pay in monthly installments 月賦で払う

□ 549 **down payment** /dáun/ /péimənt/
（分割払いの）**頭金**
関 pay down （分割払いの）頭金として払う

□ 550 **balance** /bǽləns/
名 差額、差引勘定
関 bank account balance 銀行預金の残高

continued
▼

Telephone and electric companies are examples of public utilities. The government regulates public utilities to make sure they provide adequate services at reasonable prices.	電話会社や電気会社は公共事業の一例である。政府は公共事業が間違いなく適正なサービスを手ごろな値段で提供するよう、規制を加えている。
American business firms may be organized as single proprietorships, partnerships, or corporations.	米国企業には自営業、合名会社、株式会社などの組織がある。
A corporation usually is owned by many people. These people own shares of stock in the corporation.	株式会社は一般に、多数の人に所有されている。これらの人々は、その株式会社の株を所有している。
Dividends are profits paid to stockholders of a corporation.	配当金は、株式会社の株主に支払われる利益である。
Economists use the GNP as one measure of how well our economy is performing.	エコノミスト（経済学者や経済専門家）は国民総生産を、わが国の経済がどの程度うまくいっているかを調べる尺度としている。
Mass production is made possible by machine tools, standard parts, and division of labor.	大量生産は、工作機械、規格に合った部品、分業によって可能になる。
A factory often sells goods in large quantities to a wholesaler. Wholesalers sell to retailers.	工場はしばしば、商品を大量に卸売業者に販売する。卸売業者は小売業者に販売する。
Buying an article on an installment plan increases its cost. In addition to the regular price, a carrying charge as well as interest on the unpaid balance is included in the installment payments.	分割払いで品物を買うと、その費用は高くなる。通常の価格に加え、未払い額の繰越日歩や利子が払込額に加算される。
In an installment plan, the buyer initially pays part of the purchase price. This is called the down payment.	分割払いでは、買い手は購入価格の一部を最初に支払う。これは頭金と呼ばれる。
The rest of what the buyer owes after making the down payment is called the balance.	頭金を支払った後に買い手が支払うべき額の残額は、差額と呼ばれる。

continued
▼

Day 56 経済 3 社会・人文科学300語

CD-B16

□ 551 **barter** /bɑ́ːrtər/
名**物々交換**、交換貿易　動〈物資・役務など〉交換する、物々交換をする、交換による売買をする

□ 552 **deposit** /dipɑ́zit/
動〈金を〉**預ける**　名 積立金、保証金、手付金、(銀行)預金(額)
熟 deposit money in a bank 銀行に預金する　名 depositor 預け主、預金者

□ 553 **time deposit** /tɑ́im/ /dipɑ́zit/
定期預金、有期預金
関 demand deposit 要求払い預金、当座預金(預金者が要求次第払い戻されるもの)

□ 554 **broker** /bróukər/
名**仲買人**
名 brokerage 仲買[斡旋](業)、仲買手数料　関 brokage firm 仲買会社

□ 555 **premium** /príːmiəm/
名**保険料**、掛け金

□ 556 **social insurance** /sóuʃəl/ /inʃúərəns/
社会保険

□ 557 **Medicare** /médikèər/
名**メディケア**、老人医療保険(制度)
● medical と care の混成語。主に65歳以上の高齢者を対象とした、米国連邦政府の医療保証。カナダでは「国民健康保険」

□ 558 **Medicaid** /médikèid/
名**メディケード**、国民医療保険(制度)
● medical と aid の混成語。州と米国連邦政府が共同で行う低所得者や身障者のための医療扶助(制度)

□ 559 **recession** /riséʃən/
名〈一時的な〉**景気後退**(=slump)

□ 560 **collective bargaining** /kəléktiv/ /bɑ́ːrɡəniŋ/
〈労使間の〉**団体交渉**

continued
▼

Barter was used in early societies before money became the basis of trade.	貨幣が貿易の基礎となるまで、初期の社会では物々交換が行われた。
Automatic teller machines make it possible to deposit money, withdraw money, or transfer money from one account to another, even when the bank is closed.	自動現金引出・預入装置により、銀行が閉まっているときでも、お金を預けたり、引き出したり、あるいはお金をある口座から別の口座に移したりすることができるようになった。
The money that a depositor puts in a savings account is called a time deposit. On certain types of time deposits, which pay higher interest rates, money may be withdrawn only at the end of a 90-day period.	預金者が貯蓄預金口座に預けるお金は、定期預金と呼ばれる。高い利息が支払われるある種のタイプの定期預金では、90日が経過したときにようやく引き出せるようになる。
The organizations that buy and sell stocks for their customers are called brokerage houses, and the people who work there are called brokers.	顧客のために株を売買する組織は仲買業者と呼ばれ、そこで働く人は仲買人と呼ばれる。
Premiums may be paid yearly, or at regular times throughout the year.	保険料は年1回、あるいは年間の決まった時期に支払える。
Social insurance is required by state and federal laws. Individuals and companies must pay for social insurance programs.	社会保険は州または連邦の法律で命じられている。個人や企業は社会保険制度に加入しなければならない。
In 1965, Congress passed the health insurance program known as Medicare. This helps people 65 years of age and older to pay for hospital care and for some home nursing care.	1965年、議会はメディケアと呼ばれる健康保険制度を採択した。これにより65歳以上の国民は病院での治療や自宅での看護に対する支払いに補助が与えられる。
The Medicaid health insurance program was also passed by Congress in 1965. Under this program the federal government provides money to help the states pay the medical costs of poor people.	メディケード健康保険制度もまた、議会を1965年に通過した。この制度のもと、連邦政府は、各州が貧しい人々の医療費を支払うのを助けるための資金を提供している。
Sometimes the economy begins to slow down or stays in a decline for several months. Economists call this period a recession.	時に経済は停滞し始めたり、数カ月間も下降を続けたりする。エコノミストたちはこのような期間を景気後退と呼ぶ。
The right to settle differences with management through collective bargaining was a goal that labor unions struggled for — and eventually won.	(労使間の)団体交渉を通して経営者側との不一致を解決するという権利を得ることは、労働組合がそのために奮闘し、そしてついに勝ち取った目標だった。

continued

復習テスト 経済

解答は P.244

1 1〜10の単語の定義を a〜j から選びなさい。

1. capital
2. capitalism
3. Gross National Product
4. premium
5. barter
6. monopoly
7. conglomerate
8. stock
9. down payment
10. mass production

---

a. a company that produces and markets all or most of the total supply of a product or service

b. a share of ownership in a corporation

c. the money that people invest in business

d. the total value of the goods and services produced in a nation each year

e. the initial payment made on an item bought on an installment plan

f. a large company that controls many different kinds of smaller companies

g. the payments made for insurance protection

h. an economic system based on private ownership of the means of production

i. producing large amounts of goods rapidly by machine to supply the needs and wants of large numbers of people

j. the swapping of one product for another

2 選択肢 a、b のうち正しい語を選んで文を完成させなさい。

1. A nation's (a. Gross National Product   b. standard of living) is the material well-being of its population, based on the amount of goods and services they can afford.

2. A (a. patent   b. copyright) is the exclusive right, granted by law, to publish or sell a written, musical, or art work for a certain number of years.

3. A company has (a. a monopoly   b. dividends) if it is the only firm selling a product or providing a service.

4. A (a. balance   b. conglomerate) is formed by the merger of businesses that produce, supply, or sell a number of unrelated goods and services.

5. In some industries, monopolies are legal. These legal monopolies are (a. stock exchanges   b. public utilities), companies that provide essential services to the public.

6. There are over 11 million small businesses owned by one person. These small businesses, owned by one person, are called (a. single proprietorships   b. partnerships).

7. (a. Mass production   b. Capitalism) refers to making huge amounts of goods rapidly by machines to supply the needs and wants of the nation's large population.

8. A /An (a. installment plan   b. time deposit) is a system of buying in which the buyer makes a down payment and then pays the balance over a period of time.

9. (a. Barter   b. The free enterprise system) is an economic system in which people are free to run their businesses as they see fit.

10. (a. Collective behavior   b. Collective bargaining) is a process in which representatives of a labor union and an employer work to reach an agreement about wages and working conditions.

Day 57 社会・人文科学 300語

CD-B17

□ 561 **archaeologist** /à:rkiálədʒist/
名 考古学者
名 archaeology 考古学 形 archaeológical 考古学の

□ 562 **ethnologist** /eθnálədʒist/
名 民族学者、〈広く〉文化人類学者
名 ethnólogy 民族学、文化人類学　（注）ethno-「人種、民族」の意

□ 563 **ethnic group** /éθnik/ /grú:p/
民族集団（=ethnos）
● 人種的系統のみならず、言語・宗教・慣習などの文化的諸特徴をも共有する成員より成る集団

□ 564 **ethnocentrism** /èθnouséntrizəm/
名 自民族中心主義
● 多民族に対し排他的・蔑視的な思想
関 ethnicism 民族性重視主義、民族分離主義

□ 565 **symbolic** /simbálik/
形 象徴的な、表象的な
名 symbol 象徴、表象

□ 566 **norm** /nɔ́:rm/
名 規範、〈特定人間集団の〉典型的行動様式

□ 567 **humanitarianism** /hju:mænətέəriənizm, hju:-/
名 人道主義、博愛（主義）
形 humanitarian 博愛主義の、人道主義の

□ 568 **Amish** /á:miʃ, ǽmiʃ/
名 アマン派（の人々）
● 17世紀のスイス人牧師 J. Ammann が創始したメノー派の分派。米国 Pennsylvania に移住し、きわめて質素な服装を身につけ、電気・自動車を使用しないことなどで知られる

□ 569 **masculinity** /mæskjəlíniti/
名 男らしさ
形 másculine 男らしい、力強い、勇ましい　反 femininity 女らしさ　関 féminine 女らしい

□ 570 **prescription** /priskrípʃən/
名 規定、規範、法規
動 prescribe 規定する、命令する　関 proscríption 規則、禁止、追放　関 proscribe〈習慣などを〉禁止する

continued ▼

Archaeologists are scientists who study the life and culture of ancient people.	考古学者は古代の人々の生活と文化を研究する科学者である。
Ethnologists are scientists who study living cultures.	文化人類学者は現存の文化を研究する科学者である。
Ethnic groups are often identified by their patterns of family life, language, forms of recreation, religion, and other customs.	民族集団は、その家庭生活、言語、娯楽、宗教、その他の習慣の様式によって見分けられることが多い。
Ethnocentrism is used to describe a people's sense of superiority and use of its own cultural standards to judge others.	自民族中心主義は人々の優越感や、他者を判断するのに自分たちの文化的基準を使うことを表すのに使われる。
Dress is a form of symbolic language. The necktie, for example, may signal one's membership in white-collar society.	衣服は象徴言語のひとつの形である。たとえばネクタイはホワイトカラー(頭脳労働者)社会に属していることを示している。
Norms are rules or standards of behavior. They tell people how to act.	規範とは、行動の規則や基準である。これらは人々に、どうやって行動すべきかを教える。
A number of sociologists have found humanitarianism to be an important American value. Helping others and giving to the poor are ways in which Americans show their humanitarian concern.	人道主義は米国の重要な価値観である。他者を助け、貧しい人に施すのは、アメリカ人が彼らの人道主義的関心を示す方法である。
The Amish refuse to send their children to public schools because Amish values stress religious education.	アマン派の人々の価値観は宗教教育に重きを置いているので、自分たちの子どもを公立学校に送るのを拒む。
In general, the Mexican-American subcultures seem to place more importance on "masculinity" than do the Japanese-American subcultures.	一般的に、メキシコ系アメリカ人のサブカルチャーのほうが日系アメリカ人のサブカルチャーよりも、「男らしさ」により重きを置いているようだ。
Cultural norms include prescriptions, or things one must do, and proscriptions, or things one must not do.	文化的規範には規定、つまり人がしなければいけないこと、および禁止、つまり人がしてはいけないことが含まれる。

continued
▼

Day 58 社会 2 — 社会・人文科学 300 語

CD-B18

□ 571 **mores** /mɔ́:reiz/
名 〈一集団・一社会の〉**社会的慣行**、習俗、習律

□ 572 **codify** /kάdəfài/
動 **成文化する**、体系化する、法典に編む

□ 573 **legislate** /lédʒislèit/
動 **法律を規定する**、〈……に〉必要な法的規定を設ける
名 legislation 法律規定、立法、法律　形名 legislative 法律を規定する、立法上の。立法府［部］

□ 574 **affirmative action** /əfə́:rmətiv/ /ǽkʃən/
差別撤廃措置
● 差別されてきた少数民族や女性の雇用・高等教育などを積極的に推進する計画

□ 575 **conform** /kənfɔ́:rm/
動 〈模範・範例に〉**従わせる**、〈行為を法律・風俗などに〉適合させる、順応させる、〈人が規則・習俗に〉従う

□ 576 **deviant** /dí:viənt/
形 **基準[常軌]からはずれた[逸脱した]**、〈知能・社会適応・性行動における〉異常者
動 deviate 〈進路・常軌・原則などから〉はずれる

□ 577 **anomie** /ǽnəmì:/
名 **没価値状況**、アノミー
● 社会的基準や価値が見失われたり混乱している状態

□ 578 **social stratification** /sóuʃəl/ /strǽtəfikéiʃən/
社会成層
関 stratify 〈人々を〉階層化する

□ 579 **closed system** /klóuzd/ /sístəm/
閉鎖制

□ 580 **caste system** /kǽst/ /sístəm/
カースト制度、身分制度、階級制、社会的階級
● インドの世襲的階級で Brahman（司祭者）、Kshatriya（貴族・武士）、Vaisha（庶民）、Sudra（賤民）に大別される

continued
▼

Paying back borrowed money and keeping promises to friends are mores of American society.	借金を返すことと友人との約束を守ることは、米国社会の習律である。
Many laws not only codify mores but also specify gradations of "offensiveness." In our criminal codes, a distinction is made between a major crime, or felony, and a minor one, or misdemeanor.	多くの法律が習律を成文化するだけでなく、「危害性」の等級付けを規定している。米国の刑法では、大きな犯罪つまり重罪と、小さな犯罪つまり軽犯罪の区別が成されている。
In democratic societies, attempts to legislate morality have had mixed results. For example, in the United States, opposition to liquor in the 1920s led to the passage of the Eighteenth Amendment, which prohibited the manufacture, sale, and consumption of alcohol.	民主的な社会では、道徳を法律化しようとする試みは相反する結果をもたらしてきた。たとえば米国では、1920年代のアルコール飲料への反対論が修正18条の採択につながり、アルコールの製造、販売、飲用が禁止された。
Under affirmative action, persons from minority groups are given preferential treatment in admission and hiring policies, to compensate for discrimination in the past.	差別撤廃措置のもと、少数民族出身の人々に過去の差別を補償するため、入学や雇用政策を通して優先的扱いが与えられている。
Not everyone behaves in ways that society expects or approves. Even children may fail to conform to their parents' values.	だれもが社会が望み、認める方法で行動するわけではない。子どもたちでさえ、両親の価値観に従わないことがある。
What is deviant behavior in one place or at one time may be acceptable in another place or at another time.	ある場所、あるいはある時代に逸脱した行動は、別の場所、あるいは別の時代に受け入れられることもある。
Anomie is a situation in which either there are no rules of behavior or there are so many rules that no one knows which ones to follow.	没価値状況とは、行動に何の規則もないか、あまりにもたくさんの規則があり過ぎて、だれもどの規則に従ったらよいのかわからない状況のことである。
Societies can be placed along a continuum of social stratification.	各社会は、社会成層におけるひとつの連続体として並べることができる。
At one end of the stratification continuum are the closed systems, in which social position is determined by birth and there is little chance of moving from one stratum to another.	社会成層の連続体の一方の極にあるのは閉鎖制で、そこでは社会的地位は生まれながらに決められ、ひとつの階層から別の階層に移動する機会はほとんどない。
India has a caste system based on the Hindu religion. Under this system, people remain at the same level of wealth, power, and influence occupied by their parents.	インドはヒンドゥー教に基づくカースト制度を採用している。この制度のもと、人々は富、権力、影響力において両親と同じ水準にとどまる。

continued
▼

Day 59

CD-B19

社会・人文科学 300語

□ 581 meritocracy
/mèritákrəsi/

名 **能力主義（社会）**、実力社会
名 méritocrat〈育ちや富の力でなく〉個人の実力で権力をふるう者、実力者　関 merit system 実力［成績］本位制、能力主義任用制

□ 582 extended family
/iksténdid/ /fǽməli/

拡張［拡大、複合］家族（核家族の他に近親を含むもの）
関 nuclear family 核家族（父母とその家族から成る）

□ 583 patriarchal
/pèitriá:rkəl/

形 **家父長制度の**
名 pátriarchy 家父長制度、父権制、父権社会　名 pátriarch 家父長　関 matriárchal 女家長の　関 mátriarch 女家長　関 mátriarchy 女家長制、母権制、母権社会

□ 584 egalitarian
/igæ̀lətéəriən/

形 **平等主義の**　名 平等主義者
名 egalitárianism 平等主義

□ 585 division of labor
/divíʒən/ /əv/ /léibər/

分業

□ 586 apprentice
/əpréntis/

名（昔の）**徒弟**、年季奉公人、見習い

□ 587 socialize
/sóuʃəlàiz/

動 **社会化する**
名 socialization 社会化

□ 588 upward social mobility
/ápwərd/ /sóuʃəl/ /moubíləti/

社会での上昇志向
関 mobile〈人・階層などが〉移動性のある

□ 589 stereotype
/stériətàip/

名 **固定観念**、紋切り型、ステレオタイプ

□ 590 collective behavior
/kəléktiv/ /bihéivjər/

集団行動
● 社会的相互作用の結集である刺激の影響のもとにある個人の行動
関 collective 集団的な、集団

continued
▼

In a system called a meritocracy, a person's social position depends solely on merit, or achievement.	能力主義と呼ばれる制度においては、人の社会的地位は能力、すなわち業績に全面的に依存する。
The family in the era of our great-great-grandparents was usually an extended family — three generations living under one roof, or perhaps in separate houses on the same street.	祖父母の祖父母の時代の家族は、一般に拡大家族、つまり同じ屋根の下かあるいは同じ街路の別々の家に住む3世代家族だった。
Many families today are more democratic and less patriarchal than families in earlier times.	今日の多くの家族は昔の家族より民主的で、家父長制度的なところが少ない。
Few marriages today are truly egalitarian. Women still do most of the housework, even when they are also employed at jobs outside the home.	今日の結婚において、真に平等主義といえるものはほとんどない。女性は、家庭外の仕事に就いている場合でも、いまだに家事のほとんどを行っている。
Couples who challenge the traditional division of labor often depend on social supports outside the family: friends and relatives who give assistance, and child care facilities.	伝統的な役割分担に挑戦する夫婦は、家族以外からの社会的援助、すなわち手助けしてくれる友人や親戚や育児施設に依存することが多い。
In early America, the practical knowledge needed to make a living was often taught via the apprentice method.	初期の米国のおいては、生活していくのに必要な実践的知識は徒弟方式で教えられることが多かった。
As students are socialized and taught skills, they are also selected and channeled for various roles in life.	学生たちは社会化され、技能を教わるにつれ、人生におけるさまざまな役割に向けて選抜され、方向付けられてもいく。
Upward social mobility is a goal of many students and parents in the United States, and schools can help them achieve it.	社会での上昇志向は、米国の多くの学生や両親の目標であり、学校は彼らがそれを達成するのを助けることができる。
"Feminine" and "masculine" images are what social scientists call sex stereotypes.	「女らしい」とか「男らしい」とかいうイメージは、社会科学者たちが呼ぶところの性的ステレオタイプ（固定観念）である。
John Lofland has analyzed collective behavior that is not really goal-directed, such as that of a crowd.	ジョン・ロフランドは、群衆の行動のような、あまり目標志向でない集団行動を分析した。

continued
▼

復習テスト 社会

解答は P.245

1 1〜10の単語の定義をa〜jから選んで答えなさい。

1. ethnocentrism
2. proscriptions
3. ethnologist
4. norms
5. prescriptions
6. anomie
7. mores
8. deviant behavior
9. upward social mobility
10. archaeologist

a. a scientist who studies groups of people to learn about their cultures — folkways, customs, beliefs, and so on
b. a scientist who studies ancient life and culture by digging in ruins to uncover pots, bones, tools, weapons, and so on
c. rules stating what one must do
d. behavior that violates a fundamental social norm or set of norms
e. norms that express a society's ideas of right and wrong
f. the belief that one's group is superior to others in its moral standards, beliefs, or ways of behaving
g. movement into a higher stratum, or level, of society
h. rules forbidding certain behavior
i. normlessness
j. the rules that reflect the values of a society and govern the behavior of its members

2 選択肢 a、b のうち正しい語を選んで文を完成させなさい。

1. Groups whose members share a unique social and cultural heritage passed on from one generation to the next are known as (a. ethnic b. racial) groups.

2. Members of ethnic groups often see their ways of life as better than those of others. This attitude was given the name (a. ethnocentrism b. humanitarianism) by sociologist William Graham Sumner.

3. (a. Amish b. Deviants) are people who go beyond the limits of socially acceptable behavior.

4. The arrangement of a society into levels, called strata, based upon class, prestige, or power is called (a. social stratification b. affirmative action).

5. A family structure that includes many relatives or three or more generations, often living together or near one another, is called a/an (a. nuclear b. extended) family.

6. The process of learning the rules, beliefs, values, and acceptable ways of behaving in a culture or society is called (a. collective behavior b. socialization).

7. A (a. norm b. stereotype) is a set of oversimplified, exaggerated, and often negative ideas about a group of people. It implies that all members of the group are exactly alike and does not take individual differences into account.

8. A (a. closed system b. meritocracy) is a social system in which a person's social position is supposed to depend solely on merit, or achievement.

9. A (a. stratified system b. closed system) is a system in which a person is born to a definite station in life and has no chance of changing his or her social position.

10. The philosophy that people are morally obligated to help those in need is called (a. ethnocentrism b. humanitarianism).

Day 60 法律 1 — 社会・人文科学 300 語

CD-B20

□ 591 law-abiding
/lɔ́:əbàidiŋ/

形 法を守る
関 law-abiding citizens〈法律をよく守る〉善良な市民

□ 592 statutory law
/stǽtʃutɔ̀:ri/ /lɔ́:/

成文法、制定法
関 statutory 法定の、法令の、制定法上の

□ 593 common law
/kámən/ /lɔ́:/

普通法、コモンロー
● 英国に発達した判例法で、特に非成文的慣習法

□ 594 administrative law
/ædmínəstrèitiv, -strə-/ /lɔ́:/

行政法
関 administrative 行政（上）の、管理上の

□ 595 constitutional law
/kànstətjú:ʃənl/ /lɔ́:/

憲法
関 constitutional 憲法上の、立憲的な

□ 596 accuse
/əkjú:z/

動 告発［告訴］する、非難する
名 the accused (=deféndant) 被疑者、〈特に〉(刑事) 被告人（反 accuser 告発人）　関 plaintiff 原告

□ 597 bail
/béil/

名 保釈（金）　動〈判事が拘留中の被告人を〉保釈する

□ 598 trial
/tráiəl/

名 裁判、公判
関 criminal trial 刑事裁判　熟 bring ... to trial ……を告発［検挙］する

□ 599 grand jury
/grǽnd/ /dʒúəri/

大陪審
● 23 人以下の陪審員から成り告訴状の予審を行い、12 人以上が証拠十分と認めれば正式告訴を決定する

□ 600 indict
/indáit/

動 起訴する、〈大陪審が正式に〉起訴する
名 indictment 起訴（手続き）、告発、〈大陪審による正式の〉起訴（状）　関 bring in an indictment against ... ……を起訴する

continued

The law-abiding citizen realizes that laws are passed for the good of all.	法を守る市民は、法律は全員の利益のために（議会を）通過したのだと認識している。
Laws that are passed by lawmaking bodies are known as statutory laws. They are passed by Congress and by state and local governments.	立法機関によって採択された法律は、制定法の名で知られる。これらの法律は連邦議会、そして州および地方政府によって採択される。
Common law is a customary law that develops from judges' decisions. The judge applies the rule of common sense and common practice in making a decision.	普通法は、裁判官の判決から発達していった慣習法である。裁判官は判決を下すにあたり、常識や一般慣習の規則を採用する。
The Consumer Product Safety Commission is making an administrative law when it rules that a toy is unsafe and must immediately be taken off the market.	消費者製品安全委員会が、あるオモチャを安全でなく、ただちに市場から回収されるべきだと判定したとき、同委員会は行政法を制定していることになる。
Constitutional law is law based on the Constitution and on Supreme Court decisions made by interpreting the Constitution.	憲法は、憲法と、憲法を解釈した最高裁の判決とから成る。
All persons accused of a crime are entitled to the services of a lawyer.	犯罪を告発された人はすべて、弁護士の奉仕を受ける権利を与えられる。
A person accused of a crime does not ordinarily have to spend months in prison waiting for the case to come to trial. Usually the accused person may be released if he or she can put up bail.	犯罪を告発された人は普通、事件が裁判にかけられるのを待って、何カ月も拘置所で過ごさなければならないということはない。普通、保釈金を納めれば被告は出獄できる。
When a person is arrested on suspicion of a crime, this does not mean that the person must go to trial.	ある人がある犯罪の容疑で逮捕されたからといって、その人が裁判を受けなければならないということはない。
The grand jury examines the evidence against the accused person. It questions witnesses and investigates the facts in the case.	大陪審は被告人に対して事件の証拠を調査する。証人に質問したり、当該事件の事実を調べるのである。
If a majority of the grand jury decides that the evidence against the accused is strong enough, the person is indicted, or formally accused of a crime.	大陪審の過半数が、被告人に対して事件の証拠が強力なものであると判定したら、その人は起訴、すなわち正式に犯罪を告発されたことになる。

continued
▼

Day 61

法律 ② 社会・人文科学 300 語

CD-B21

□ 601
trial jury
/tráiəl/ /dʒúəri/

審理陪審、小陪審（=petit jury）

□ 602
verdict
/vɚ́ːrdikt/

名〈陪審員の〉**評決**、答申
熟 bring in [return] a verdict of guilty [not guilty] 有罪［無罪］の評決を下す

□ 603
testimony
/téstəmòuni/

名**証言**
動 testify 証人となる、証明［立証］する　熟 testify to [against] ... ……に有利［不利］な証言をする

□ 604
appeal
/əpíːl/

動**上訴［告訴・上告］する**　名 上訴［告訴・上告］

□ 605
jurisdiction
/dʒùərisdíkʃən/

名**司法権**、裁判権、管轄区
熟 have jurisdiction over ... ……を管轄する

□ 606
district court
/dístrikt/ /kɔ́ːrt/

地方裁判所
• 1) 連邦第一審裁判所、2) 諸州の下級裁判所
関 district〈行政・司法・選挙・教育などの目的で区分された〉地区、管区、行政区

□ 607
court of appeals
/kɔ́ːrt/ /əv/ /əpíːlz/

上訴裁判所
• 通常、州の supreme court の次に位置する中間上訴裁判所　《米》フロリダ州など一部の州では court of appeal

□ 608
the Supreme Court
/ðə/ /səpríːm/ /kɔ́ːrt/

最高裁判所

□ 609
impeachment
/impíːtʃmənt/

名**弾劾**、告発
動 impeach〈重大な罪で〉告発［非難］する、〈公職にある者を法的に〉弾劾する

□ 610
suspect
/sʌ́spekt/

名**容疑者**
動 suspéct〈人に〉疑いをかける

continued
▼

The Sixth Amendment to the Constitution guarantees an accused person the right to be tried before a trial jury. The men and women of the trial jury, who judge the evidence, are called jurors.	憲法の修正６条は、被告人に小陪審の審理を受ける権利を保障している。証拠を審理する小陪審の男女は、陪審員と呼ばれる。
Usually the jury's verdict must be decided by a unanimous vote. This means that all the members must agree on whether the accused person is guilty or innocent.	通常、陪審員の評決は全員一致の投票で決められなければならない。このことは、被告人が有罪か無罪かについて、全員の意見が一致していなければならないことを意味する。
Accused persons cannot be forced to testify against themselves. Their lawyers have the right to question all witnesses to make sure their testimony is accurate and honest.	被告人は自分に不利な証言を強制されることはない。彼らの弁護士は、証人全員に対して、その証言が正確で偽りがないかどうかを確かめるために、尋問を行う権利をもつ。
If there is reason to doubt that justice was done in a court trial, the convicted person can appeal to a higher court.	公判において正当に扱われなかったと思われる理由があれば、有罪判決を受けた人は上級裁判所に上訴できる。
Lawsuits between citizens of different states come under federal jurisdiction. District courts are the only federal courts in which juries are used.	異なる州の住民間の訴訟は、連邦裁判権のもとに入る。地方裁判所は、陪審を使う唯一の連邦裁判所である。
At the base of our federal court system are the district courts. There is at least one district court in each of the 50 states and the District of Columbia.	わが国（米国）の連邦裁判制度で下位にあるのは、地方裁判所である。50のそれぞれの州とコロンビア特別区に、少なくともひとつの地方裁判所がある。
The next level of the federal court system consists of courts of appeals. These courts review cases from the district courts that are appealed.	連邦裁判制度の次の段階は、各上訴裁判所から成る。これらの裁判所は地方裁判所から上訴されてきた事件を再検討する。
The highest court in the land is the Supreme Court of the United States. It works chiefly as an appeals court. It reviews cases that have been tried in lower federal courts and in state courts.	わが国で最上級の裁判所は米国最高裁判所である。これは主に上訴裁判所として機能する。ここでは下級の連邦裁判所や州裁判所で審理された事件を再検討する。
Federal judges are appointed for life by the president. They can be removed from office only by impeachment.	連邦裁判官は大統領によって終身職として任命される。彼らは弾劾によらない限り、免職されることはない。
In the 1966 case of Miranda vs. Arizona, the Supreme Court declared that the police must inform suspects of their rights before they question them.	最高裁は1966年のミランダ対アリゾナ事件で、警察は容疑者たちにその権利を知らせない限り、彼らを尋問することはできないと宣言した。

continued
▼

Day 62 法律 3

611 juvenile delinquent
/dʒúːvənl/ /dilíŋkwənt/

非行少年
関 juvenile 少年[少女]の 関 delinquent 法律違反者（の） 関 juvenile delinquency 未成年非行[犯罪]、少年非行[犯罪]

612 life imprisonment
/láif/ /imprízṇmənt/

終身刑
関 imprison 刑務所に入れる、拘束する 関 imprisonment 投獄、監禁、拘留、禁固（刑）

613 execute
/éksikjùːt/

動（判決に基づいて）〈罪人の〉**死刑を執行する**、処刑する
名 execution 処刑、死刑執行

614 manslaughter
/mǽnslɔ̀ːtər/

名 **殺人**、（特に）殺意なき殺人、故殺（一時の激情によるなど）
反 murder 謀殺、殺意ある殺人

615 aggravated assault
/ǽɡrəvèitid/ /əsɔ́ːlt/

加重暴行
● 婦女子に対する暴行など、普通の暴行より刑を加重される
関 aggravate〈負担・罪などを〉一層重くする 関 assault 暴行、暴行未遂、強姦

616 burglary
/bə́ːrɡləri/

名〈犯罪を目的とする〉**住居侵入（罪）**、（特に）押し込み、夜盗（罪）

617 white-collar crime
/hwáitkɑ̀lər/ /kráim/

ホワイトカラーの犯罪
● 横領・脱税・贈収賄・不当広告などホワイトカラーの職務に関連した罪

618 civil law
/sívəl/ /lɔ́ː/

民法、民事法
反 criminal law 刑事法

619 parole
/pəróul/

名 **仮釈放（許可証）**、執行猶予 形 仮釈放の
動 仮釈放する
熟 on parole 仮釈放されて

620 capital punishment
/kǽpətl/ /pʌ́niʃmənt/

死刑、極刑（=death penalty）

continued ▼

Americans have long debated the proper role of the police, the justice of court and prison systems, and the treatment of juvenile delinquents.	アメリカ人は警察の適切な役割、裁判および刑務所制度の正当性、そして非行少年の扱いについて討論を重ねてきた。
Most states define a first-degree murder as one that is planned and carried out deliberately. It may be punished by life imprisonment.	大半の州は第一級殺人を、計画され、故意に実行された殺人と規定している。第一級殺人は終身刑によって罰せられることもある。
A number of states have laws that permit some first-degree murderers to be executed.	多くの州に、一部の第一級殺人犯を死刑に処することを認める法律がある。
A murder that is carried out on the impulse of the moment is called a second-degree murder. This type of murder is sometimes called manslaughter.	時のはずみで実行された殺人は、第二級殺人と呼ばれる。この種の殺人は時に故殺と呼ばれる。
Aggravated assault is any kind of physical injury that is done intentionally to another person.	加重暴行は他者に対して故意になされた、あらゆる種類の身体への傷害のことである。
Examples of crimes against property are burglary, larceny, robbery, vandalism, and arson.	所有物に対する犯罪の例には、住居侵入罪、窃盗罪、強盗罪、公共物などの汚損罪、放火罪などがある。
White-collar crimes range from stealing paper clips to embezzlement and fraud.	ホワイトカラー犯罪は、クリップを盗むことから、横領や詐欺にまで及ぶ。
States have the power to establish their own systems of criminal and civil laws, with the result that each state has its own laws, prisons, police force, and state court.	州は独自の刑法および民法体系を制定する権限を持っており、その結果として、各州は独自の法律、刑務所、警察力、そして州裁判所を備えている。
After serving only a part of their sentence, prisoners may be eligible for parole, or release, on condition that they obey certain rules and keep out of trouble.	刑期の一部のみを務めた後、囚人は特定の規則に従い、悶着を起こさないとの条件で仮釈放、すなわち釈放の資格を得ることができる。
In 1976 the United States Supreme Court ruled that capital punishment as a penalty for murder is constitutional.	1976年、米国最高裁は殺人に対する刑罰として、死刑を合憲と判定した。

continued
▼

復習テスト 法律

解答は P.246

1 1〜10の単語の定義をa〜jから選びなさい。

1. statutory law
2. administrative law
3. indictment
4. verdict
5. jurisdiction
6. the Supreme Court of the United States
7. manslaughter
8. capital punishment
9. accuse
10. trial

---

a. the unplanned killing of a person; also known as second-degree murder

b. the decision of a jury

c. bring charges against (someone) for a misdeed

d. judging a criminal case in court

e. the death penalty

f. a formal charge against an accused person

g. the authority to judge and administer laws

h. the highest court in the U.S.

i. a law passed by Congress or by a lawmaking body of a state or local government

j. a law made by a government agency

2 選択肢 a、b のうち正しい語を選んで文を完成させなさい。

1. (a. Verdict   b. Bail) is a sum of money deposited with the court as a pledge that the accused will appear in court at the time of trial.

2. The group of people that hears the evidence in a criminal case and decides whether there is reason to bring the accused person to trial is called a (a. grand jury   b. trial jury).

3. To make sure that justice is done, the United States court system provides the right to (a. indict   b. appeal), or ask for a review of a case.

4. The constitution gives the federal courts (a. testimony   b. jurisdiction), or authority, to conduct trials for a wide variety of cases and to judge these cases.

5. The conditional release from prison of a convicted person before the completion of the person's sentence is called (a. bail   b. parole).

6. The (a. grand jury   b. trial jury) are the people who hear the evidence and decide the verdict in a court case. Between six and 12 people may serve on a jury.

7. Bringing a formal charge, or indictment, against a government official is called (a. imprisonment   b. impeachment).

8. The harshest punishment is (a. aggravated assault   b. capital punishment) putting the criminal to death for a serious crime.

9. Most states define juveniles as people under 18. Juveniles become (a. delinquents   b. suspects) when they are found guilty of breaking a law.

10. (a. White-collar crimes   b. Burglaries) are crimes committed by white-collar workers while on the job.

Day 63 — 教育 1 / 社会・人文科学 300 語

CD-B23

621 attendance /əténdəns/
名 出席、出席者数、出席率
熟 take attendance 出席をとる 動 attend 出席する

622 compulsory /kəmpʌ́lsəri/
形 義務的な、強制的な、必修の
関 compulsory education 義務教育

623 kindergarten /kíndərgà:rtn/
名 幼稚園 (4〜6歳)
関 university 総合大学 関 college 単科大学 関 junior college 短大 関 occupátional school 実業校
関 vocational school 専門学校 関 núrsery school 保育園

624 diploma /diplóumə/
名〈学位・資格の〉免状、卒業［修了］証書

625 college-bound /kɑ́lidʒbàund/
形 大学進学志望の
・（注）-bound「〜行きの、〜を目指す」の意

626 grant /grǽnt/
動 与える、許可する、認める、是認する（=admit）
名 許可、助成金

627 academic standard /ækədémik/ /stǽndərd/
学術水準

628 reputable /répjutəbl/
形 評判のよい、りっぱな
名 reputation 評判 関 a person of high reputation 評判のよい人

629 board of education /bɔ́:rd/ /əv/ /èdʒukéiʃən/
教育委員会
関 board 委員（会） 関 teachers' union 教職員組合

630 elective /iléktiv/
形〈科目が〉随意選択の 名 選択科目
関 elective course 選択科目 関 elective system 選択科目制度 関 required course〈学校で〉必修科目［単位］ 関 prerequisite 基礎必須科目

continued

Improved attendance is a major goal of high schools, because it results in students' learning more and getting better grades.	出席率の向上は、生徒がより多くを学び、より良い成績を得る結果となるので、高等学校の重要な目標となっている。
By the middle of the 20th century, the education of children from about 6 to 16 was free and compulsory in most countries of the world.	20世紀半ばには、世界のほとんどの国で、約6歳から16歳までの子どもの教育が無料・義務化された。
Public education from kindergarten through grade 12 is tax-supported; no tuition is required.	幼稚園から第12級までの公教育は税金に支えられており、授業料は不要である。
In 1970, the City University of New York (CUNY) began admitting almost any student with a high school diploma.	1970年、ニューヨーク市立大学（CUNY）が、高校の卒業証書をもっている学生のほとんどすべてを受け入れ始めた。
College-bound students may be enrolled in college-preparatory courses such as chemistry, political science, or advanced writing.	大学進学志望の学生は、化学、政治科学、あるいは上級ライティングなどの大学入学準備課程を履修している。
Arts colleges grant degrees to students who concentrate in specialized fields such as ballet and filmmaking.	芸術大学はバレエや映画製作などの特殊な分野を専攻する学生に学位を与えている。
Besides the diversified course offerings at all levels, there is also variety in schools' academic standards and reputations.	あらゆる種類の大学には、多様なコースが提供されているだけでなく、学術的水準や評価にも多様性が見られる。
Highly reputable colleges such as Harvard and Yale accept only students of exceptional ability.	ハーバードやイェールなどの非常に評価の高い大学は、抜きんでた能力をもつ学生だけを受け入れる。
In public schools, decisions about school curriculum, teacher certification, and student achievement standards are made by boards of education at the state and/or district level.	公立学校におけるカリキュラム、教師の資格、生徒の学業水準に関する決定は、州ないし地域あるいはその両方の教育委員会によってなされる。
Most secondary schools require students to take English, mathematics, science, social studies, and physical education. In addition to this "core" curriculum, students choose "elective" courses in their areas of interest.	大半の中等学校は、生徒に英語、数学、科学、社会、そして体育を受けるよう要求している。この「コア」カリキュラムに加えて、生徒は自分たちが興味のある分野から「選択」科目を選ぶ。

continued
▼

Day 64 教育 2

631 integration
/ìntəgréiʃən/
名 人種的統合、〈軍隊・学校などの〉人種差別廃止（による教育［公共］施設の統合）
動 íntegrate 〈人種集団・学校・地域に対する〉人種［宗教的］差別を廃止する、……における差別施設を統合する **名形** integrationist 人種差別廃止論者（の）

632 dropout
/drápàut/
名 〈高校などの〉**中途退学者**
関 drop out 中途退学する

633 illiteracy
/ilítərəsi/
名 無学、読み書きの能力がないこと
形 illiterate 非識字の、読み書きのできない

634 tardiness
/táːrdinis/
名 遅刻すること
形名 tardy 遅れた、遅刻した。遅刻

635 motivate
/móutəvèit/
動 動機を与える、動機づける
名 motivátion 動機づけ、熱意 **名形** motive 動機、動因、〈行動の〉目標。行動を起こさせる、動機となる

636 competency
/kámpətənsi/
名 能力（=competence）
形 competent 有能な、十分な

637 bureaucracy
/bjuərákrəsi/
名 官僚政治［主義、制度、支配］
名 búreaucrat 官僚、官僚主義者 **形** bureaucrátic 官僚政治の、官僚的な **動** buréaucratize 官僚化する、官僚体制［組織］にする

638 uniformity
/jùːnəfɔ́ːrməti/
名 一様、均質、均一、一律
形 úniform 一様な、均質の、同一基準に一致する

639 maximize
/mǽksəmàiz/
動 最大限に強化［拡大、活用］する、最大限に活用［重要視］する

640 orderly
/ɔ́ːrdərli/
形 きちんとした、規律正しい、整頓された

continued

One measure introduced to speed up integration was the compulsory "busing" of black children to schools in white areas and white children to schools in black areas.	人種的統合を促進するために導入されたひとつの措置は、白人居住地域の学校への黒人の子どもたち、そして黒人居住地域の学校への白人の子どもたちの「強制バス通学」の義務付けだった。
If education is the pathway into the societal mainstream, lack of education is a road to nowhere. Today's dropouts are tomorrow's unemployed and poverty-stricken.	教育が社会的主流への道であるとすれば、教育の欠如は失敗への道である。今日の中途退学者たちは、明日の失業者、貧困に悩む人々である。
Illiteracy affects all of us. A person who cannot read enough to hold a decent job contributes little or nothing to the national wealth.	無学はわれわれ全員に影響を与える。まともな仕事をこなすのに十分な読解力がない人は皆、国の豊かさにほとんどあるいはまったく貢献しない。
Tardiness is a bad habit for students to develop. When a student is tardy three times, it will be counted as a one-day absence.	遅刻は、生徒が身につけてはならない悪い習慣である。生徒が3回遅刻したら、それは1日分の欠席と数えられる。
A teacher's expectations often serve as a positive or negative motivating factor for students.	教師の期待は生徒にとって、積極的または消極的な動機付けの要因となることがしばしばある。
As more and more Americans complained about poor student competency, many school systems began to stress more strongly the teaching of fundamental reading, writing, and math skills.	より多くのアメリカ人が生徒の能力の貧弱さに不満の声をあげるにつれ、多くの教育機関が基本的な読み・書きと数学の技能に、より重点を置き始めた。
As a bureaucracy, the school system allows little flexibility in its hierarchy of authority.	官僚制度と同じように、教育機関は権限の階層の中で、柔軟性がほとんどない。
Curiosity, creativity, and individualism decline with the insistence on uniformity, obedience, and conformity to a structured approach.	均質性や従順性、構造主義的アプローチへの服従を強調すると、好奇心や創造力、そして個性が低下する。
If education is to achieve its goal of maximizing individual development, it must allow all students equal educational opportunities.	教育が、個人の成長を最大限まで拡大させるというその目標を達成しようとするものであるなら、すべての生徒に平等な教育機会を与えなければならない。
The most effective schools are those that achieve a balance between discipline and self-expression, treating students as mature, responsible persons in a cooperative, orderly, and democratic atmosphere.	最も効果的な学校は、協力的で、規律正しく、そして民主的な雰囲気の中で、生徒を成熟した、責任ある人間として扱いながら、規律と自己表現のバランスを達成している学校である。

continued
▼

Day 65

教育 ③ 社会・人文科学 300 語

CD-B25

641 Scholastic Assessment Test
/skəlǽstik/ /əsésmənt/ /tést/

SAT（学力適正検査）
- 米国で高校生が大学に入るために受ける全国統一試験

642 attainment
/ətéinmənt/

名 到達、達成
動 attain〈目的・望みなどを〉（努力して）成し遂げる、達成する、獲得する **関** achieve〈技術・能力・努力などによりある目標を〉達成する **関** accomplish〈ある特定の仕事・目標などを努力を払って〉完成・達成する

643 challenging
/tʃǽlindʒiŋ/

形〈物事が〉**興味をかき立てる**、刺激的な、やりがいのある

644 progressivism
/prəgrésəvìzm/

名 進歩主義教育理論
関 progressive education 進歩主義教育（生徒の個性・自主性を尊重する教育法） **関** essentialism《米教育》本質主義（ある文化の根幹を成す思想・技能を体系的にすべての生徒に与えることを主張する）

645 enrollment
/inróulmənt/

名 入学、登録、登録者名簿、登録（者）数
動 enroll 登録する、入学する

646 punctuality
/pʌ̀ŋktʃuǽləti/

名 時間を守ること
形 púnctual 時間［期限］を固く守る、規則的な

647 peer
/píər/

名 仲間、同僚、同等の者
関 peer group 仲間集団、ピアグループ（年齢・地位のほぼ等しい同一価値観をもつ社会学上の集団）

648 ability grouping
/əbíləti/ /grú:piŋ/

能力別編成
関 tracking 能力［適性］別クラス編成

649 IQ test
/ái/ /kjú:/ /tést/

知能テスト
関 intelligence quotient 知能指数

650 credential
/kridénʃəl/

名 資格、学業証明書（卒業する大学生に渡す）
- 複数形で表すことが多い
形 資格認定の
名 credentialism 証明書［学歴］偏重主義 **関** diplomaism 学歴主義、学歴偏重

continued
▼

In 1988 the average scores on the verbal and mathematical sections of the Scholastic Assessment Test were 428 and 476, respectively in the U.S.	1988年、SAT（学力適正検査）の英語と数学部門の平均点は、米国においてそれぞれ428点と476点だった。
It is well known that educational attainment is strongly correlated with socioeconomic status.	教育的達成が社会経済的地位と強い相関関係にあることは、よく知られている。
Schools and colleges should adopt more rigorous standards and higher expectations of academic performance. Students will learn more in a more challenging environment.	学校や大学は学問上の目標達成に対して、より厳格な基準とより高い期待をもつべきである。より刺激的な環境におかれると、生徒たちはより多くを学ぶ。
Progressivism emphasizes vocational training, "daily-living skills," and a "child-centered curriculum."	進歩主義教育理論は職業訓練、「日常生活に必要な技能」、そして「子ども中心のカリキュラム」に重点を置いている。
Preschool education improved cognitive performance in early childhood and increased high school graduation and college enrollment rates.	就学前教育は幼児期における認知能力を向上させ、高校卒業率や大学入学率を高めた。
In early grades teachers place emphasis upon cleanliness, neatness, quiet, orderliness, punctuality and conformity.	低学年では、教師たちは清潔にすること、整頓すること、静かにすること、規律を守ること、時間を守ること、素直に従うことに重点を置く。
Family and peers play an important role in an individual's educational motivation.	家族と仲間は、教育に関する個人の動機付けにおいて重要な役割を果たす。
Ability grouping and teacher expectations affect self-esteem, motivation, and achievement.	能力別編成と教師の期待は、自尊心、やる気、成績に影響を与える。
Critics argue that only certain intellectual aptitudes are tested in IQ tests: language, mathematical reasoning, and spatial and symbolic relationships.	評論家は、知能テストでは言語、数学的推理力、そして空間的・記号的関係性といった特定の知的素質しか検査されないと主張している。
Over half the states in the U.S. now require a minimum competency test (MCT) as a condition of earning a high school diploma. In a credential-oriented society, the MCT is emerging as another necessary credential.	現在では米国の半分以上の州が、高校の卒業証書を得る条件としてMCT（最小限能力テスト）を課している。資格優先の社会では、MCTは新たな必要資格として台頭しつつある。

基本語彙200語

自然科学300語

社会・人文科学300語

continued
▼

復習テスト 教育

1 1〜10の単語の定義をa〜jから選びなさい。

1. compulsory
2. reputable
3. illiteracy
4. tardy
5. motivate
6. uniformity
7. orderly
8. attainment
9. challenging
10. peer

> a. well-behaved, well-organized
> b. requiring the full use of one's abilities and effort; difficult, but in an interesting way
> c. late, not punctual
> d. sameness
> e. achievement, accomplishment
> f. a person of the same age, class, position, etc., as oneself
> g. obligatory, required
> h. the condition of being unable to read and write
> i. stimulate to action; provide with an incentive or motive
> j. having a good reputation; honorable

2 選択肢 a、b のうち正しい語を選んで文を完成させなさい。

1. (a. Elective   b. Busing) is a compulsory integration measure of carrying students by bus to a school in a different area, where the pupils are of a different race.

2. The attempts of the last 30 years to achieve fully (a. reputable   b. integrated) schools have resulted in some successes and some failures. In some cities, compulsory busing has worked. Yet in many areas, people have reacted strongly against it.

3. In some cities and rural areas, more American students (a. drop out of   b. complete) than graduate from high school.

4. At least 21 million American adults, 13 percent of the population, are (a. reputable   b. illiterate), that is, unable to read and write.

5. Because schools are (a. challenging   b. bureaucracies), they function through a multitiered stratification of personnel wherein the limits of authority are clearly set and specific procedures are delineated for various situations.

6. The plans and actions of one's school or (a. punctuality   b. peers) affect a student's aspirations, regardless of teachers' efforts at motivation.

7. (a. Ability grouping   b. Integration) is a system that puts students of similar ability in the same class to provide a proper standard of instruction.

8. (a. Scholastic Assessment Tests   b. IQ tests) are widely used as a basis for ability grouping, because most people associate educational achievement with intelligence.

9. To weed out incompetence, 30 states now require teachers to pass a (a. competency test   b. attendance) before being certified.

10. (a. Progressivism   b. Essentialism) is associated with the educational philosophy of John Dewey, who believed that education should stress the expression of individuality and learning through experience.

Day 66

社会・人文科学300語 — 心理 ①

CD-B26

□ 651 psychology
/saikálədʒi/

名心理学、〈個人・群衆などの〉心理、心理状態、〈人の〉性格
名psychólogist 心理学者 **形**psychológical 心理学の [を用いた]、心理 (的) な、精神の **関**psychiatrist /saikáiətrist/ 精神病医 [学者] **関**psychiatry 精神医学

□ 652 experimental group
/ikspèrəméntl/ /grúːp/

実験群
関control group 対照群（同一実験で実験要因を加えないグループ） **関**expériment 実験。実験をする

□ 653 behavioral
/bihéivjərəl/

形行動の、習性の
名behaviorism 行動主義（客観的観察の可能な行動のみを対象に限定する） **関**behavioral science 行動科学（人間の行動の一般原理を探る社会科学）

□ 654 reasoning
/ríːzəniŋ/

名推論、論法
関a reasoning creature 人間

□ 655 classical conditioning
/klǽsikəl/ /kəndíʃəniŋ/

古典的条件づけ
関conditioning 条件づけ（条件反応、条件反射を形成すること）

□ 656 operant conditioning
/ápərənt/ /kəndíʃəniŋ/

オペラント条件づけ
関operant 自発的な、操作的な

□ 657 artificial intelligence
/àːrtəfíʃəl/ /intélədʒəns/

人工知能
●推論・学習など人間の能力に似た動作を計算機が行う能力

□ 658 cybernetics
/sàibərnétiks/

名サイバネティックス
●制御と通信を扱う学問、特に生物体の通信・制御機構と電子機器のそれとを比較研究する

□ 659 cognition
/kɑɡníʃən/

名認識、認知、認識力
形cognitive 認識の [に関する]、経験的事実認識に基づいた

□ 660 developmental psychology
/divèləpméntl/ /saikálədʒi/

発達心理学

continued

Psychology is formally defined as the study of the behavior of organisms.	心理学は正式には、生物の行動の研究と定義される。
A typical experiment involves two groups of subjects: an experimental group and a control group. The independent variable is manipulated for the experimental group, but held constant for the control group.	典型的な実験では実験群と対照群のふたつの被験者群を用いる。独立変数は実験群に対し手を加えられるが、対照群に対しては一定に保たれる。
Ivan Pavlov, a Russian physiologist, studied conditioned reflexes in animals. His work greatly influenced behavioral and learning theory.	ロシアの生理学者、イワン・パブロフは動物の条件反射を研究した。彼の研究は行動理論と学習理論に偉大な影響を及ぼした。
Jean Piaget, a Swiss psychologist, studied the development of thought, concepts of space and movement, logic, and reasoning in children.	スイスの心理学者、ジャン・ピアジェは子どもにおける思考の発展、空間及び運動概念、論理、推論を研究した。
A bell repeatedly associated with food will eventually trigger salivation, even if presented without food. This is an example of classical conditioning.	食餌のたびにベル音を繰り返すと、ついには食餌なしでもベル音だけで唾液分泌を引き起こす。これは古典的条件付けの例である。
Children will be more likely to say "Thank you." if they have been repeatedly praised for doing so when given something. This is an example of operant conditioning.	子どもたちは何かをもらって「ありがとう」と言ったことを繰り返しほめられると、「ありがとう」をもっと口にするようになる。これはオペラント条件付けの例である。
Artificial intelligence refers to the computer simulation of cognitive processes, such as language and problem-solving.	人工知能とは言語や問題解決といった認知過程のコンピューター・シミュレーションのことをいう。
Cybernetics is the study of feedback control and communications in machines and living systems.	サイバネティックスとは、機械と生物におけるフィードバック制御と通信の研究である。
The study of cognition covers a number of functions — for example, perception, attention, memory and language.	認知の研究では種々の機能、たとえば、知覚、注意、記憶、言語などを扱う。
Developmental psychology is the study of the development of cognition and behavior from birth to adulthood.	発達心理学とは、誕生から成人に至る認知と行動の発達の研究である。

continued
▼

Day 67

心理 2 — 社会・人文科学 300 語

661 psychoanalysis
/sàikouənǽlisis/
名 精神分析（学、法）
名 psychoánalyst 精神分析学者　形 psychoanalytic 精神分析の

662 neurosis
/njuəróusis/
名 神経症、ノイローゼ
形名 neurótic 神経の、神経症の、【口語】神経過敏な。神経症患者

663 neuroticism
/njuərátəsìzm/
名 神経症的性格［性質、傾向］

664 psychosis
/saikóusis/
名 精神障害
名 psychotic /saikάtik/（【俗語】psycho /sáikou/）精神障害者　関 psychopath〈反社会的または暴力的傾向の〉精神病質者　関 psychópathy 精神病質　関 psychopathic 精神病質の

665 schizophrenia
/skìtsəfríːniə/
名 統合失調症
形名 schizophrénic 統合失調症の、統合失調症的な。統合失調症患者　【口語】schizo /skítsou/

666 obsession
/əbséʃən/
名 脅迫観念、脅迫現象、忘念
関 be obsessed by ... ……に取りつかれている
形 obsessional 脅迫観念［妄想］に取りつかれた。脅迫観念に取りつかれた［脅迫神経症の］人
関 obsessional neurosis 脅迫神経症　動 obséss 悩ます

667 phobia
/fóubiə/
名 恐怖症、病的恐怖、

668 stress
/strés/
名 ストレス、緊張

669 unconscious
/ʌnkάnʃəs/
形 自意識のない、無意識の
副 unconsciously 無意識に

670 meditation
/mèdətéiʃən/
名 瞑想、黙想、沈思黙考
動 méditate 黙想する

continued
▼

Sigmond Freud, an Austrian psychiatrist, developed psychoanalysis.	オーストリアの精神病医、シグムント・フロイトは精神分析を発展させた。
The main disturbance in neurosis tends to be one of mood. Perception of reality, however, is relatively unaffected.	神経症における主な障害は気分であることが多い。しかし現実の認識という点では、それほど影響を受けない。
People with a high level of neuroticism are worriers, emotional and moody.	神経症的性格の強い人は、心配性で感情的でそううつ的である。
In a paranoid psychosis, an individual may believe that others are plotting against him or her.	妄想症的精神障害にかかった人は、他人が自分に対し陰謀を企んでいると信じ込む。
Schizophrenia may develop in early adulthood, and can lead to profound changes in personality and behavior.	統合失調症は青少年期に発病し、人格と行動に激しい変化をもたらす。
A person excessively troubled by fears of contamination by dirt or disease may engage in continuous hand-washing for four or five hours every day. This is an example of a patient suffering from obsession.	ほこりや病気による汚れに対し過度な恐怖に取りつかれた人は、1日に4、5時間も続けざまに手を洗ったりする。これは脅迫観念を被った患者の例である。
A phobia is an excessive, irrational fear of an object or situation. Examples of phobias are agoraphobia, acrophobia, and claustrophobia.	恐怖症とはあるものや状況に対する過度で不合理な恐怖である。恐怖症の例に、広場恐怖症、高所恐怖症、閉所恐怖症がある。
Individual reactions to stress are varied, and may include irritability, fatigue, anxiety or physical health problems, such as stomach ulcers or high blood pressure.	ストレスに対する個人の反応は、短気、疲れ、不安、または胃潰瘍や高血圧といった身体上の健康問題と、さまざまである。
Emotional problems and irrational actions are believed by psychoanalysts to stem from unconscious conflicts.	情緒障害と不合理な行動は無意識な葛藤から生じると、精神分析学者は考えている。
People with high blood pressure can learn methods to lower it, such as relaxation, meditation, and lifestyle changes.	高血圧の人は、リラクゼーション、瞑想、ライフスタイルの変化といった方法を身に付けるといい。

基本語彙200語

自然科学300語

社会・人文科学300語

continued
▼

Day 68 — 心理 3 社会・人文科学300語

CD-B28

□ 671
introspection
/ìntrəspékʃən/
- 名 **内省**、内観、自己反省（=self-examination）
- 形 introspective 内省的な、内観的な、自己反省の
- 名 introspectionism 内観主義（心理学）

□ 672
psychotherapy
/sàikouθérəpi/
- 名 **精神療法**（特に催眠術による）
- 形 psychotherapéutic 精神療法の

□ 673
trauma
/tráumə, trɔ́:-/
- 名 **(精神的)外傷**（精神に持続的な影響を与える衝撃）
- 形 traumátic 外傷(性)の、深く傷ついた

□ 674
dementia
/diménʃiə/
- 名 **認知症**
- 関 senile dementia 老年性認知症 形 demented 認知症になった 関 amentia 〈先天的な〉知的障害

□ 675
depression
/dipréʃən/
- 名 **うつ病**、抑うつ（症）
- 関 be depressed 意気消沈した

□ 676
empathy
/émpəθi/
- 名 **感情移入**、共感
- 動 empathize 感情移入する

□ 677
extrovert
/ékstrəvə̀:rt/
- 名 **外向型の人**、外向者
- 名 extrovérsion 外向（性） 形 éxtroverted 外向性の強い、外向型の

□ 678
introvert
/íntrəvə̀:rt/
- 名 **内向型の人**、内向者
- 名 introvérsion 内向（性） 形 introverted 内向的な

□ 679
long-term memory
/lɔ́:ŋtə̀:rm/ /méməri/
- **長期間記憶**
- 反 short-term memory 短期間記憶

□ 680
amnesia
/æmní:ʒə/
- 名 **健忘(症)**、記憶喪失
- 形 名 amnesiac 健忘症の（人）

continued ▼

John Watson, an American founder of behaviorism, rejected introspection, and regarded psychology as the study of observable behavior.	行動主義を提唱したアメリカ人、ジョン・ワトソンは内観を拒否し、心理学を観察可能な行動の研究とみなした。
Psychotherapy is a method of treating mental problems which involves talking, rather than using drugs or other physical treatments.	精神療法は、精神障害に対する治療法であり、薬物を使ったり他の物理的治療法よりも、むしろ対話のような方法を使う。
Brain damage can be caused by trauma or a disease, or it may be present at birth.	脳の損傷は精神的外傷や病気が原因となりうるし、または生まれたときに損傷を負っていることもある。
Dementia is typically a problem of old age.	認知症は老年期に典型的な障害である。
Clinical depression is often treated with electro-convulsive therapy (ECT), in which an electrical current is passed through the brain.	臨床的うつ病では電気ショック療法が必要となることが多い。この療法では電流が脳を通過する。
Carl Rogers emphasized the importance of certain qualities, such as empathy, warmth and genuineness, in a psychological counselor.	カール・ロジャーズは感情移入、心の温かさ、誠実さといった心理カウンセラーの人格の重要性を強調した。
Extroverts are sociable, outgoing, active, impulsive, "tough-minded" people.	外向型の人は、社交的で親しみやすく、活発で直情的で「現実的な」人である。
Introverts are "tender-minded" individuals, noted for being withdrawn, inner-directed, passive, cautious, and reflective.	内向型の人は、引っ込み思案で内にこもり、受動的で用心深く思慮深いといった性格が顕著で、「気が弱い」人である。
Long-term memory uses semantic processing: as the level of processing becomes more meaningful, memory becomes more effective.	長期記憶は意味をいかに処理するかを利用する。処理の程度が意味あるものになればなるほど、記憶は効果的となる。
The patient suffering from amnesia could converse normally, except that he couldn't remember what happened a few seconds before.	健忘症にかかった患者は正常に会話することができたが、数秒前に起こったことを思い出すことができなかった。

continued
▼

復習テスト　心理

1　1〜10の単語の定義を a〜j から選びなさい。

1. reasoning
2. psychology
3. agoraphobia
4. acrophobia
5. claustrophobia
6. unconscious
7. introspection
8. empathy
9. extrovert
10. introvert

> a. the observation by an individual of his or her own mental processes
> b. fear of enclosed places
> c. realistic thinking directed toward problem-solving
> d. fear of open spaces and crowded places
> e. without awareness
> f. a sociable, impulsive and active person
> g. the ability to imagine oneself in the position of another person, and so to share and understand that person's feelings
> h. a quiet, inward-looking, and thoughtful person
> i. the scientific study of the behavior and experiences of organisms
> j. fear of heights

2 選択肢 a、b のうち正しい語を選んで文を完成させなさい。

1. A/An (a. experimental   b. control) group is a group of subjects for whom the experimenter alters the independent variable, the influence of which is being investigated.

2. In (a. classical   b. operant) conditioning, as described by Pavlov, a new stimulus can evoke an automatic response by being repeatedly associated with a stimulus that naturally provokes that response.

3. In (a. classical   b. operant) conditioning, as described by Thorndike and Skinner, the frequency of a voluntary response can be increased by following it with a reinforcer, or reward.

4. (a. Neurosis   b. Psychosis) is a general term for a serious mental disorder in which the individual commonly loses contact with reality and may experience hallucinations or delusions.

5. (a. Neurosis   b. Psychosis) is a general term referring to emotional disorders, such as anxiety, depression and obsessions.

6. A/An (a. obsession   b. cognition) is a repetitive, unwanted thought that is often recognized by the sufferer as being irrational, but which nevertheless causes him or her distress.

7. (a. Meditation   b. Stress) refers to a wide range of situations or events which can tax the individual's physical or mental coping abilities.

8. (a. Depression   b. Dementia) is a progressive loss of mental abilities, such as memory and orientation.

9. In (a. short-term   b. long-term) memory, limited amounts of information are stored for brief periods of time. Content that is to be retained for longer periods of time is transferred to (a. short-term   b. long-term) memory.

10. (a. Depression   b. Obsession) is an emotional state characterized by sadness, unhappy thoughts, apathy and dejection.

Day 69 文学語学 1 社会・人文科学 300語

CD-B29

□ 681 **mythic** /míθik/
形 **神話の**、架空の（=mythical）
名 myth 神話、作り話 名 mythólogy 神話、神話集、神話学［研究］ 名 mythicism 神話的解釈、神話主義

□ 682 **literary** /lítərèri/
形 **文学の**、文学的な
関 literary works 文学作品、著作物

□ 683 **aesthetic** /esθétik/
形 **審美的な**、美学の、芸術的な 名 美学的原理、美的価値観
名 aesthetics《哲学》美学

□ 684 **poetry** /póuitri/
名 **韻文**、詩、詩歌
名 poem /póuəm/ （一遍の）詩 名形 poétic 詩。詩的な 名 póet 詩人

□ 685 **prose** /próuz/
名 **散文**、散文体
反 verse 詩形、詩の一行、韻文

□ 686 **epic** /épik/
名 **叙事詩**、史詩、エピック、〈映画・小説などの〉大作
• Iliad（『イーリアス』）など英雄の冒険・業績・民族の歴史などを歌った長唄
関 a Hollywood epic ハリウッドの（超）大作

□ 687 **lyric** /lírik/
名 **叙情詩** 形 叙情的な、音楽的な
• lyrics と複数にすると「歌詞」という意になる
関 lyric poetry 叙情詩

□ 688 **fiction** /fíkʃən/
名 **小説**（=novels）、作り話、作り事（=invention）
関 Fact [Truth] is stranger than fiction.《諺》事実は小説よりも奇なり

□ 689 **figurative** /fígjurətiv/
形 **比喩的な**（=metaphórical）、比喩の多い

□ 690 **novel** /návəl/
名 〈作品としての〉**（長篇）小説**
名 novelist 小説家 動 novelize 小説化する

continued
▼

In the ancient oral traditions, literature had a mainly public function — mythic and religious.	古代の口承の時代には、文学は人々にとって主に、神話と宗教の役割を持っていた。
As literary works came to be preserved in writing, their role became that of a vehicle for the exploration and expression of emotion and of the human situation.	文学作品が文章に残されるようになると、それは人間の感情や境遇を探究し表現する役割を担うこととなった。
Aesthetic criteria came increasingly to the fore; the English poet and critic Coleridge, for example, defined prose as words in their best order.	英国の詩人で批評家のコールリッジが散文を最もまとまりの良い文章表現と定義したように、審美的な基準がどんどん目立つようになった。
Poetry has traditionally been distinguished from prose, although the distinction is not always clear-cut.	詩は古くから散文と区別されてきた。ただしその区別は必ずしも明確ではない。
Poetry tends to be metrically formal, whereas prose corresponds more closely to the patterns of ordinary speech.	詩は韻律の形式にこだわる傾向がある。一方、散文はより日常の会話体に近い。
The Iliad and *The Odyssey* are epic works attributed to Homer — works probably intended to be chanted in sections at feasts.	『イーリアス』と『オデュッセイア』はホメロス作とされる叙事詩である。それはたぶん宴会などの席でうたわれた作品である。
Over the centuries poetry has taken on a wide range of forms, from the lengthy narrative such as the epic, to the lyric, which expresses personal emotion in songlike form.	何世紀もの間に、詩は叙事詩のような長大な物語詩から歌曲のような形式で個人の感情を表現する叙情詩まで、広範な形式をとってきた。
The term fiction is usually used to refer to imaginative works of narrative prose such as the novel or the short story.	小説とは一般に、長編、短編どちらでも想像に基づく散文体物語のことである。
Poetry is the imaginative expression of emotion or thought, often in metrical form, and often in figurative language.	詩は想像に基づく感情や思考の表現であり、韻を踏んだり、比喩的な言葉を使ったりすることが多い。
By the 19th century the novel had become the main form of narrative fiction in Europe and the U.S.	19世紀には欧州や米国で、長編小説が物語小説の主流形式となった。

continued
▼

Day 70 文学語学 2

691 **allegory** /ǽligɔ̀ːri/	名 **寓話物語** 動 állegorize 寓話化する、〈寓話物語として〉表現［説明］する 形 allegóric 寓話物語の（ような）
692 **biography** /baiágrəfi/	名 **伝記**、一代記、伝記文学 形 biográphic 伝（体）の 関 a biographic dictionary 人名辞典 関 autobiógraphy 自伝
693 **fairy tale** /féəri/ /téil/	**おとぎ話**、うその話、作り話
694 **children's literature** /tʃíldrənz/ /lítərətʃər/	**児童文学**
695 **adventure story** /ædvéntʃər/ /stɔ́ːri/	**冒険小説**
696 **detective fiction** /ditéktiv/ /fíkʃən/	**推理小説**（=detective story [novel]） 関 detective 探偵。探偵の 関 private detective 私立探偵
697 **fantasy** /fǽntəsi/	名 **空想物語**（特に科学小説のこと）、空想的作品
698 **oral literature** /ɔ́ːrəl/ /lítərətʃər/	**口承文学**
699 **satire** /sǽtaiər/	名 **風刺文学**、風刺 形 satirical /sətírikəl/ 風刺的な 名 satirist /sǽtərist/ 風刺家
700 **parody** /pǽrədi/	名 **パロディー**、風刺的もじり詩文 動 もじる、へたにまねる

continued

Allegory is often used for moral purposes, as with John Bunyan's *Pilgrim's Progress* (1678).	ジョン・バニヤンの『天路歴程』(1678)に見られるように、寓話物語は教訓を目的としたものが多い。
Biography was firmly established as a literary form in the 18th century in England with *Lives of the English Poets* (1779-81) by Samuel Johnson, and Samuel Boswell's *Biography of Johnson* (1791).	英国におけるサミュエル・ジョンソンの『詩人伝』(1779～81)とジェームズ・ボズウェルの『サミュエル・ジョンソン伝』(1791)の発表とともに、18世紀に伝記ははっきりと文学ジャンルのひとつとして確立された。
Fairy tales were originally part of a vast range of oral literature, credited only to the writers who first recorded them, such as Charles Perrault.	おとぎ話はもともと、膨大な口承文学の一部を成すものだが、シャルル・ペローのように、最初にそれを記録した作家にだけ功績が認められた。
The late 19th century was the great era of **children's literature** in the UK, with the publications of works by Lewis Carroll.	19世紀後半、英国ではルイス・キャロルの作品が出版されて、児童文学の黄金時代を形成した。
Adventure stories have often appealed to children even when they were written for adults. Examples include *Robinson Crusoe* by Daniel Defoe, and the satirical *Gulliver's Travels* by Jonathan Swift.	冒険小説は大人向けに書かれたときですら、子どものお気に入りとなることが多い。たとえば、ダニエル・デフォーの『ロビンソン・クルーソー』やジョナサン・スウィフトの風刺に富んだ『ガリバー旅行記』などがそうだ。
The earliest work of **detective fiction** was *Murders in the Rue Morgue* (1841) by Edgar Allen Poe, and his detective, Dupin, became the model for those who detected by deduction from a series of clues.	最初の推理小説はエドガー・アラン・ポーの『モルグ街の殺人』(1841)であり、彼が創造した探偵デュパンは一連の手がかりから推理して犯人を見破る探偵のモデルとなった。
Fantasy started to thrive in the late 1960s, after the success of Tolkien's *Lord of the Rings* (1954-55).	空想物語は、トールキンの『指輪物語』(1954～55)の成功以後、1960年代後半にその隆盛が始まった。
Most preliterate societies seem to have had a tradition of **oral literature**, including short "folk tales," legends, proverbs, and riddles, as well as longer narrative works.	文字のなかった社会のほとんどは、より長大な物語と同様に短い民話、伝説、諺、なぞなぞなど口承文学の伝統を持っていたようだ。
A **satire** is a work, in poetry or prose, which uses wit, humor, or irony, to ridicule human pretensions or expose social evils.	風刺文学は、人間の自惚れを嘲笑したり社会悪を暴露するために機知、ユーモア、皮肉を取り入れた韻文または散文である。
A **parody** mocks a particular work, such as a poem, by imitating its style, often with purely comic intent rather than to make a moral point.	パロディーは文体を似せて詩などの作品をまねたものであるが、教訓的であるよりもむしろ純粋に笑いを誘うことを意図したものが多い。

continued
▼

Day 71 文学語学 3

社会・人文科学 300 語

□ 701 parts of speech
/pɑ́ːrts/ /əv/ /spíːtʃ/

品詞

□ 702 punctuation
/pʌ̀ŋktʃuéiʃən/

名 句読点

□ 703 acronym
/ǽkrənìm/

名 頭字語

□ 704 antonym
/ǽntənìm/

名 反意語、反義語
名 antónymy 反意性　形 antónymous 反意語の関係にある

□ 705 synonym
/sínənìm/

名 類義語、同義語
形 synónymous 類義語の、同意語の、同義の、同じことを意味する　名 synónymy 類義語の比較研究、同意語集、同義性

□ 706 homonym
/hámənìm/

名 同音異義語、同綴同音異義語
形 homónymous 同義の、同音異義の　名 homónymy 同義

□ 707 dialect
/dáiəlèkt/

名 方言、〈標準語をはずれたとされる〉方言、お国なまり、〈語派の一部を成す〉言語
関 local dialect 地域方言　関 class dialect 階級方言
形 dialéctal 方言の　名 dialectólogy 方言学

□ 708 etymology
/èṭəmálədʒi/

名 語源学、〈語の〉語源的意味

□ 709 jargon
/dʒɑ́ːrgən/

名 〈同業者・同一集団内だけに通ずる〉専門用語、職業語、仲間言葉、わけのわからない言葉

□ 710 rhetoric
/rétərik/

名 修辞的技巧、修辞学、華麗な文体
形 rhetórical 修辞学の、修辞的な、修辞効果をねらった、表現が凝った

continued ▼

The four major parts of speech are the noun, verb, adjective and adverb.	品詞には大きく分けて、名詞、動詞、形容詞、副詞の4つがある。
Punctuation contributes to the effective layout of visual language; if a work is not adequately punctuated, there may be problems of ambiguity and unclear association among words.	句読点により、目で見る言語の割り振りが良くなる。句読点のつけ方が悪いと、意味があいまいになったり、語句の関係が不明瞭になったりと問題が出てくる。
Examples of acronyms are NATO (North Atlantic Treaty Organization), and radar (radio detecting and ranging).	頭字語の例に NATO（北大西洋条約機構）や radar（レーダー）がある。
Antonyms may vary according to content and situation. In a discussion of the weather, "dull" and "bright" are antonymous, but when one is talking about knives and blades, the opposite of "dull" is "sharp."	反意語は内容と状況によって異なる。たとえば天気の話をしているときに "dull"「曇った」と "bright"「晴れた」は反意語の関係にあるが、ナイフや刃について話しているときは "dull"「切れ味の悪い」の反意語は "sharp"「よく切れる」である。
"Good" and "evil" are antonyms; "good" and "bad" are also antonyms; and therefore, "evil" and "bad" are synonyms in this context.	"good"「良い」と "evil"「邪悪な」は反意語である。"good"「良い」と "bad"「悪い」も反意語である。よって "evil" と "bad" はこの場合、類義語である。
Homonyms are an aspect of language in which two or more words may sound and look alike (proper homonyms), may sound the same but look different (homophones), or may look the same but sound different (homographs).	言語における同音異義語には、ふたつ以上の語が発音と綴りがどちらも同じである同綴同音異義語、発音は同じだが綴りが異なる同音異義語、綴りは同じだが発音が異なる同綴異義語がある。
"Dialect" is often used in a judgmental and dismissive way, as in "the locals have a harsh, ugly dialect."	方言は「地方の人間は荒く聞き苦しい方言を使う」といったような、軽蔑的な評価をするのに利用されることが多い。
Research in etymology has been particularly successful in tracing the development of words and word elements within the Indo-European language family.	語源学における研究は特に、印欧語族の語彙と語の要素の発展をたどることに成功している。
Jargon is language usage that is complex and hard to understand, usually because it is technical or occupational.	専門用語は一般に、専門または職業上の用語であるため、複雑で難解な語法である。
Nowadays, "rhetoric" is often a pejorative term as in "Cut the rhetoric and tell us what you really think!"	今日、「修辞的技巧」は、「修辞的技巧を使わずに、考えていることをはっきり言いなさい！」などといわれるように、しばしば軽蔑的な用語である。

continued
▼

復習テスト 文学語学

解答は P.248

1 1〜10の単語の定義を a〜j から選びなさい。

1. biography
2. children's literature
3. fantasy
4. antonymy
5. synonym
6. jargon
7. rhetoric
8. allegory
9. figurative
10. aesthetic

> a. near or identical meaning between or among words
> b. an account of a person's life
> c. a story, poem, painting, etc., in which the characters and actions represent general truths, good and bad qualities, etc.
> d. works specifically written for children
> e. near or precise oppositeness between or among words
> f. the specialized or technical language of a group or profession
> g. non-realistic fiction
> h. of or showing a highly developed sense of beauty; artistic
> i. metaphorical, not literal
> j. traditionally, the art of the orator or of public speaking and debate

2 選択肢 a、b のうち正しい語を選んで文を完成させなさい。

1. An (a. epic   b. essay) is a narrative poem or cycle of poems dealing with some great action, often the founding of a nation or the forging of national unity, and often using religious or cosmological themes.

2. (a. Non-fiction   b. Fiction) is a general term for any work or type of work whose content is completely or largely invented.

3. (a. Prose   b. Poetry) is often divided into the categories of lyric, or song-like poetry (sonnet, ode, elegy, pastoral); and narrative, or story-telling poetry (ballad, lay, epic).

4. A (a. novel   b. parody) is an extended fictional prose narrative, often including some sense of the psychological development of the central characters and of their relationship with the world.

5. The term (a. biography   b. detective fiction) refers to novels and short stories in which mysteries are solved, mainly by professional or amateur detectives.

6. Stories which are or have been transmitted in spoken form, such as public recitation, rather than through the written word, are called (a. children's literature   b. oral literature).

7. (a. Punctuation   b. Parts of speech) is the system of conventional signs and spaces by means of which written and printed language is organized so as to be as readable, clear, and logical as possible.

8. An (a. antonymy   b. acronym) is a word formed from the initial letters and/or syllables of other words, intended as a pronounceable abbreviation.

9. A (a. dialect   b. jargon) is a variety of a language, spoken either in a particular area (The "Yorkshire dialect", by a particular social group ("the dialect of educated Standard English"), or both ("The Black American dialects of English").

10. (a. Rhetoric   b. Etymology) is the study of the origin and history of words within and across languages.

Day 72

歴史 1 — 社会・人文科学 300 語

CD-B32

□ 711
colony
/kάləni/

名**植民地**、殖民、入植者
動colonize ……に植民地をつくる [移住する]　形colonial 植民 (地) の　名colonialism〈経済・政治・社会政策としての〉植民地主義

□ 712
settlement
/sétlmənt/

名**定住**、植民、移民、植民地、開拓地
動settle 植民する、移住させる　名settler 移民、移住者、開拓者、入植者

□ 713
diverse
/divə́:rs/

形**多様な**（=varied）、別種の、種々の
名diversity 種々、雑多、多様性　動diversify 多様化させる

□ 714
Puritan
/pjúəritn/

名**清教徒**、ピューリタン
● 16～17 世紀に英国国教内に現れた新教徒の一派。厳格な信仰から教義・礼拝儀式の改革を要求し、迫害されて一部は 1620 年 Pilgrim Fathers となってアメリカ大陸に移住した

□ 715
Protestant
/prάtəstənt/

名**プロテスタント**、新教徒　形プロテスタントの、新教徒の
関Protestantism プロテスタンティズム　関Protestant ethic プロテスタンティズムの倫理：労働への献身・倹約・労働の成果を上げることを強調する　関Catholic〈Protestant に対して〉〈ローマ〉カトリック教会 (の)、旧教 (の)

□ 716
mercantilism
/mə́:rkəntilizm/

名**重商主義**、〈一般に〉商業本位 [主義]

□ 717
the American Revolution
/ði/ /əmérikən/ /rèvəlú:ʃən/

アメリカ革命
● = the Revolutionary War：米国独立戦争（1775～83）のことで、英国では the War of American Independence という

□ 718
slavery
/sléivəri/

名**奴隷制度**
名slave 奴隷

□ 719
immigration
/ìməgréiʃən/

名**(入国) 移住**、入植、入国
名immigrant〈外国・他地域からの〉移民、(入国) 移住者　関émigrant〈他国・他地域への〉(出国) 移民

□ 720
frontier
/frʌntíər/

名**開拓前線 [地帯]**、フロンティア（開拓地と未開拓地の境界地域）

continued ▼

The history of the United States began on July 4, 1776, when the 13 English colonies declared their independence from Great Britain.	米国の歴史は、13のイギリス植民地が英国からの独立を宣言した1776年7月4日に始まった。
The native American Indians resisted the expansion of European settlement.	原住民であるネイティブ・アメリカンは、ヨーロッパ人定住の拡大に抵抗した。
Colonies were founded by various kinds of people for different reasons, and consequently were very diverse.	植民地は多種多様な人々によりさまざまな理由で建設された。その結果、形態も多様なものとなった。
Massachusetts was colonized by Puritans, religious dissenters from the Church of England.	マサチューセッツには、英国国教会の非国教徒である清教徒が植民地をつくった。
Except for Maryland, the English colonies were overwhelmingly Protestant, and often Catholics could neither vote nor hold public office.	英国植民地は、メリーランドを除いて、圧倒的に新教徒が多かった。カトリック教徒はしばしば、投票もできなければ公職に就くこともできなかった。
The British government adopted the economic philosophy called mercantilism. According to this philosophy, colonies existed for the benefit of the mother country.	英国政府は重商主義という経済政策を採用した。この政策に従って、植民地は母国の利益のために存在した。
The written constitution was an American invention. No nation had ever had one before the American Revolution.	成文憲法は米国の発明だった。アメリカ革命以前に成文憲法をもつ国はひとつもなかった。
In 1787, Congress ruled that the states to be formed from the Northwest Territory should never allow slavery or involuntary servitude.	1787年、米国議会は北西部領地で形成される州では奴隷制も強制労働もけっして許さないと規定した。
Between 1790 and 1860, the population increased from four million to almost 31.5 million, to which large-scale immigration contributed a good share.	1790年から1860年の間に、人口は400万人から3,150万人近くまで増加した。かなりの部分、大規模な移住がその要因となった。
In American history, the concept of "rugged individualism" is commonly identified with frontier heroes such as Daniel Boone and Davy Crockett, men who braved the wilderness alone.	米国史において、「武骨な個人主義」は一般に、ひとりで勇敢に荒野に立ち向かった男たち、ダニエル・ブーンやデイヴィ・クロケットといったフロンティアの英雄に当てはまる考え方である。

continued
▼

Day 73

社会・人文科学 300語 / 歴史 2

CD-B33

□ 721 the Civil War
/ðə/ /sívəl/ /wɔ́:r/

南北戦争（1861〜65）

□ 722 the Emancipation Proclamation
/ði/ /imænsəpéiʃən/ /pràkləméiʃən/

奴隷解放令
- 1862年9月にリンカーンが発し、1863年1月1日発効

□ 723 Reconstruction
/rìkənstrʌ́kʃən/

名 再編入
- 南北戦争直後の南部諸州の再統合（1865〜77）

□ 724 segregation
/sègrigéiʃən/

名 人種差別（=racial discrimination）
動 segregate 差別待遇をする **関** desegregate 人種差別を廃止する

□ 725 poll tax
/póul/ /tæks/

人頭税
関 poll 投票、投票結果、投票数、世論調査

□ 726 separate but equal
/sépərèit/ /bət/ /í:kwəl/

分離すれども平等
- 《米》人種分離平等政策で、黒人と白人の分離はするが教育・乗り物・職業などでは差別をしないこと

□ 727 agrarian
/əgréəriən/

形 農地の、農業の、農民の **名** 農地改革論者
関 Agrarianism 土地均分論

□ 728 reservation
/rèzərvéiʃən/

名 〈ネイティブ・アメリカンのための〉政府指定保留（地）、居留地

□ 729 the Prohibition movement
/ðə/ /pròuhəbíʃən/ /mú:vmənt/

禁酒運動
関 Prohibition 《米》禁酒法（憲法修正第18条）、禁酒法期間（1920〜33）

□ 730 conservative
/kənsə́:rvətiv/

形 保守的な **名** 保守的傾向の人、保守派

continued
▼

Slavery was the main factor in the Civil War, which lasted from 1861 to 1865. The South fought the Civil War to preserve slavery: the north to preserve the Union.	奴隷制は1861年から1865年まで続いた南北戦争の主な原因だった。南部は奴隷制を維持するため、北部は国家統一を維持するために南北戦争を戦った。
Black slaves were freed by Abraham Lincoln's Emancipation Proclamation and by the Thirteenth Amendment to the Constitution.	黒人奴隷はアブラハム・リンカーンの奴隷解放令と憲法修正第13条により自由の身となった。
After the death of Lincoln, radical Republicans who wanted to punish the South imposed a policy called Reconstruction.	リンカーンの死後、南部の処罰を望む共和党急進派は再編入という政策を課した。
By the end of 1877, southern whites had nullified the legal protections Reconstruction had tried to provide for blacks, and had made segregation of the races in every area of public life official policy.	1877年末までに、南部白人は再編入が黒人に与えようとした法的保護を無効にし、社会生活のあらゆる領域において人種差別を公的政策とした。
Between 1890 and 1910, the southern states imposed legal qualifications for voting, such as literacy tests and poll taxes.	1890年から1910年の間に、南部諸州は読み書き能力試験や人頭税など、投票への法的資格を課した。
In 1896 a Supreme Court decision, Plessy vs. Ferguson, declared that legal segregation of the races was constitutional as long as "separate but equal" facilities were provided for both.	1896年の連邦最高裁判所プレッシー対ファーガソン判決は、「分離すれども平等な」施設が白人黒人双方に提供される限り、法的人種差別は憲法に違反しないと宣言した。
The South remained predominantly agrarian until World War I.	南部では第一次世界大戦まで圧倒的に農業が中心だった。
There was a series of Indian wars in which the Indians were driven from their ancestral homelands and, in the end, were herded onto reservations on the poorest land.	一連のネイティブ・アメリカンと政府軍との戦争により、ネイティブ・アメリカンは先祖代々の土地を追われ、最後には最も不毛な土地にある政府指定保留地に集められた。
Women were especially active in the Prohibition movement.	禁酒運動では、特に女性が活躍した。
Several conservative southern states passed laws forbidding the teaching of evolution in the public schools.	南部でも特に保守的ないくつかの州は、公立学校で進化論を教えることを禁止する法律を制定した。

continued
▼

Day 74

CD-B34

□ 731
organized crime
/ɔ́ːrɡənàizd/ /kráim/

組織犯罪

□ 732
the Ku Klux Klan
/ðə/ /kjúː kláks klǽn/

クー・クラックス・クラン
- 第一次世界大戦後米国に結成された白人秘密テロ結社で、旧教徒・ユダヤ人・黒人・進化論者などを排斥する

□ 733
prosperity
/prɑspérəti/

名 繁栄、成功
形 prosperous 繁栄する (=thriving)、裕福な **動** prosper 繁栄する、〈事業などが〉成功する

□ 734
the Great Depression
/ðə/ /gréit/ /dipréʃən/

大恐慌
- 1929年米国に始まった。the Slump ともいう

□ 735
the New Deal
/ðə/ /njúː/ /díːl/

ニューディール政策
- F. D. ルーズベルト大統領の社会保障と経済復興を主とした革新政策 (1933 〜 39)

□ 736
welfare
/wélfɛər/

名 福祉 [厚生] 事業
関 welfare state 福祉国家 (社会保障制度の整った国)

□ 737
pension
/pénʃən/

名 年金、恩給、老齢年金 (=old age pension 扶助料)
名 pensioner 年金受給者、恩給生活者

□ 738
self-reliance
/sèlfriláiəns/

名 独立独行、自分を頼むこと、自信

□ 739
turmoil
/tə́ːrmɔil/

名 混乱、動揺、騒動

□ 740
the Equal Rights Amendment
/ði/ /íːkwəl/ /ráits/ /əméndmənt/

男女平等憲法修正案 (略 ERA)

---

continued
▼

Prohibition increased the scope and profits of organized crime syndicates, and led to the corruption of police and public officials through bribery.	禁酒法は組織犯罪の活動範囲の拡大と利益の増大を生み、贈賄による警察と役人の腐敗を導いた。
The widespread fear that American culture was being threatened led to a resurgence of the Ku Klux Klan in the 1920s. It aimed its activities against Catholics, Jews and blacks.	アメリカ文化が脅かされているという不安が広がり、1920年代にクー・クラックス・クランの復活を招いた。それはカトリック教徒、ユダヤ人、黒人に対する迫害を目的とした。
The period between 1922 and 1929 was one of great prosperity, in which a free-spending, pleasure-seeking spirit was encouraged.	1922年から1929年に至る年代は、消費三昧、快楽追求の精神がもてはやされた偉大なる繁栄の時代だった。
In October of 1929, the stock market crashed. In a few weeks, 30 billion dollars vanished into thin air. The period that followed is known as the Great Depression.	1929年10月、株式市場が大暴落した。数週間にして、300億ドルという額が泡と消えた。これに続く期間は大恐慌として知られている。
The New Deal used monetary and fiscal policy to try to stimulate and control the economy.	ニューディール政策は金融・財政政策を採用し、経済の刺激と管理に努めた。
The New Deal marked the beginning of a welfare state in America.	ニューディール政策によって、米国は福祉国家としてのスタートを切った。
In 1935, Congress passed the Social Security Law. This provided pensions for the needy elderly, old-age insurance, unemployment insurance, aid to the blind, and support for dependent mothers and children.	1935年、米国議会は社会保障法を可決した。これにより貧困老年層に対する年金、老齢保険、失業保険、盲人援助、生活難の母子家庭助成が定められた。
Individualism, understood as self-reliance and economic self-sufficiency, has been a central theme in American society.	独立独行とか経済的自立と解釈される個人主義は、米国では常に中心テーマとなってきた。
Turmoil over civil rights issues increased during Kennedy's administration and continued through the 1960s.	公民権問題に関する混乱はケネディ政権の間に強まり、それは1960年代を通して続いた。
Early in 1972, the Equal Rights Amendment was proposed by Congress in response to lobbying by feminist groups. This amendment, however, encountered strong opposition, and it became a dead issue.	1972年初め、議会は女性解放論を唱えるグループの圧力に応じて、男女平等憲法修正案を提出した。しかし、この修正案に対する反対は強く、廃案となった。

continued
▼

復習テスト　歴史

解答は P.248

1　1〜10の単語の定義を a〜j から選びなさい。

1. poll tax
2. conservative
3. reservation
4. Prohibition
5. diverse
6. mercantilism
7. prosperity
8. welfare
9. turmoil
10. the Equal Rights Amendment

> a. a state of confusion, excitement, and trouble
> b. good fortune and success, especially in material terms
> c. a legal bar on the making or sale of alcoholic drinks
> d. a philosophy that values trade and business
> e. a proposed change in American law, intended to give women the same legal rights as men
> f. a tax of a fixed amount collected from every citizen
> g. preferring old and established ways; resisting change, especially sudden change
> h. health, comfort, and happiness; well-being; help given by the government to people especially in need
> i. different from each other; showing variety
> j. a piece of land set apart for American Indians to live in

2 選択肢 a、b のうち正しい語を選んで文を完成させなさい。

1. Each (a. Puritan   b. colony) had a character of its own, which subsequently contributed something unique to the new American nation.

2. In 1896, the Supreme Court ruled that racial (a. emancipation   b. segregation) was legal as long as "separate but equal" facilities were provided.

3. (a. Protestantism   b. Agrarianism) is a division of the Christian church that separated from the Roman Catholic Church in the 16th century.

4. Worsening economic conditions led to steady (a. exploitation   b. immigration) from Ireland, and the Irish Potato Famine of 1845-46 led to a mass exodus to avoid starvation.

5. (a. Slavery   b. Turmoil) was the main factor in the Civil War, but economic and regional conflicts contributed to it.

6. English Puritans — Protestants who disagreed with the teachings of the Church of England established (a. reservations   b. settlements) in the northeastern region of America.

7. The inconsistency of the presence of black slavery in a society supposedly dedicated to freedom and equality plagued the nation from the very beginning, and was not resolved until the (a. Reconstruction   b. Civil War).

8. In American history the (a. frontier   b. settlement) was the edge of the settled country where unlimited cheap land was available, attracting pioneers who were willing to live the hard but independent life in the West.

9. The war between Great Britain and her colonies in North America (1775-83) by which the colonies won their independence is called the (a. Civil War   b. Revolutionary War).

10. The economic crisis and worldwide decline in business activity which began with the stock market crash in October 1929 and continued through the 1930s is called the (a. Great Depression   b. New Deal).

Day 75 — 社会・人文科学 300 語 文化 1

CD-B35

---

741 fitness /fítnis/

名 **フィットネス**、〈健康状態の〉良好、健康、元気であること
関 stay [keep] fit よい健康状態でいる　形 fit 健康で、元気で、〈特に運動選手など〉良い調子［コンディション］で　熟 feel fit 〈身体の具合が〉とても良い

---

742 sports analyst /spɔ́ːrts/ /ǽnəlist/

スポーツ解説者（=《英》sport analyst）
関 sportscast スポーツ放送

---

743 play-off /pléiɔ(ː)f/

名 〈引き分け・同点時の〉**決勝試合**
● シーズン終了後の優勝決定戦シリーズ、プレーオフ

---

744 accessible /æksésəbl, ək-/

形 **利用しやすい**、便利な、近づきやすい
関 have access to ... ……に接近［出入り］できる

---

745 pursue /pərsúː/

動 〈目的を〉**追求する**、従事する、続行する
名 pursuit /pərsjúːt/ 追求、続行、従事

---

746 gymnasium /dʒimnéiziəm/

名 **体育館**、屋内競技場

---

747 exclusive /iksklúːsiv/

形 **会員制の**、会員［顧客］を厳選する、上流向けの、高級な、全面的な、唯一の、限定的な
副 exclusively もっぱら（=only; solely）

---

748 indoor /índɔ̀ːr/

形 **屋内の**、室内の
反 outdoor 屋外の

---

749 competitive /kəmpétətiv/

形 **競争的な**、競争の
名 competitor 競争相手、商売がたき　名 competition 競争、競技、試合　動 compete /kəmpíːt/ 競争する

---

750 premises /prémisiz/

名 **土地**、構内、屋敷
● この意味の場合は複数形を用いる。premise は「前提」

---

continued ▼

For many people who have an overriding desire to stay healthy, fitness has become a science of quantification involving weighing, measuring, monitoring, graph charting, and computer printouts.	健康を維持したいと切に望む者にとって、フィットネスは、体重その他の測定、モニター観察、グラフ図表化、コンピューター出力など計量・測定を採用した科学にまで高められている。
The station's sports analyst reports on local, regional, and national sports events.	放送局のスポーツ解説者は地方レベルから地域レベル、全国レベルまでのスポーツ競技を報じる。
For those who cannot afford to buy tickets or travel to the sites of expensive play-offs, a flick of the television dial provides close-up viewing that beats front row seats.	プレーオフの高い入場券を買ったり出かけたりする余裕のない人たちでも、テレビのチャンネルを回せば前列席にも負けないクローズアップで試合を見ることができる。
Jogging is extremely popular, perhaps because it is the cheapest and most accessible sport.	ジョギングは非常に人気がある。たぶん最も安価かつ利用しやすいスポーツだからだろう。
Aerobic exercise and training with weight-lifting machines are two activities which more and more men and women are pursuing.	エアロビック運動とウェートリフティングのマシンを使ったトレーニングは、ますます多くの男女が追求する2大活動である。
Some large corporations, hospitals, and churches have indoor gymnasiums and organize informal team sports events.	大企業、病院、教会の中には、屋内体育館を所有し、楽しむことに重点を置いた団体スポーツ競技を組織しているところもある。
For those who can afford membership fees, there are the exclusive country club and the health and fitness center.	会員料金を支払う余裕がある人は、会員制カントリー・クラブ、ヘルスセンター、フィットネスセンターを利用できる。
Members of these fitness clubs have access to all kinds of indoor and outdoor sports.	これらのフィットネス・クラブの会員は屋内でも屋外でもありとあらゆるスポーツを楽しめる。
Teams and competitions in schools are highly organized and competitive and generally receive substantial local publicity.	学校のチームや競技は、高度に組織化され、激しい競争を繰りひろげ、一般に地域での知名度はかなり高い。
Practices and games are generally held on the school premises after classes are over.	一般に練習や試合は授業が終わった後、学校の校庭で行われる。

continued
▼

Day 76

社会・人文科学 300 語
文化 2

CD-B36

□ 751 **athlete** /ǽθliːt/
名 **運動選手**、運動競技者、スポーツマン、陸上競技選手
形 athletic 運動選手［競技者］の、運動競技の、運動選手らしい、活発な

□ 752 **spectator** /spékteitər/
名 **観衆**、観客、見物人、傍観者、目撃者
関 spectator sport（大観衆を集める）見るスポーツ、観客動員力のあるスポーツ

□ 753 **broadcast** /brɔ́ːdkæst/
動 **放送［放映］する** 名 放送、(1 回の) 放送［放映］（番組）
名形 broadcasting〈ラジオ・テレビの〉放送(の) 関 radio broadcasting ラジオ放送 関 a broadcasting station 放送局 関 broadcast journalism 放送ジャーナリズム：ラジオ・テレビなど放送を媒体とするジャーナリズム

□ 754 **lucrative** /lúːkrətiv/
形 **富をもたらす**、もうかる（=profitable）

□ 755 **intercollegiate** /ìntərkəlíːdʒiət/
形 **大学間の**、大学連合［対抗］の
●〈複数形で〉(大学連盟主催の) 対抗競技会

□ 756 **media** /míːdiə/
名 **マスコミ媒体**（=mass media）(テレビ・新聞など)
● medium の複数形

□ 757 **audience** /ɔ́ːdiəns/
名 **聴衆**、観衆、〈テレビの〉視聴者、〈ラジオの〉聴取者、読者

□ 758 **periodical** /pìəriɑ́dikəl/
名〈日刊新聞を除く〉**定期刊行物**、雑誌 形 定期刊行の、定期刊行物の
副 periodically 定期的に

□ 759 **readership** /ríːdərʃip/
名〈雑誌・新聞などの〉**読者層［数］**

□ 760 **circulation** /sɜ̀ːrkjuléiʃən/
名〈特に新聞の〉**発行部数**、売れ行き、普及高
関 has a large [small, limited] circulation 発行部数が多い [少ない]

continued
▼

Student athletes in high schools and colleges receive strong community support.	高校や大学の学生運動選手は地域の強力な支持を受ける。
Although many spectator sports are aggressive and sometimes even bloody, American spectators are generally less violent than spectators in other countries.	大観衆を集めるスポーツの多くは攻撃的で、時には流血する場合もあるが、米国の観客は一般的に他の国々の観客ほどは暴力的ではない。
The major television networks negotiate with professional sports leagues for the rights to broadcast their games.	テレビの主要キーステーションは試合の放映権を獲得するために、プロスポーツ競技連盟と交渉する。
Football and basketball are the most lucrative college sports because they attract many fans.	アメリカン・フットボールと野球はファンが多いので、最もお金になる大学スポーツである。
Some athletes enroll in college to play sports, and use intercollegiate sports as a springboard to a professional career.	運動選手の中にはスポーツをするために大学に入学する者もいる。彼らは大学対抗の競技を、プロになるための足がかりとして利用する。
The broadcast media in some countries have been largely responsible for homogenizing cultural and regional characteristics.	放送メディアはいくつかの国において、文化的、地域的特質を均質化する大きな力となってきた。
Most newspapers, magazines, radio and television networks that are private commercial enterprises must be responsive to their audiences' demands if they are to stay in business.	民間の営利事業である新聞、雑誌、ラジオ、テレビのほとんどは、もし事業を続けるつもりなら、読者や視聴者の要求に応えなければならない。
Periodicals are published in either weekly, monthly, bimonthly, quarterly, or semiannual issues.	定期刊行物は、週刊、月刊、隔月刊、季刊、または半年ごとに出版される。
Readership levels are not as high as they once were.	読者数はかつてほど多くない。
Newspapers have suffered a decline in circulation because of the trend of urban populations moving to the suburbs.	新聞は都市人口が郊外へ移動する傾向が続いているので、発行部数を落としている。

continued
▼

Day 77

社会・人文科学 300 語 ③ 文化

CD-B37

□ 761
feature
/fíːtʃər/

名〈新聞・雑誌などの〉**特集 [特別] 記事**
関 feature story フィーチャーストーリー（ニュース以外の記事・小論文・随筆・連載漫画など） 関 feature program 特別番組

□ 762
publication
/pʌ̀bləkéiʃən/

名 **出版物**、刊行物、出版、刊行、発行

□ 763
syndicate
/síndəkèit/

動 **配給する** 名 新聞雑誌用記事 [写真、漫画] 配給企業
●同一経営の下にある新聞社グループ。〈記事などを〉多くの新聞、雑誌に同時に配給する

□ 764
subscribe
/səbskráib/

動〈新聞・雑誌の〉**購買契約 [申し込み] をする**、（前もって）購読料を支払う、申し込む、予約する

□ 765
objectivity
/ʌ̀bdʒiktívəti/

名 **客観（的妥当）性**、客観主義的傾向 [志向]、客観的実在
形 objective 実在の、客観的な（反 subjéctive）

□ 766
editorial
/èdətɔ́ːriəl/

形 **社説の**、論説の、編集者による、編集（上）の 名 社説、論説
名 éditor 編集者、〈新聞・雑誌の〉編集発行人 動 édit〈書籍・新聞・雑誌などを〉編集（発行）する 名 edítion 版

□ 767
censorship
/sénsərʃìp/

名 **検閲（の方針 [計画、制度]）**
名動 censor〈出版物・映画などの〉検閲官。検閲する、検閲して修正 [一部削除、発禁処分に] する

□ 768
investigative reporting
/invéstigèitiv/ /ripɔ́ːrtiŋ/

〈犯罪・汚職などに関する〉**マスコミ [記者] 独自の調査による報道**（=investigative journalism）
関 investigative 調査の、研究の

□ 769
commercial
/kəmɔ́ːrʃəl/

形〈テレビ・ラジオの〉民間放送の**コマーシャルの** 名 広告放送、コマーシャル、CM、広民間放送の告主をスポンサーとする番組

□ 770
network
/nétwəːrk/

名 **放送網**、キーステーション 形 ネットワーク放送の 動 放送網に載せる

continued
▼

To meet the public demand for more **feature** material, some publishers add "lifestyle" and "home living" sections to their papers.	もっと多くの特集記事を望む大衆の要求をかなえるため、新聞に「ライフスタイル」や「家庭生活」といった欄を加える新聞社もある。
One result of the decline in readership and number of **publications** is the dramatic decline in competition.	読者数や出版物の部数が減少した結果、出版社間の競争も激減している。
Both the *New York Times* and the *Washington Post* **syndicate** their staff-written stories to regional newspapers all over the country.	『ニューヨーク・タイムズ』と『ワシントン・ポスト』はともに、スタッフが書いた記事を全国の地方新聞に同時に配信している。
Most newspapers rely heavily on wire copy from the two major news services, the Associated Press (AP) and United Press International (UPI), which gather national and international news stories and sell them to **subscribing** newspapers.	ほとんどの新聞は、多くをアソシエイティッド・プレス（AP）とユナイティッド・プレス・インターナショナル（UPI）の２大通信社が電送してくるニュースに頼っている。これら通信社は国内外のニュースを集め、それを契約している新聞社に送る。
The American press has insisted on **objectivity** in news reports, imposing a rigorous separation of fact from opinion.	米国の報道機関はニュース報道において、事実と主観的見解を厳密に区別すべきだとし、客観性を強く主張してきた。
Opinion is excluded from news columns and is presented on separate **editorial** pages.	主観的見解はニュース欄から切り離され、別枠の社説ページに掲載される。
The mass media in the United States claim explicit recognition of their right to be free from government control and **censorship**.	米国のマスメディアは、政府の取り締まりと検閲を受けない権利をはっきりと認めるよう主張している。
Investigative reporting with the aim of uncovering injustice and corruption in American institutions often leads to confrontations between government and media.	米国の各種団体内部の不正や腐敗を暴露しようとするマスコミの独自調査による報道は、政府とメディアを対立状態に導くことがある。
TV advertisements are usually in the form of 15-, 30-, or 60-second **commercial** announcements broadcast before, during and after programs.	広告は普通、番組の前中後に、15秒、30秒、あるいは60秒のコマーシャルとして、流される。
Most commercial television stations are affiliated with one of the three major **networks** — ABC, CBS, or NBC. Networks are essentially program distribution companies.	民間テレビ局のほとんどは、ABC、CBS、NBCの３大放送網のいずれかと系列関係にある。放送網は本質的に、番組配給会社である。

continued
▼

復習テスト 文化

解答は P.249

1 1〜10の単語の定義を a〜j から選びなさい。

1. feature
2. subscribe
3. objectivity
4. censorship
5. intercollegiate
6. readership
7. circulation
8. gymnasium
9. premises
10. periodical

- a. among members of different colleges
- b. a room or building equipped for gymnastics and sports
- c. the average number of copies of a newspaper, magazine, etc. that is regularly sold
- d. pay regularly to receive a magazine, newspaper, etc.
- e. a special long article in a newspaper or magazine
- f. published at regular intervals of more than one day
- g. the number or type of people who read a newspaper or magazine
- h. the quality of not being influenced by personal feelings or opinions
- i. removing material considered offensive from books, films, etc.
- j. land and the buildings on it

2 選択肢 a、b のうち正しい語を選んで文を完成させなさい。

1. The term (a. broadcast   b. media), understood broadly, includes any channel of information through which information can pass.

2. It is with passion that Americans pursue the latest (a. fitness   b. athlete) fads, convinced that staying fit requires much more than regular exercise and balanced meals.

3. The football season starts in early autumn and is followed by basketball, an (a. outdoor   b. indoor) winter sport, and then baseball, played in spring and summer.

4. Ice hockey, boxing, golf, car racing, horse racing, and tennis have been popular for decades and attract large (a. playoffs   b. audiences).

5. Fighting, bottle throwing, and rioting are not common among American (a. editorials   b. spectators).

6. Team owners usually sign up individual players for (a. lucrative   b. exclusive) long-term contracts.

7. The commercial aspects of American professional sports can make or break a/an (a. athlete's   b. sports analyst's) career.

8. American sports are becoming more (a. periodical   b. competitive) and more profit-oriented.

9. The United States has become what social observers sometimes call a media state, a society in which (a. access   b. exclusive) to power is through the media.

10. The print and (a. accessible   b. broadcasting) media not only convey information to the public, but also influence public opinion.

Day 78

芸術 1 — 社会・人文科学 300 語

CD-B38

□ 771
architecture
/ɑ́ːrkətèktʃər/

名 **建築術**、建築学、建築様式［方法］
名 árchitect 建築家　形 architéctural 建築学の、建築上の

□ 772
coverage
/kʌ́vərɪdʒ/

名 **報道［取材］**、〈テレビ・ラジオの〉受信可能範囲
動 cover《ジャーナリズム》〈事件などを〉取り扱い［報道］範囲に入れる、ニュースとして報道する、取材する

□ 773
sculpture
/skʌ́lptʃər/

名 **彫刻（術）**、彫刻品　動 彫刻する
名 sculptor 彫刻家

□ 774
abstract expressionism
/ǽbstrækt/ /ɪkspréʃənìzm/

《美術》**抽象表現主義**
• Jackson Pollock, Mark Rothko などによって代表される
関 abstractionist 抽象主義画家［作家］

□ 775
mixed media
/míkst/ /míːdiə/

《絵画》〈絵の具・クレヨンなど〉**異なった材料で描いた絵**

□ 776
pop art
/pɑ́p/ /ɑ́ːrt/

ポップアート
• 1950 年代後半米国を中心に興った美術。広告・漫画など大衆文化の産物を使用する

□ 777
op art
/ɑ́p/ /ɑ́ːrt/

オップアート（=optical art)
• 光学的トリックを採り入れた 1960 年代に盛んになった抽象美術

□ 778
performance art
/pərfɔ́ːrməns/ /ɑ́ːrt/

パフォーマンスアート
• 肉体の行為を音楽・映像・写真などを通じて表現しようとする 1970 年代に始まった芸術様式：body art、video art など

□ 779
ragtime
/rǽgtàɪm/

名 **ラグタイム**
• 1890 年～ 1910 年ごろ、黒人ピアニストたちの間で起こったシンコペーションを効かせた演奏のリズム、その曲

□ 780
blues
/blúːz/

名 **ブルース**
• 米国南部黒人民謡から興った歌曲の一形式で主として悲痛な心情を歌う

continued
▼

The architecture seen in new designs of museums and theaters suggests the elevated status of the arts in America today.	博物館や劇場に見られる新しいデザインの建築術は、今日の米国において芸術が高い地位にあることを示している。
Television has generated a broad base of interest in and enthusiasm for the arts through regular promotion and coverage of cultural events.	テレビは文化的行事を定期的に宣伝し報道することで、芸術に対して広範囲な関心と情熱の基盤を生み出してきた。
Until the 1940s, America's visual arts — painting and sculpture — were primarily influenced by European trends.	1940年代まで、米国の視覚芸術、つまり絵画と彫刻は主にヨーロッパの動向に左右された。
Abstract expressionism became the first American art movement to command the attention of artists abroad.	抽象表現主義は海外の芸術家の注目を集めた米国最初の芸術運動となった。
In the late 1950s and early 1960s, young artists reacted to abstract expressionism by producing works of "mixed media."	1950年代後半と1960年代初期には、若い芸術家が抽象表現主義に反発して、「ミクストメディア」なる作品を作った。
The reaction to abstract expressionism continued with a movement called "pop art" ("pop" is short for "popular").	抽象表現主義への反動はさらに、「ポップアート」(「ポップ」は「ポピュラー」の省略形)と呼ばれた運動を引き起こした。
"Pop" art was followed by "op" art, based on the principle of optical illusion.	「ポップ」アートの後には、光学的錯覚の法則に基づいた「オップ」アートが続いた。
Movements of the 1970s and '80s included performance art, earth art, conceptual art, graffiti art, and neo-geo art.	1970年代と80年代の運動には、パフォーマンスアート、アースアート、コンセプチュアルアート、グラフィックアート、ネオジオアートなどがあった。
Ragtime was the first black American music to gain wide popularity.	ラグタイムは広範な人気を博した最初のアメリカ黒人音楽であった。
Sung by soloists or featuring solo instruments, blues music often expresses disappointment or regret.	ブルースは歌手や器楽奏者がソロで歌ったり演奏したりするが、失望や後悔の念を表現することが多い。

continued
▼

Day 79

CD-B39

□ 781 **jazz** /dʒǽz/
名 ジャズ
関 Jazz Age ジャズエイジ（F. Scott Fitzgerald に象徴されるような米国の1920年代）

□ 782 **fusion** /fjúːʒən/
名 フュージョン
● ジャズとロックなどが混じった音楽

□ 783 **country and western** /kʌ́ntri/ /ǽnd/ /wéstərn/
カントリーミュージック（=country music）
● 米国南部［西部のカウボーイ］の音楽から発生［を模倣］したフォークミュージック

□ 784 **musical** /mjúːzikəl/
名 ミュージカル、喜歌劇［映画］　**形** 音楽の、音楽的な、音楽好きな

□ 785 **appeal** /əpíːl/
名 魅力、人の心を動かす力　**動**〈物事が人心に〉訴える、うける、興味をそそる
● Jazz appealed to young people.（ジャズは若者にうけた）のように使用する。

□ 786 **choreographer** /kɔ̀ːriɑ́grəfər/
名 振り付け師、バレエ編成家
名 choreography〈バレエの〉舞踊法、振り付け

□ 787 **motion picture** /móuʃən/ /píktʃər/
映画（=moving picture, film, movie）

□ 788 **rugged individualism** /rʌ́gid/ /ìndəvídʒuəlìzm/
無骨な個人主義
関 rugged ごつごつした、ぶかっこうな、粗野な

□ 789 **comedy** /kɑ́mədi/
名 喜劇、人生劇（悲喜の両面から人生の真相を描いた作品）
反 tragedy 悲劇

□ 790 **moviegoer** /múːvigòuər/
名 よく映画に行く人、映画好き［ファン］
名形 moviegoing 映画見物。よく映画に行く

continued ▼

Jazz originated around the turn of the century among black musicians in the American South.	ジャズは20世紀に入ったころに、米国南部の黒人ミュージシャンの間で生まれた。
In the 1960s and '70s, jazz musicians began combining the rhythms of rock'n'roll and electronic instruments with traditional elements of jazz, to form a blend of music called "**fusion**."	1960年代と70年代に、ジャズ・ミュージシャンはロックンロールのリズムと電子楽器をジャズの伝統的要素と組み合わせ、「フュージョン」という混合音楽を作った。
The style of **country and western** music has its roots in the folk songs and ballads of the early Scottish and English settlers in the southern colonies.	カントリーミュージックのスタイルは、南部植民地においてスコットランドやイングランドからの初期の植民者が歌った民謡やバラードを起源とする。
The **musical** was inspired by the Anglo-Irish musical theater, the central European operetta, and the American vaudeville minstrel show.	ミュージカルは英国系アイルランドの音楽劇、中央ヨーロッパのオペレッタ、米国のボードビル・ミンストレル・ショーの影響を受けた。
Rock'n'roll quickly won intense and sustained **appeal** with young people not only in America, but all over the world.	ロックンロールはまたたく間に米国のみならず世界中の若者の間で、強力でしかも衰えることのない魅力を発散した。
America's modern dance **choreographers** include Alvin Ailey, whose works feature African dance elements and black music.	米国の現代ダンス振り付け師には、アフリカのダンス要素と黒人音楽を取り入れたアルヴィン・エイリーがいる。
Born in Hollywood after the turn of the century, the **motion picture** became the monumentally popular art form of the century.	20世紀初頭にハリウッドで生まれた映画は、今世紀不滅の人気を得た芸術形態となった。
The western fused violence and **rugged individualism** into larger, mythical themes of taming the frontier, curbing lawlessness, and forging a nation.	西部劇は暴力および無骨な個人主義を、フロンティアを開拓し無法を抑え、国家建設に邁進するという壮大で神話的なテーマと融合させた。
Entertaining **comedies** and musicals carried messages of aspiration and optimism.	娯楽喜劇とミュージカルには大志と楽観主義のメッセージがあった。
The movies have changed since the advent of television. Today's **moviegoers** are mostly teenagers.	映画はテレビの登場以来、変化してきた。今日の映画ファンは、ほとんど10代の若者である。

continued
▼

Day 80

CD-B40

社会・人文科学 300 語 — 芸術 3

□ 791
vernacular
/vərnækjulər/

形〈建築様式などが〉**その土地[時代、集団]に特有の**

□ 792
landscape
/lændskèip/

名**景色**、風景、風景画、風景画法
関 seascape 海の風景、海の風景画、海の絵

□ 793
portray
/pɔːrtréi/

動〈人物・風景を〉**描く**、……の肖像を描く
名 pórtrait 肖像(画)、似顔絵　名 portráyal 描画、描写、記述、肖像(画)

□ 794
retain
/ritéin/

動**保持する**、維持する

□ 795
skyscraper
/skáiskrèipər/

名**摩天楼**、超高層ビル、高層建築

□ 796
Art Deco
/àːrt/ /dékou/

アールデコ
● 1920〜30 年代の一種のデザイン運動(大胆な輪郭、流線、直線形、プラスチックなどの新素材の使用が特徴)

□ 797
flamboyant
/flæmbɔ́iənt/

形〈建築〉**フランボワイヤン様式の**(15〜16 世紀ごろフランスで流行した)、火炎式の、燃えるような、けばけばしい、どぎつい

□ 798
drawing
/drɔ́ːiŋ/

名**製図**、図形、図面、素描、デッサン(鉛筆・ペン・クレヨン・木炭などで描く)

□ 799
cubism
/kjúːbizm/

名**立体派**、キュービズム
● 初め Cézanne が、のちに Picasso、Braque が主唱した

□ 800
gentrification
/dʒèntrəfikéiʃən/

名〈下層[労働]階級の居住地域などの〉**高級化**、上流化
動 gentrify 高級化させる、上流化させる

continued

"Vernacular architecture" refers to traditional buildings, such as the cottages and farms of particular areas, that have no individual designer.	「土地特有の建築物」とは、特定のデザイナーがいないある特定地域の小住宅や農場のような伝統的な建物のことを指す。
Landscape painting was conceived as a vehicle for the articulation of the new republic's unique historical and moral position in world history.	風景画は新しい共和国（米国）の独特な歴史的、道徳的地位を明確にする手段と考えられた。
Dorothea Lange's photographs honestly and sympathetically portray families who were victims of drought and the Great Depression.	ドロシア・ラングの写真は、干ばつと大恐慌の犠牲となった家族を正直に、かつ同情を込めてとらえている。
Nearly all of the 19th-century buildings were retained and refurbished.	19世紀建築物のほとんどすべては保持され改装された。
The skyscraper became a popular symbol of our national character: a soaring, upward-aspiring image as powerful as a moon rocket.	摩天楼は、月ロケットのように強力な上昇指向のイメージで表されるわが国（米国）の特徴を示す人気シンボルとなった。
Art Deco, which originated in France in 1925, uses a rather heavy, geometric simplification of form. Examples of Art Deco are the Chrysler Building and Radio City Music Hall.	1925年フランスで生まれたアールデコは、かなり重厚で、幾何学的で、簡素化された形式を用いる。クライスラービルやラジオシティ・ミュージックホールなどがアールデコの例である。
Antonio Gaudi (1852-1926) is a Spanish architect who is noted for his flamboyant style. His Church of the Holy Family, Barcelona, begun in 1883, was still under construction when he died.	アントニオ・ガウディ（1852～1926）はフランボワイヤン様式で知られるスペインの建築家である。彼が手がけたバルセロナのサグラダファミリア教会（聖家族贖罪教会）は1883年に建築が始まり、彼が死亡したときもまだ建築中だった。
It was very much a "how-to-do-it" book, since it contained plans and detailed drawings for various private and public structures.	それはさまざまな民間および公共建造物の見取り図や詳細な製図を含んでいて、まさに「初心者向け案内書」とでもいうべきものであった。
The picture blends elements of two European styles: cubism, which shows objects from a number of different angles of vision, and futurism, which portrays speed and objects in motion.	写真はヨーロッパで生まれたふたつの様式の要素を融合している。ひとつはさまざまな視点から物体を示す立体派であり、もうひとつはスピードと動く物体を描く未来派である。
"Gentrification" leaves some of urban renewal's more difficult questions unanswered.	居住地域の高級化には、都市再開発に関する未解決の難問がある。

continued
▼

復習テスト　芸術

1　1〜10の単語の定義を a〜j から選びなさい。

1. architecture
2. landscape
3. portray
4. retain
5. flamboyant
6. appeal
7. comedy
8. coverage
9. moviegoer
10. motion picture

- a. a wide view of country scenery; a picture of such a scene
- b. a funny play, film, or other work in which the story and characters are amusing and which ends happily
- c. brightly colored and noticeable
- d. the art of building structures
- e. keep possession of; avoid losing
- f. movie
- g. one who often goes to the movies
- h. depict pictorially
- i. the amount of time or space given by television, a newspaper, etc., to a particular subject or event
- j. attraction, interest

2 選択肢 a、b のうち正しい語を選んで文を完成させなさい。

1. (a. Classical   b. Ragtime), blues, jazz, country and western, rock'n'roll, and the musical are all American-born.

2. The (a. rock'n'roll   b. blues) evolved from African folk songs and church music.

3. (a. Abstract expressionism   b. Mixed media) rejected traditional subject matter, such as the human body, still life, or rural scenes. Instead, it focused on such things as the utilization of space, dimension, and surface texture, and the interrelationship of colors.

4. (a. Musicals   b. Country and western music) developed over a long period, with melodies and lyrics reflecting rural life in the Southeast and Southwest.

5. In the 1930s, another native American-born art form emerged. (a. The musical   b. Op art) was a new form of entertainment which combined acting, music, and ballet.

6. The (a. skyscraper   b. vernacular) is a type of tall building first developed in 1868 in New York, where land prices were high and the geology adapted to such methods of construction.

7. The process by which a street or area, formerly inhabited by poor people, is changed to cater to wealthy people who want to live there, is called (a. gentrification   b. vernacular).

8. (a. Cubism   b. Futurism) is a 20th-century art style in which the subject matter is represented by geometric shapes.

9. One who makes up or arranges the steps and dances for a ballet or piece of music is called a (a. comedian   b. choreographer).

10. The art of making three-dimensional representations of people, animals, or objects out of stone, wood, clay, metal, etc. is called (a. op art   b. sculpture).

基本語彙200語　**復習テスト 解答・訳例**

>>> 動詞　P.26

【解答】

1
| 1. NO | 2. YES | 3. YES | 4. NO | 5. YES | 6. NO | 7. YES |
| 8. YES | 9. YES | 10. NO |

1. 「友だちと仲直りをしたので、彼との関係が悪くなった」
   正解は NO。もし友だちと仲直りをした（reconciled）のであれば、彼との関係は悪くなる（aggravate）のではなくよくなるはず。
4. 「警察は麻薬産業を拡大することによって犯罪を撲滅しようとしている」
   正解は NO。麻薬産業を拡大する（expand）ことによって犯罪を撲滅する（eradicate）ことができるとは考えられない。
6. 「ふたつともとても異なっているので区別しにくい」
   正解は NO。ふたつとも異なっていたら区別する（distinguish）のは簡単。
10. 「たくさん消費すれば出費を減らすことができる」
    正解は NO。消費する（consume）ことで出費を削減する（reduce）ことはできない。

2　1. d　2. e　3. h　4. b　5. c　6. a　7. g　8. j　9. f　10. i

3
| 1. estimate | 2. imply | 3. indicate | 4. interact | 5. prevail |
| 6. respond | 7. survive | 8. verify | 9. absorb | 10. apply |

4　1. b　2. a　3. c　4. b　5. c

>>> 名詞　P.38

【解答】

1
| 1. NO | 2. YES | 3. YES | 4. NO | 5. YES | 6. YES | 7. YES |
| 8. YES | 9. NO | 10. NO |

1. 「雄弁家は話し方に欠点がある」
   正解は NO。話し方に欠点があったら雄弁な（eloquent）話し手とはいえない。
4. 「彼と意見が一致しているので彼にはたくさん不満がある」
   正解は NO。彼に不満（grievance）がたくさんあったら彼と意見の一致（concord）はみられない。
9. 「混沌とはすべてが秩序正しいことを意味する」
   正解は NO。chaos は「無秩序、大混乱」の意。
10. 「彼女の顔色のよさは彼女の健康状態の悪化を意味するものだ」
    正解は NO。顔色（complexion）がいいのに健康状態が悪化（deterioration）しているのはおかしい。

| 2 | 1. e | 2. c | 3. h | 4. b | 5. a | 6. f | 7. d | 8. i | 9. j | 10. g |

3	1. conjecture	2. decade	3. glossary	4. precaution	5. settlement
	6. burden	7. famine	8. prejudice	9. core	10. eloquence

| 4 | 1. c | 2. b | 3. a | 4. c | 5. b |

>>> 形容詞　P.50

【解答】

1	1. NO	2. YES	3. NO	4. NO	5. NO	6. YES	7. YES
	8. NO	9. YES	10. YES				

1. 「倹約家は浪費家である」
   正解は NO。倹約な（thrifty）人が浪費する（extravagant）人というのはおかしい。
3. 「信じやすい人はいつも疑わしく思っている」
   正解は NO。credulous は「信じやすい」という意味。疑わしく思う（doubtful）人が信じやすいというのはおかしい。
4. 「気の合う人とうまくやっていくのは難しい」
   正解は NO。congenial は「性分に合う」という意味。気が合う人とはうまくやっていけるはず。
5. 「明白に表すにはあいまいな言葉を使う」
   正解は NO。equivocal は「あいまいな」の意。明白に（explicitly）表すためにあいまいな言葉は使わない。
8. 「多目的に使用できるものは役に立たない」
   正解は NO。versatile は「多目的に利用できる」の意。用途の広いものが、役に立たない（useless）というのはおかしい。

| 2 | 1. d | 2. b | 3. f | 4. c | 5. g | 6. h | 7. a | 8. e | 9. j | 10. i |

3	1. eccentric	2. constant	3. extinct
	4. intensive	5. obsolete	6. plausible
	7. prolific	8. sophisticated	9. sympathetic
	10. unanimous		

| 4 | 1. b | 2. a | 3. c | 4. b | 5. c |

>>> 副詞 P.62

【解答】

1
1. YES 2. YES 3. NO 4. YES 5. NO 6. YES 7. YES
8. NO 9. NO 10. NO

3. 「わたしはあなたにまったく賛成ですが、いくつか異議があります」
   正解は NO。entirely は「まったく、完全に」の意。異議があったら、I entirely agree with you とはいえない。
5. 「人口が急激に増加した。ということは人口が徐々に増えたということである」
   正解は NO。rapidly は急激に (fast、quickly)、gradually は徐々に (slowly、by degree) の意。
8. 「それは疑う余地もなく真実である。ほんの少し疑いがあるだけである」
   正解は NO。undoubtedly は「疑う余地のないほどに」の意。疑い (doubt) があったら undoubtedly とはいえない。
9. 「彼らは彼に会議を出るようにいった。彼はそれに応じてそこに残った」
   正解は NO。accordingly は「したがって、それに応じて」の意。accordingly ときたら he left とならなくてはおかしい。
10. 「きょうはきのうと比べてかなり冷え込んでいる。気温が少し下がった」
    正解は NO。considerably は「かなり」の意。気温が少し (a bit) 下がっただけで、きょうはきのうと比べてかなり冷え込んでいるというのはおかしい。

2
1. f 2. d 3. g 4. i 5. h 6. e 7. a 8. c 9. j 10. b

3
1. namely   2. slightly   3. immediately
4. inherently   5. initially   6. definitely, undoubtedly
7. literally   8. primarily   9. commonly
10. eventually

4
1. a 2. c 3. b 4. c 5. b

>>> 総復習テスト P.64

【解答】

1
1. d   2. f   3. g   4. b   5. e   6. c   7. a   8. h

2
1. explicit
2. abstract
3. extravagant
4. reluctant
5. contemporary
6. futile
7. constant
8. impromptu
9. ambiguous
10. credulous
11. intricate
12. eccentric
13. conspicuous
14. ordinary
15. strong

3
1. c   2. d   3. e   4. b   5. a

4
1. escription
2. distinction
3. expansion
4. implication
5. inspiration
6. consumption
7. application
8. absorption
9. exploitation
10. extension
11. conference
12. portrait, portrayal
13. prevalence
14. production
15. response
16. reconciliation
17. reduction
18. restraint
19. survival
20. completion

5
1. chaotic
2. concordant
3. concurrent
4. defective
5. defensive
6. eloquent
7. extravagant
8. burdensome
9. hypothetical
10. progressive
11. prospective
12. conjectural
13. regional
14. spontaneous
15. significant

6
1. d   2. a   3. c   4. e   5. f   6. i   7. b   8. h   9. j   10. g

7
1. c   2. b   3. a   4. b   5. c   6. b   7. a   8. c   9. a   10. c
11. b   12. c   13. a   14. b   15. c

8
1. b   2. b   3. a   4. c   5. b   6. c   7. a   8. b   9. c   10. a
11. b   12. c   13. a   14. b   15. a

9
1. c   2. b   3. c   4. b   5. c   6. b   7. a   8. c   9. a   10. b
11. a   12. c   13. c   14. a   15. c

10
1. c   2. b   3. a   4. c   5. b   6. a   7. c   8. a   9. a   10. b

自然科学 300 語　**復習テスト 解答・訳例**

>>> 宇宙　P.78

【解答】

1　1. d　2. e　3. g　4. c　5. h　6. i　7. f　8. a　9. b　10. j

2　1. b　2. a　3. b　4. a　5. b　6. a　7. b　8. a　9. b　10. b

1. 恒星の想像上の分類を星座という。
2. 物体間の引きつけ合う力を引力という。
3. 太陽の周囲を回る地球や、地球の周囲を回る月や宇宙船の曲線の通路を軌道という。
4. 地球は地軸を中心に自転する。
5. 地上に達する流星を隕石という。
6. 夜にしばしば明るい雲のように見える、恒星間のガスや塵のかたまりを星雲という。
7. 科学的研究と検査のための設備が整った場所を実験室という。
8. 地球が太陽と月の間にあるときに月食は起こる。
9. 裸眼では見られないくらいに微小な物体を拡大して見せる器具を光学顕微鏡という。
10. 月が太陽光を遮りながら太陽と地球の間を通過するときに、日食は起こる。

>>> 気象　P.86

【解答】

1　1. c　2. h　3. b　4. g　5. a　6. i　7. j　8. f　9. e　10. d

2　1. b　2. b　3. a　4. a　5. a　6. a　7. b　8. b　9. a　10. b

1. 暖かい空気が冷たい空気に押し上げられる過程を対流という。
2. 温室効果は気温の上昇を引き起こす。
3. 暖かい空気は冷たい空気より密度が低い。
4. 水蒸気が表面に凝結する温度を露点という。
5. 雷雨は雷、稲光、強風、ときにはひょうも伴った豪雨のことである。
6. 温帯気候はすごく暑くもなく寒くもない。
7. 低気圧は前線と雲や雨の天気と関連がある。
8. 移動性気団の先端部分は寒冷前線または温暖前線という。
9. 天気予報は今後の天気を伝える。
10. 気圧計は気圧を測るために使われる。

>>> 地学　P.94

【解答】

1　1. c　2. e　3. a　4. f　5. b　6. g　7. d

2　1. b　2. a　3. a　4. a　5. b　6. a　7. b　8. a　9. b　10. b

1. 経度はある地点が本初子午線からどの程度東または西かを示す。
2. 緯度は赤道から何度北または南かを示す。
3. 水の蓄えに利用する自然の、または人口の湖を貯水池という。
4. 間欠泉は熱水と蒸気が噴水のように噴出するものである。
5. 農作物は土壌で育つ。
6. 地熱力は地球内部の熱から出るエネルギーである。
7. 震央は地下の震源地から真上の地表の点である。
8. 地震計は地震波の計測器である。
9. 氷河は雪線内で積雪から生じた膨大な氷の集まりである。
10. マントルは地球の地殻の下にある層である。

>>> 環境　P.102

【解答】

1　1. e　2. a　3. f　4. b　5. d　6. c

2　1. a　2. b　3. b　4. a　5. b　6. b　7. b　8. b　9. a　10. a

1. 石油は輸送、暖房、発電のためのエネルギー源として使用される。
2. 大気は太陽からの有害な紫外線を遮断する。
3. 化学ガス、粉塵、煙は汚染物である。
4. 排泄物、ごみ、汚水は下水汚物の例である。
5. 魚は海からの収穫物の90%を占める。
6. オゾンは有害な紫外線が大気に侵入するのを防ぐ。
7. 大気汚染は汚染物質が引き起こす。
8. 石炭を燃やすと発生する二酸化硫黄は、大気中の水と化合して酸性雨を生じる。
9. 天然資源は地球から入手できる物質で、水、食物、木材、そして鉱物などがある。
10. 石油と石炭は大昔に死んだ植物や動物からできるので、化石燃料という。

>>> 生物   P.110

【解答】

1   1. b   2. i   3. e   4. j   5. g   6. d   7. h   8. c   9. a   10. f

2   1. b   2. a   3. b   4. b   5. a   6. a   7. a   8. b   9. b   10. b

1. 動植物の病気の多くはウイルスによって起こる。
2. チーズとヨーグルトは一部、細菌の細胞から成っている。
3. 針葉樹は水分をほとんど失わない幅の狭い葉を持つので、乾燥地帯でも成長する。
4. 花や野菜には毎年種をまかなければならないものがある。これらの植物を一年生植物という。
5. 緑色植物が太陽エネルギーを使って養分を生産する過程を、光合成という。
6. 生物が生物同士および非生物環境といかなる影響を与え合っているかを研究する学問を、生態学という。
7. ウイルスは細胞をもたないし、生物のように成長したり動いたりもしない。
8. 同じ種の仲間は同じ界の仲間よりも、構造的に共通した特質を多くもっている。
9. ひとつの母体のみによる生殖を無性生殖という。
10. 食物連鎖における消費者はすべて、食料を他の生物に依存している。

>>> 動物   P.118

【解答】

1   1. j   2. g   3. h   4. i   5. a   6. b   7. c   8. f   9. d   10. e

2   1. a   2. a, b   3. b   4. b   5. a, b   6. b   7. a   8. b   9. a   10. b

1. ほとんどの昆虫は卵から成虫へと成長するときに、体の大きさや形において一連の変化を経験する。この一連の変化、つまり成長段階を変態という。
2. 反射運動と本能は先天的な行動形態である。反射運動は単純で反射的な行為である。本能は一連の段階を伴う複雑な行動パターンである。
3. 淡水と海水が混じり合う、海岸に近い区域を河口域という。
4. 魚類、両生類、爬虫類は冷血である。これは、体温が周囲の気温とともに変化することを意味する。
5. 条件付けにおいて、動物は刺激と反応を関係付ける。試行錯誤はひとつの行動を何度も繰り返し練習することを含む。
6. 両生類は休眠によって、極端な寒さや暑さから身を守る。寒いときに、彼らはぬかるみや池の底に体を埋める。この冬の休眠を冬眠という。
7. 1年に数回、ヘビは外皮を脱ぎ落とす。これを脱皮という。
8. 体温が高く、一定している脊椎動物は温血である。
9. 鳥は温血なので、まだ卵の中にいる間は常に温かくしてやらなければならない。巣を守る母鳥が体温で卵を温めて卵をかえす。
10. サルや人間は霊長類である。どれも大きな脳、物をつかむことのできる指、一点に焦点の合う目を備えている。

>>> 生理学 P.126

【解答】

1　1. a　2. h　3. c　4. g　5. i　6. f　7. j　8. d　9. e　10. b

2　1. b　2. b　3. b　4. a　5. b　6. b　7. a　8. b　9. b　10. a, a

1. 母親の子宮の筋肉は緊張、または収縮を始め、次に弛緩する。子宮の収縮を分娩という。
2. 医者には、反射波を利用して子宮内にいる赤ん坊を見る超音波という新しい道具がある。
3. 性とは親から子へ受け継がれる特徴である。
4. 遺伝とは親から子へと特性が受け継がれることである。
5. 遺伝子は DNA から成り、染色体上に配列される。
6. 血友病患者にとっては小さな切傷ですら大事に至ることがある。なぜなら凝血に時間がかかるためである。
7. 突然変異は世代間で受け継がれる遺伝子に、たまたま突発的な変化が起こることである。
8. 環境によく適応した生物が生き残り繁殖する過程を自然淘汰という。
9. 膵臓は消化液を生産する大きな腺である。
10. 新陳代謝は体内で起こる化学作用の過程すべてが含まれる。新陳代謝によって生じる排泄物には、二酸化炭素、水、塩、熱、尿素がある。

>>> 健康 P.134

【解答】

1　1. d　2. h　3. b　4. a　5. e　6. i　7. j　8. g　9. c　10. f

2　1. a　2. a　3. b　4. b　5. a　6. a　7. b　8. b　9. a　10. b

1. 糖尿病は米国では、心臓病、癌に次いで死因の第 3 位である。それはインシュリンを生成する膵臓の機能障害によって起こる。
2. 特定の病気への免疫を得るにはふたつの方法がある。ひとつはその病気にかかること。もうひとつはワクチンを受けることである。
3. ワクチンとなる病原の微生物には、死んでいるものと弱っているものがある。ワクチンの微生物は病気を引き起こさずに、体内で抗体の生成をもたらす。
4. 必要以上にカロリーを摂取すると太る。
5. 食品添加物は腐敗を防止したり、見かけと味をよくしたり、栄養を加えたりするために食品に添加される化学薬品である。
6. 大脳は脳の中で占める割合が最も大きい。大脳は感覚器官からメッセージを受け取り、それを解明する。また、体の動き、思考、記憶、言語を調節する。
7. 小脳は平衡を維持し、筋肉運動を調整する。
8. 大脳と小脳からのニューロンの多くは、脳幹を通って情報を伝える。脳幹の下方部分を延髄という。
9. 脊髄は延髄から背中の下まで続く。
10. 大腸が水をほとんど吸収しないため糞便が水っぽい状態を、下痢という。

>>> 化学 P.142

【解答】

1 1. a   2. c   3. h   4. j   5. b   6. e   7. d   8. f   9. i   10. g

2 1. b   2. a, a   3. b, b   4. a   5. b   6. b   7. a   8. b   9. b   10. b

1. ほとんどの物質は2個以上の元素が化学的に結合した化合物である。
2. 物質は原子から成る。種類が同じ原子の集まりは元素である。(2個以上の元素が化学的に結合した)化合物の最小単位は分子である。
3. 拡散とは、ある場所から別の場所へ分子が無秩序に移動することである。匂いは拡散によって起こる。
4. 興奮薬、つまり「覚醒剤」は神経系の機能亢進と心拍数および呼吸数の増加を引き起こす。
5. 抑制薬、つまり「鎮痛剤」は中枢神経系の機能を抑制する薬である。この薬は心拍数と呼吸数を減少させ、眠気をもたらす。
6. 脂肪は炭水化物と同様に、エネルギー源となる栄養素である。
7. コカインはコカの葉から作る興奮薬である。それは興奮状態を引き起こす。しかし、興奮がおさまるや、神経過敏、混乱、憂うつの気分が残る。
8. ニコチン以外に、煙草の煙には有毒ガスとタール(ある種の癌の原因ともいわれる化学物質)が含まれる。
9. 麻薬を乱用する者は、それなしではいられなくなることが多い。このように麻薬を必要とすることを麻薬依存という。
10. LSDとマリファナは幻覚薬であり、調整の喪失、いつもと違う振る舞いや、とっぴな行動、幻覚に加えて、しばしばパニックまたは憂うつ状態を引き起こす。

>>> 物理 P.150

【解答】

1 1. f 2. i 3. a 4. b 5. j 6. e 7. d 8. c 9. g 10. h

2 1. a 2. b 3. a 4. a 5. b 6. b 7. b, a 8. a 9. a 10. a

1. 落下する物体はすべて同じスピードで加速する。地表近くを落下する物体は 9.8m/s/s 加速する。これは物体の落下速度が 1 秒ごとに秒速 9.8m 速くなることを意味する。
2. 空気がなければ空気抵抗はありえない。
3. 一般に、ふたつの物体が同じ速度で動いているなら、質量の大きな物体のほうが運動量が大きい。
4. 重力は物体間の距離が開くにつれて、小さくなる。
5. 髪の間にくしを走らせ、小さく切り裂いた新聞紙の上にくしを持ってくると、新聞紙はくしへと引きつけられ、くっつくこともある。この引きつける力は電力によって生じる。
6. 車が走っているときに運転手が急ブレーキをかけると、慣性によって乗客は何か他の力が作用して動きが遅くなるまで一定の速度で動き続ける。シートベルトは慣性の法則の影響から身を守る。
7. 求心性とは「中心に近づこうとする」ことを意味する。求心力は常に、円の中心に向く。
8. ふたつの磁石の N 極を近づけると、反発し合う。しかし、ひとつの磁石の N 極を別の磁石の S 極に近づけると、磁石同士が引きつけ合う。これを磁極の法則という。
9. 電子が移動しやすい物質を伝導体という。電子が移動しにくい物質を絶縁体という。
10. 車が近づいてきて、通りすぎ、そして遠ざかっていくときに聞こえる音の調子の変化は、ドップラー効果の例である。

社会・人文科学300語　復習テスト 解答・訳例

>>> 政治　P.160

【解答】

1　1. d　2. i　3. j　4. a　5. c　6. g　7. h　8. b　9. e　10. f

2　1. b　2. a　3. a　4. b　5. b　6. b　7. a　8. a　9. b　10. b

1. 均衡と抑制は、政府の各部門に他の2部門の権力を抑制、すなわち制限する権限を与えている。
2. 下院、あるいはときに呼ばれるところに従えばザ・ハウス（the House）は、435人の議員から成る。全議員が2年の任期で選出される。
3. 下院議員選挙区は州の地域区分で、それぞれの選挙民が下院議員1人を選出する。
4. 拒否権とは、大統領ないし知事が法案に署名することを拒否することで、拒否された法案はその後、破棄の理由を記した教書とともに、連邦議会ないし州議会に差し戻される。
5. 現在、上院の定員は100人、すなわち50州のそれぞれから選出された上院議員2名ずつから成る。
6. ロビイストとは、議会の（常任）委員会の聴問会において、特定集団の意見、すなわち利益を代表するために雇われている人物である。
7. 大統領の顧問としても活動する連邦政府の各省の長官は、内閣と呼ばれる。
8. 多数決原理とは、半分以上の人々の決定が全員によって受け入れられるという制度である。
9. 郡とは州法を実施し、税金を徴収し、選挙を監視するために制定された、州政府の1区分である。
10. 代表民主制とは、住民が自分たちのために政治の仕事を行う代表を選出する政治制度である。

>>> 経済　P.168

【解答】

1　1. c　2. h　3. d　4. g　5. j　6. a　7. f　8. b　9. e　10. i

2　1. b　2. b　3. a　4. b　5. b　6. a　7. a　8. a　9. b　10. b

1. ある国の生活水準とは、その国の国民が手に入れることのできる財とサービスの量に基づく、国民の物質的な幸福のことである。
2. 著作権とは法律によって与えられた、特定の年数にわたって著作、音楽、または芸術作品を独占的に公刊ないし販売する権利のことである。
3. ある企業がある製品を販売したり、あるサービスを提供したりする唯一の企業なら、その企業は独占権を握っていることになる。
4. コングロマリットは、複数の無関係な財やサービスを生産、供給、ないし販売している企業の合併によって形成される。

5. 一部の産業では、独占企業は合法である。これらの合法的な独占企業とは、公共事業、つまり公衆に基本的サービスを提供する諸企業である。
6. 1100万以上の小企業が、ひとりの人間によって所有されている。ひとりの人間に所有されたこれらの小企業は、自営業と呼ばれる。
7. 大量生産品とは、国家の大人口が必要としているものや望んでいるものを供給するために、機械によって迅速に製造される莫大な量の商品のことである。
8. 分割払いは買い手が頭金を払い、その後、ある期間で差額を支払うという購入方法である。
9. 自由企業制は、人々が自由に、自分たちの思いどおりに事業を経営できる経済制度である。
10. (労使間の) 団体交渉とは、労働組合の代表と経営者が、賃金や労働条件について合意を結ぶべく努力する過程である。

>>> 社会 P.176

【解答】

1 1. f 2. h 3. a 4. j 5. c 6. i 7. e 8. d 9. g 10. b

2 1. a 2. a 3. b 4. a 5. b 6. b 7. b 8. b 9. b 10. b

1. ある世代から次の世代へと受け継がれる独特な社会的、文化的遺産を共有するような集団は、民族集団と呼ばれる。
2. 民族集団の構成員は、自分たちの生活様式のほうが他の集団のそれより優れているとみなすことが多い。この態度は、社会学者ウィリアム・グレアム・サムナーにより、自民族中心主義と命名された。
3. 逸脱者とは、社会的に受容できる行動の限界を超えていく人々である。
4. ひとつの社会を階級や名声、あるいは権力に基づいて、階層と呼ばれる複数の段階に分けることを社会成層化と呼ぶ。
5. 多数の親戚、あるいは3世代以上を含み、しばしば同居ないし近隣に住む家族組織は、拡大家族と呼ばれる。
6. 規則や信念、価値観、そしてある文化ないし社会において受容される振る舞いを学ぶ過程は、社会化と呼ばれる。
7. ステレオタイプ (固定観念) とは、ある集団に対する、過度に単純化され、誇張され、そしてしばしば否定的な一連の観念のことである。それは暗に、その集団全員がまったく同じようなものであることを示唆し、個人間の差異を無視するものである。
8. 能力主義とは、人の社会的地位は全面的に能力、すなわち業績によるものと考える社会制度である。
9. 閉鎖制とは、人が特定の身分に生まれつき、自分の社会的地位を変える機会がまったくない制度のことである。
10. 人は道義上、困っている人々を助ける義務があるという哲学は、人道主義と呼ばれる。

>>> 法律   P.184

【解答】

1 1. i   2. j   3. f   4. b   5. g   6. h   7. a   8. e   9. c   10. d

2 1. b   2. a   3. b   4. b   5. b   6. b   7. b   8. b   9. a   10. a

1. 保釈金とは、容疑者が公判時に出廷することの保証として、裁判所に預託される金額のことである。
2. 刑事事件において証言を聞き、被告人を裁判にかけるのに十分な理由があるかどうかを判定する一群の人々は大陪審と呼ばれる。
3. 正当に取り扱われたかどうかを確認するために、米国の司法制度は上訴、すなわち事件の再検討を要求する権利を認めている。
4. 憲法は連邦裁判所に、広範に及ぶ事件の審理を行い、それらの事件を裁定する裁判権、すなわち権限を与えている。
5. 有罪判決を受けた人の、刑期終了以前の刑務所からの条件付き釈放は、仮釈放と呼ばれる。
6. 小陪審は法廷事件において証言を聞き、評決を決める人々である。ひとつの陪審に、6～12人が参加できる。
7. 政府の役人に対して行われた正式の告発、すなわち起訴は、弾劾と呼ばれる。
8. 最も厳しい刑罰は死刑、すなわち重罪のために犯罪者を死に至らしめることである。
9. 大半の州は少年を18歳以下の人々と定義している。法律に反する罪を犯したことがわかったとき、少年は非行者となる。
10. ホワイトカラー犯罪は、ホワイトカラー（頭脳労働者）が仕事中に犯す犯罪である。

>>> 教育   P.192

【解答】

1 1. g   2. j   3. h   4. c   5. i   6. d   7. a   8. e   9. b   10. f

2 1. b   2. b   3. a   4. b   5. b   6. b   7. a   8. b   9. a   10. a

1. 強制バス通学は、生徒たちを異なる人種の生徒のいる他地域の学校に輸送するという、義務的な人種差別撤廃措置である。
2. 完全に人種差別をなくした学校を実現しようとする、ここ30年来の試みは、成功と失敗の両方をもたらした。一部の都市では強制バス通学の義務付けが成功した。しかし多くの地域では、人々はこれに激しく反発している。
3. 一部の都市や田園地帯では、高校を卒業するより、中途退学するアメリカ人生徒のほうが多い。
4. 人口の13％にあたる、少なくとも2,100万人のアメリカの成人が非識字、すなわち読み書きができない。

5. 学校は官僚制であるため、権限が明確に規定され、さまざまな状況に対して特定の手続きが定められた、多岐に分化した職員の階級組織を通して機能している。
6. 動機付けに対する教師の努力とは無関係に、自分の学校の計画や活動、あるいは仲間たちが生徒の熱意に影響を与える。
7. 能力別編成は、教育上適正な基準が得られるように、似たような能力の生徒を同じクラスに入れる方式である。
8. 大半の人々が教育上の成績を知能と結びつけているため、知能テストは能力別編成の基礎として広く用いられている。
9. 無能力を根絶するために、現在 30 の州で新人教師に免許を与える前に能力テストを実施している。
10. 進歩主義教育理論はジョン・デューイの教育哲学と結びつけられる。デューイは、教育は個性の表現と経験を通した学習に重点が置かれるべきだと考えた。

>>> 心理　P.200

【解答】

1　1. c　2. i　3. d　4. j　5. b　6. e　7. a　8. g　9. f　10. h

2　1. a　2. a　3. b　4. b　5. a　6. a　7. b　8. b　9. a, b　10. a

1. 実験群とは、実験者が独立変数の影響を調査するために独立変数を変える被験者群である。
2. 古典的条件付けでは、パブロフが述べているように、新しい刺激は、自然にある反応を引き起こす刺激と繰り返し結びつけられると、自動的にその反応を引き出すことができるようになる。
3. オペラント条件付けでは、ソーンダイクとスキナーが述べているように、反応に対して強化あるいは報酬を行うと、自発的な反応をますます繰り返すようになる。
4. 精神障害は一般に現実とのつながりを失い、幻覚や妄想を経験する重い障害についての一般用語である。
5. 神経症は不安、うつ病、脅迫観念といった情緒障害についての一般用語である。
6. 脅迫観念は望んでもいない考えに繰り返しとらわれることで、不合理なことであるとしばしば認識できるのに、苦悩を引き起こす。
7. ストレスとは、心身の処理能力に負担をかけるさまざまな状況やできごとである。
8. 認知症は記憶や見当識といった精神能力の喪失が進行することである。
9. 短期記憶では、限られた量の情報が短時間しか保たれない。長期間保持される内容は長期記憶へ移される。
10. うつ病は寂しさ、悲しい思い、無感動、意気消沈により特徴付けられる感情状態である。

>>> 文学語学 P.208

【解答】

1 1. b 2. d 3. g 4. e 5. a 6. f 7. j 8. c 9. i 10. h

2 1. a 2. b 3. b 4. a 5. b 6. b 7. a 8. b 9. a 10. b

1. 叙事詩は物語詩、つまりある偉大な行為を語った一群の詩歌である。宗教的または宇宙的テーマを掲げて国家の建設や国家統一の達成を伝えるものが多い。
2. 小説は内容のすべて、または大部分が創作である作品またはジャンルを指す一般用語である。
3. 詩は叙情詩、つまり歌曲のような詩（ソネット：十四行詩、オード：頌詩、エレジー：哀歌調の詩、田園詩）と物語詩、つまり話を語る詩（バラード：民間伝説・民話などの物語詩、レイ：吟詠用の短い抒情［物語］詩、叙事詩）に区分されることが多い。
4. 長編小説は創作による長大な散文物語であり、中心人物の心理展開や周囲との関係を伝えることが多い。
5. 探偵小説は、不可思議な事件が主にプロまたはアマチュアの探偵の活躍によって解決される長編または短編小説である。
6. 書かれたりすることなく、民衆による復唱のように語り伝えられる、または語り伝えられてきた話を口承文学という。
7. 句読点は慣習として用いられる符号とスペースの規則であり、これにより書かれた、つまり印刷された言葉をできるだけ読みやすく明確かつ論理的に構成する。
8. 頭字語は複数の語の頭文字と音節、または頭文字か音節だけから形成されるひとつの語であり、発音しやすく省略することを意図したものである。
9. 方言は特定地域で使われたり（ヨークシャー方言）、特定の社会階級で使われたり（教育程度の高い標準英語の方言）、または特定地域の特定社会で使われる（アメリカ黒人の英語方言）言葉の一形式である。
10. 語源学とはある言語において、または言語間で、語彙の起源と歴史を研究することである。

>>> 歴史 P.216

【解答】

1 1. f 2. g 3. j 4. c 5. i 6. d 7. b 8. h 9. a 10. e

2 1. b 2. b 3. a 4. b 5. a 6. b 7. b 8. a 9. b 10. a

1. 各植民地はそれぞれに特色を持っていた。それはのちにアメリカ新国家の独自性に貢献した。
2. 1896年、連邦最高裁判所は「分離すれども平等な」施設が提供されていれば、人種差別は合法であるとの判決を下した。
3. プロテスタンティズムはキリスト教の一派で、16世紀にローマ・カトリック教会から

分離した。
4. 経済状態の悪化が進むアイルランドからの移住は一定して続いていたが、1845～46年のアイルランド・ジャガイモ飢饉では、餓死を逃れて集団移住が起こった。
5. 奴隷制は南北戦争の主要原因となったが、経済摩擦や地域対立も影響した。
6. 英国国教会の教義に異を唱えたプロテスタント、清教徒がアメリカ北西部に植民した。
7. 自由と平等を目指すはずの社会が黒人奴隷制の存在を保持するという矛盾が、建国当初から国家の悩みの種であり、南北戦争まで解決されなかった。
8. 米国史において、フロンティアは安価で限りない土地が手に入る移民国家の境界地域であり、西部での困難だが独立した人生を求める開拓者を魅了した。
9. 英国と北米植民地間の戦争（1775～83）は植民地側に勝利と独立をもたらし、米国独立戦争といわれる。
10. 1929年10月の株式市場の大暴落に始まり、1930年代を通して続いた経済危機と世界的な経済活動の衰退を大恐慌という。

>>> 文化 P.224

【解答】

1　1. e　2. d　3. h　4. i　5. a　6. g　7. c　8. b　9. j　10. f

2　1. b　2. a　3. b　4. b　5. b　6. a　7. a　8. b　9. a　10. b

1. 広く理解されている意味でのメディアには、情報の通過するあらゆるルートが含まれる。
2. アメリカ人は情熱を傾けて、最近流行のフィットネスにいそしむ。健康でいるには、普通の運動やバランスのとれた食事程度ではまったく足りないと確信している。
3. アメリカン・フットボールのシーズンは初秋に始まり、屋内のウィンター・スポーツであるバスケットボールに引き継がれ、それはさらに春と夏に行われる野球に引き継がれる。
4. アイス・ホッケー、ボクシング、ゴルフ、カー・レース、競馬、テニスは過去何十年にもわたって人気を保ち、多くの観衆を集めている。
5. ケンカをしたりビンを投げたり、暴動を起こすといった類は、米国の観衆の間ではあまり見られない。
6. 普通、チームのオーナーは有利な長期契約を結ぶため、選手ひとりひとりと契約を交わす。
7. 米国プロスポーツの営利本位な側面は、運動選手の経歴をつくりもすれば、壊すことにもなりかねない。
8. 米国のスポーツはますます競争が激しく、営利志向が強くなっている。
9. 米国は社会評論家がときに呼ぶところのメディア主体の国家となった。これは権力への接近がマスメディアを通して行われる社会のことである。
10. 印刷と放送媒体は情報を一般大衆に伝えるばかりでなく、世論にも影響を与える。

>>> 芸術   P.232

【解答】

1   1. d   2. a   3. h   4. e   5. c   6. j   7. b   8. i   9. g   10. f

2   1. b   2. b   3. a   4. b   5. a   6. a   7. a   8. a   9. b   10. b

1. ラグタイム、ブルース、ジャズ、カントリーミュージック、ロックンロール、ミュージカルはすべて、米国で生まれた。
2. ブルースはアフリカの民謡と教会音楽から発展した。
3. 抽象表現主義画家は人体、静物、田園風景といった伝統的な主題を拒絶した。代わりに彼らは、空間、大きさ、表面の質感の活用と色彩の相互関係といったことに焦点を当てた。
4. カントリーミュージックは南東部と南西部の田舎生活を反映したメロディーと歌詞をもち、長い年月をかけて形成された。
5. 1930年代に、もうひとつ米国生まれの芸術が現れた。ミュージカルは芝居と音楽とバレエを組み合わせた新形式のショーだった。
6. 摩天楼とは一種の高層ビルであり、1868年ニューヨークで初めて発展した。ニューヨークは地価が高かったし、地質的にそのような建設手法が可能だった。
7. かつて貧困層が住んでいた通りや地域を、そこに住むことを望む裕福な人々の要求が満たされるように変えていく過程を、高級化という。
8. 立体派は20世紀の芸術様式であり、主題は幾何学的な形で表現される。
9. バレエや曲のためにステップやダンスを作ったりアレンジしたりする人を、振り付け師という。
10. 石、木、粘土、金属などから人間、動物、物体の立体彫像を作る芸術を彫刻という。

INDEX

※見出しとして掲載されている単語・熟語は赤字、それ以外のものは黒字で示されています。それぞれの語の右側にある数字は、見出し番号を表しています。赤字の番号は、見出しとなっている番号を示します。

Index

A

- [ ] a biographic dictionary 692
- [ ] a broadcasting station 753
- [ ] a Congressional district 066
- [ ] a dense fog 234
- [ ] a dense forest 234
- [ ] a dormant volcano 275
- [ ] a Hollywood epic 686
- [ ] a person of high reputation 628
- [ ] a reasoning creature 654
- [ ] a volcanic eruption 275
- [ ] **ability grouping** 648
- [ ] **abound** 102
- [ ] **abrasive** 300
- [ ] **absolute monarch** 501
- [ ] absolute monarchy 501
- [ ] **absorb** 001
- [ ] absorption 001
- [ ] **abstract** 101
- [ ] **abstract expressionism** 774
- [ ] abstractionist 774
- [ ] abundance 102
- [ ] **abundant** 102
- [ ] **academic standard** 627
- [ ] **accelerate** 476
- [ ] acceleration 476
- [ ] **accessible** 744
- [ ] **accomplish** 002, 642
- [ ] accomplishment 002
- [ ] **accordingly** 151
- [ ] **accumulate** 003
- [ ] accumulation 003
- [ ] **accuse** 596
- [ ] accuser 596
- [ ] achieve 642
- [ ] acid 310

- [ ] **acid rain** 310
- [ ] **acronym** 703
- [ ] acute pneumonia 419
- [ ] administrative 594
- [ ] **administrative law** 594
- [ ] admit 626
- [ ] **adventure story** 695
- [ ] **aesthetic** 683
- [ ] aesthetics 683
- [ ] **affirmative action** 574
- [ ] **aggravate** 004, 615
- [ ] **aggravated assault** 615
- [ ] aggravating 004
- [ ] **agrarian** 727
- [ ] agrarianism 727
- [ ] **air resistance** 477
- [ ] **akin** 103
- [ ] akin to ... 103
- [ ] **alcohol-related** 469
- [ ] alcoholic 469
- [ ] allegoric 691
- [ ] allegorize 691
- [ ] **allegory** 691
- [ ] **altitude** 257
- [ ] amalgamation 539
- [ ] ameliorate 064
- [ ] amelioration 064
- [ ] **amendment** 513
- [ ] amentia 674
- [ ] **Amish** 568
- [ ] **amnesia** 680
- [ ] amnesiac 680
- [ ] **amphetamine** 465
- [ ] **amphibian** 360
- [ ] **ample** 104
- [ ] amplification 104
- [ ] amplify 104
- [ ] amplitude 104
- [ ] amply 104
- [ ] an active volcano 275
- [ ] an extinct volcano 275
- [ ] analysis 207
- [ ] analyzation 207
- [ ] **analyze** 207

- [ ] **anemia** 416
- [ ] **anemometer** 256
- [ ] **anguish** 051
- [ ] anguished 051
- [ ] **annual** 344
- [ ] **anomie** 577
- [ ] **antibody** 408
- [ ] **antonym** 704
- [ ] antonymous 704
- [ ] antonymy 704
- [ ] **apparent** 105
- [ ] apparently 105
- [ ] **appeal** 604, 785
- [ ] **appendicitis** 413
- [ ] appendix 413
- [ ] applicability 005
- [ ] applicable 005
- [ ] applicant 005
- [ ] application 005
- [ ] **apply** 005
- [ ] **apprentice** 586
- [ ] **appropriate** 106
- [ ] appropriation 106
- [ ] **approximately** 152
- [ ] archaeological 561
- [ ] **archaeologist** 561
- [ ] archaeology 561
- [ ] architect 771
- [ ] architectural 771
- [ ] **architecture** 771
- [ ] **arid** 255
- [ ] **Art Deco** 796
- [ ] artificial incubation 365
- [ ] **artificial intelligence** 657
- [ ] **asexual** 327
- [ ] asexual reproduction 327
- [ ] assault 615
- [ ] **asteroid** 226
- [ ] **astronomer** 201
- [ ] at wholesale 547
- [ ] **athlete** 751
- [ ] athletic 751
- [ ] **atmosphere** 232
- [ ] **atom** 443

☐ attain	642
☐ **attainment**	642
☐ attend	621
☐ **attendance**	621
☐ **audience**	757
☐ autobiography	692
☐ **autonomous**	107
☐ autonomy	107
☐ **axis**	216

B

☐ **baby tooth**	388
☐ **bacteria**	326
☐ **bail**	597
☐ **balance**	550
☐ bank account balance	550
☐ **barometer**	259
☐ **barter**	551
☐ **basically**	153
☐ be absorbed in ...	001
☐ be depressed	675
☐ be obsessed by ...	666
☐ **bear**	006
☐ **behavioral**	653
☐ behavioral science	653
☐ behaviorism	653
☐ belly button	385
☐ **biennial**	345
☐ **bill**	521
☐ biographic	692
☐ **biography**	692
☐ bioluminescence	358
☐ **bioluminescent**	358
☐ bleeder	399
☐ **blues**	780
☐ board	629
☐ **board of education**	629
☐ botanical	341
☐ botanical garden	341
☐ **botanist**	341
☐ botany	341
☐ **briefly**	154

☐ bring ... to completion	008
☐ bring ... to trial	598
☐ bring in a verdict of guilty	602
☐ bring in a verdict of not guilty	602
☐ bring in an indictment against ...	600
☐ **broadcast**	753
☐ broadcast journalism	753
☐ broadcasting	753
☐ brokage firm	554
☐ **broker**	554
☐ brokerage	554
☐ bronchial	418
☐ bronchial asthma	418
☐ bronchitic	418
☐ **bronchitis**	418
☐ bronchium	418
☐ **burden**	052
☐ burdensome	052
☐ **bureaucracy**	637
☐ bureaucrat	637
☐ bureaucratic	637
☐ bureaucratize	637
☐ **burglary**	616
☐ by wholesale	547

C

☐ **cabinet**	523
☐ cal.	431
☐ **calorie**	431
☐ **camouflage**	340
☐ **capital**	536
☐ capital investment	536
☐ **capital punishment**	620
☐ **capitalism**	537
☐ capitalist	536
☐ capitalist country	536
☐ captive	007
☐ captor	007
☐ **capture**	007
☐ **carbohydrate**	446

☐ carbon	445
☐ **carbon dioxide**	445
☐ carnivora	335
☐ **carnivore**	335
☐ carnivorous	335
☐ **caste system**	580
☐ **caterpillar**	353
☐ Catholic	715
☐ celestial body	213
☐ **celestial sphere**	213
☐ **cell**	321
☐ censor	767
☐ **censorship**	767
☐ **central nervous system**	436
☐ centripetal	483
☐ **centripetal force**	483
☐ **cerebellum**	438
☐ **cerebrum**	437
☐ **challenging**	643
☐ **chaos**	053
☐ chaotic	053
☐ **characteristically**	155
☐ **checks and balances**	511
☐ **chemical formula**	444
☐ **children's literature**	694
☐ chip	488
☐ chloride	455
☐ **chlorophyll**	349
☐ **choreographer**	786
☐ choreography	786
☐ **circulation**	760
☐ **circulatory system**	366
☐ **civil law**	618
☐ **civil rights**	515
☐ class dialect	707
☐ **classical conditioning**	655
☐ **climate**	252
☐ **closed system**	579
☐ **coal**	309
☐ coal mine	309

どれだけチェックできた？ 1 ☐ 2 ☐

☐ coal miner 309	☐ concordant (with) 056	☐ constitutional 595
☐ coal mining 309	☐ concrete 101	☐ **constitutional law** 595
☐ **cocaine** 466	☐ concur 057	☐ **construct** 011
☐ **cocoon** 354	☐ **concurrence** 057	☐ construction 011
☐ **codify** 572	☐ concurrent 057	☐ **consume** 012
☐ **cognition** 659	☐ **conditioning** 378, 655	☐ consumer 012
☐ cognitive 659	☐ **conductor** 487	☐ consumption 012
☐ cold current 253	☐ **confer** 009	☐ **contain** 013
☐ cold latitudes 277	☐ conference 009	☐ contained 013
☐ **cold-blooded** 359	☐ **confiscate** 010	☐ **contemporary** 114
☐ collective 590	☐ confiscation 010	☐ continual 113
☐ **collective bargaining** 560	☐ **conform** 575	☐ continuous 113
☐ **collective behavior** 590	☐ **congenial** 109	☐ **contribute** 014
☐ college 623	☐ congeniality 109	☐ contributory 014
☐ **college-bound** 625	☐ **congenital** 110	☐ control group 652
☐ colonial 711	☐ **congest** 058	☐ **controversial** 115
☐ colonialism 711	☐ congested 058	☐ controversy 115
☐ colonize 711	☐ **congestion** 058	☐ controvert 115
☐ **colony** 711	☐ **conglomerate** 540	☐ convect 235
☐ **color-blind** 375	☐ conglomerator 540	☐ **convection** 235
☐ **comedy** 789	☐ congress 519	☐ convention 116
☐ **comet** 225	☐ **congressional district** 519	☐ **conventional** 116
☐ **commercial** 769	☐ congressman 518	☐ conventionalize 116
☐ **common law** 593	☐ **conifer** 343	☐ conversion 015
☐ **commonly** 156	☐ coniferous 343	☐ **convert** 015
☐ **comparatively** 157	☐ conjectural 059	☐ converter 015
☐ compete 749	☐ **conjecture** 059	☐ **copyright** 535
☐ competence 636	☐ conscience 111	☐ copyright reserved 535
☐ **competency** 636	☐ **conscientious** 111	☐ copyrighted 535
☐ competent 636	☐ **conscious** 112	☐ **coral** 266
☐ competition 749	☐ consciously 112	☐ **core** 060
☐ **competitive** 749	☐ consciousness 112	☐ **Coriolis effect** 258
☐ competitor 749	☐ **consequently** 158	☐ Coriolis force 258
☐ **complement** 054	☐ **conservation** 303	☐ costruct 011
☐ **complete** 008	☐ conservationist 303	☐ **country and western** 783
☐ completely 008	☐ **conservative** 730	☐ country music 783
☐ completion 008	☐ conserve 303	☐ **county** 524
☐ **complexion** 055	☐ **considerably** 159	☐ **court of appeals** 607
☐ compulsion 108	☐ **consistently** 160	☐ cover 772
☐ **compulsory** 108, 622	☐ **constant** 113	☐ **coverage** 772
☐ compulsory education 622	☐ **constellation** 212	☐ **credential** 650
☐ **concord** 056	☐ constipate 414	☐ credentialism 650
☐ concordance 056	☐ **constipation** 414	☐ **credulous** 117
	☐ **constitution** 505	☐ criminal law 618

☐ criminal trial	598	
☐ **critically**	**161**	
☐ crude	307	
☐ **crude oil**	**307**	
☐ crude petroleum	307	
☐ **crust**	**268**	
☐ **cubism**	**799**	
☐ **current**	**253**	
☐ **cybernetics**	**658**	

D

☐ date line	278
☐ death penalty	620
☐ **decade**	**061**
☐ **decibel**	**494**
☐ **dedicate**	**016**
☐ dedicated	016
☐ dedication	016
☐ **defect**	**062**
☐ defective	062
☐ defend	063
☐ defendant	596
☐ **defense**	**063**
☐ defensive	063
☐ **definitely**	**162**
☐ delinquent	611
☐ demand deposit	553
☐ demented	674
☐ **dementia**	**674**
☐ Democrat	526
☐ democrat	503
☐ democratic	503
☐ **democracy**	**503**
☐ **dense**	**234**
☐ **depict**	**017**
☐ depiction	017
☐ **deposit**	**296, 552**
☐ deposit money in a bank	552
☐ depositor	552
☐ **depressant**	**463**
☐ **depression**	**675**
☐ **describe**	**018**
☐ description	018
☐ descriptive	018

☐ desegregate	724
☐ **designate**	**019**
☐ designation	019
☐ detective	696
☐ **detective fiction**	**696**
☐ detective novel	696
☐ detective story	696
☐ deteriorate	064
☐ **deterioration**	**064**
☐ **developmental psychology**	**660**
☐ **deviant**	**576**
☐ deviate	576
☐ **device**	**065**
☐ devise	065
☐ **dew**	**239**
☐ **dew point**	**240**
☐ dewy	239
☐ **diabetes**	**427**
☐ diabetic	427
☐ **dialect**	**707**
☐ dialectal	707
☐ dialectology	707
☐ **diarrhea**	**415**
☐ **diet**	**390**
☐ dietary fiber	390
☐ **diffuse**	**452**
☐ diffusible	452
☐ diffusion	452
☐ digestion	330
☐ **digestive**	**330**
☐ digestive juice	330
☐ digestive organs	330
☐ **digestive system**	**367**
☐ dioxide	445
☐ **diploma**	**624**
☐ diplomaism	650
☐ **directly**	**163**
☐ discord	056
☐ **distinct**	**020**
☐ distinction	020
☐ distinctive	020
☐ **distinguish**	**020**
☐ distinguished	020
☐ **district**	**066, 606**

☐ **district court**	**606**
☐ **diverse**	**713**
☐ diversify	713
☐ diversity	713
☐ **dividend**	**544**
☐ **division of labor**	**585**
☐ **Doppler effect**	**491**
☐ Doppler radar	491
☐ **down payment**	**549**
☐ **drawing**	**798**
☐ drop out	632
☐ **dropout**	**632**
☐ **drought**	**260**
☐ **drug**	**461**
☐ drug abuse	461
☐ drug addict	461
☐ **dubious**	**118**
☐ **dune**	**285**
☐ durability	119
☐ **durable**	**119**
☐ **dust**	**224**

E

☐ **eccentric**	**120**
☐ eccentricity	120
☐ **eclipse**	**227**
☐ **ecology**	**350**
☐ edit	766
☐ edition	766
☐ editor	766
☐ **editorial**	**766**
☐ **efficient**	**121**
☐ **egalitarian**	**584**
☐ egalitarianism	584
☐ **elective**	**630**
☐ elective course	630
☐ elective system	630
☐ **electric discharge**	**486**
☐ **electric force**	**480**
☐ **element**	**441**
☐ **eloquence**	**067**
☐ eloquent	067
☐ embryo	382
☐ emigrant	719
☐ empathize	676

☐ **empathy** 676	☐ execution 613	☐ **federalism** 506
☐ **emphysema** 420	☐ **executive** 509	☐ **feed** 026
☐ **endangered** 380	☐ executive branch 509	☐ feel fit 741
☐ **enormously** 164	☐ Executive Mansion 509	☐ feminine 569
☐ enroll 645	☐ **expand** 023	☐ femininity 569
☐ **enrollment** 645	☐ expanse 023	☐ **fertilization** 342, 299
☐ **entirely** 165	☐ expansion 023	☐ fertilize 299, 342
☐ **enzyme** 449	☐ expansive 023	☐ **fertilizer** 299
☐ enzyme detergent 449	☐ experiment 652	☐ **fetus** 382
☐ **epic** 686	☐ **experimental group** 652	☐ **fiction** 688
☐ **epicenter** 273	☐ **explicit** 123	☐ **figurative** 689
☐ **equally** 166	☐ **exploit** 024	☐ film 787
☐ **equator** 237	☐ exploitation 024	☐ **financial** 534
☐ equatorial 237	☐ extant 379	☐ financial crisis 534
☐ **equivocal** 122	☐ **extend** 025	☐ financier 534
☐ equivocation 122	☐ **extended family** 582	☐ financing 534
☐ ERA 740	☐ extension 025	☐ **firmly** 169
☐ **eradicate** 021	☐ extensive 025	☐ first meridian 279
☐ **erosion** 289	☐ extent 025	☐ fit 741
☐ erosive 289	☐ **extinct** 124, 379	☐ **fitness** 741
☐ **esophagus** 405	☐ extinction 124, 379	☐ **flamboyant** 797
☐ essentialism 644	☐ extinguish 124	☐ fluorescence 498
☐ **essentially** 167	☐ extinguisher 124	☐ **fluorescent light** 498
☐ **estimate** 022	☐ **extravagance** 069	☐ **food additive** 432
☐ estimated 022	☐ extravagant 069, 145	☐ **food chain** 339
☐ estimation 022	☐ extroversion 677	☐ food coloring 432
☐ estivate 361	☐ **extrovert** 677	☐ food cycle 339
☐ estuarine 357	☐ extroverted 677	☐ food web 339
☐ **estuary** 357	☐ **eyesight** 389	☐ **formally** 170
☐ **ethnic group** 563		☐ **fossil** 283
☐ ethnicism 564	**F**	☐ fossil fuel 283
☐ **ethnocentrism** 564	☐ Fact is stranger than	☐ fossilize 283
☐ **ethnologist** 562	fiction. 688	☐ free economy 532
☐ ethnology 562	☐ **fairy tale** 693	☐ **free enterprise system** 532
☐ ethnos 563	☐ **famine** 070	☐ free market 532
☐ **etymology** 708	☐ famish 070	☐ **frequency** 495
☐ eulogistic 068	☐ **fantasy** 697	☐ **friction** 481
☐ eulogize 068	☐ **fat** 447	☐ **front** 245
☐ **eulogy** 068	☐ **fault** 280	☐ **frontier** 720
☐ evaporate 238	☐ **feature** 761	☐ **fusion** 782
☐ **evaporation** 238	☐ feature program 761	☐ **futile** 125
☐ **eventually** 168	☐ feature story 761	☐ futility 125
☐ **exclusive** 747	☐ federal 506	
☐ exclusively 747	☐ **federal system** 506	
☐ **execute** 613		

G

- galaxy 219
- gene 397
- gene mutation 402
- generally 171
- genetic 393
- genetic engineering 400
- genetics 393
- genotype 398
- gentrification 800
- gentrify 800
- geologist 261
- geology 261
- geotherm 290
- geothermal energy 290
- geyser 284
- glacier 282
- gloss 071
- glossary 071
- GNP 545
- gradually 172
- gram 206
- grand jury 599
- grant 626
- gravitation 479
- gravitational force 479
- greenhouse effect 233
- grief 072
- grievance 072
- grieve 072
- grind 027
- Gross National Product 545
- gymnasium 746

H

- habitat 328
- habitat group 328
- hail 251
- hailstone 251
- hallucinate 467
- hallucination 467
- hallucinogen 467
- hallucinogenic 467
- harvest 304
- has a large circulation 760
- has a limited circulation 760
- has a small circulation 760
- have access to ... 744
- have jurisdiction over ... 605
- heart attack 421
- heart disease 421
- heart failure 421
- hemophilia 399
- hemophiliac 399
- hemp 468
- herbivora 334
- herbivore 334
- herbivorous 334
- hereditary 392
- heredity 392
- hibernate 361
- hibernation 361
- high atmospheric pressure 246
- high blood pressure 423
- high latitudes 277
- hold ... in (high) estimation 022
- hold the copyright on a book 535
- homonym 706
- homonymous 706
- homonymy 706
- horizon 236
- horizontal 236
- hormone 459
- humanitarian 567
- humanitarianism 567
- humid 241
- humidity 241
- hurricane 250
- hybrid 396
- hydrocarbon 456
- hydrologic cycle 244
- hydrology 242
- hypertension 423
- hypertensive 423
- hypocenter 273
- hypotension 423
- hypothesis 073
- hypothetical 073

I

- IC 488
- iceberg 282
- ideally 173
- IDL 278
- illiteracy 633
- illiterate 633
- immediately 174
- immigrant 719
- immigration 719
- imminence 126
- imminent 126
- immune 429
- immune body 408
- immunity 429
- immunize 429
- immunology 429
- impeach 609
- impeachment 609
- implication 028
- implicit 123
- imply 028
- imprison 612
- imprisonment 612
- impromptu 127
- in anguish 051
- in good shape 434
- in poor shape 434
- in principle 085
- in response to ... 045
- in shape 434
- in substance 097
- inalienable right 529
- incidence 074
- incident 074
- incidental 074
- incidentally 175, 074

どれだけチェックできた？ 1 ☐ 2 ☐

☐ incinerate 317	☐ interaction 034	☐ **kingdom** 323
☐ **incineration** 317	☐ **intercollegiate** 755	
☐ incinerator 317	☐ internal organs 322	**L**
☐ **incubation** 365	☐ **International Date Line** 278	☐ **labor** 383
☐ **indicate** 029		☐ **laboratory** 204
☐ indication 029	☐ **intestine** 407	☐ **landscape** 792
☐ indicative 029	☐ intricacy 130	☐ **larva** 352
☐ **indict** 600, 075	☐ **intricate** 130	☐ lat. 277
☐ **indictment** 075, 600	☐ **introspection** 671	☐ **latitude** 277
☐ **indigestion** 412	☐ introspectionism 671	☐ **lava** 274
☐ **indoor** 748	☐ introspective 671	☐ **law-abiding** 591
☐ **inertia** 482	☐ introversion 678	☐ law-abiding citizens 591
☐ **infancy** 386	☐ **introvert** 678	☐ **layer** 270
☐ infant 386	☐ introverted 678	☐ **legislate** 573, 508
☐ infants 386	☐ invention 688	☐ legislation 508, 573
☐ **influence** 030	☐ **invertebrate** 331	☐ **legislative** 508, 573
☐ influential 030	☐ investigative 768	☐ legislative branch 508
☐ infrared 499	☐ investigative journalism 768	☐ legislature 508
☐ **infrared light** 499		☐ **leukemia** 417
☐ infrared radiation 499	☐ **investigative reporting** 768	☐ leukemic 417
☐ **ingredient** 433		☐ leukocyte 410
☐ **inherently** 176	☐ **IQ test** 649	☐ **life imprisonment** 612
☐ **initially** 177	☐ **irrigate** 316	☐ **light year** 218
☐ **initiate** 031		☐ lightning rod 487
☐ initiative 031	**J**	☐ liter 206
☐ **innovation** 076	☐ **jargon** 709	☐ **literally** 178
☐ **inquisitive** 128	☐ **jazz** 781	☐ **literary** 682
☐ inspiration 032	☐ Jazz Age 781	☐ literary works 682
☐ **inspire** 032	☐ jeopardize 077	☐ living standard 531
☐ installment 548	☐ **jeopardy** 077	☐ **lizard** 362
☐ **installment plan** 548	☐ **judicial** 510	☐ lobby 522
☐ **instinct** 377	☐ judicial branch 510	☐ lobbyism 522
☐ instinctive 377	☐ junior college 623	☐ **lobbyist** 522
☐ **insulin** 460	☐ **jurisdiction** 605	☐ local dialect 707
☐ **integrate** 033, 631	☐ juvenile 611	☐ **loess** 281
☐ **integrated circuit** 488	☐ juvenile delinquency 611	☐ lon(g). 276
☐ **integration** 631, 033	☐ **juvenile delinquent** 611	☐ **long-term memory** 679
☐ integrationist 631		
☐ intelligence quotient 649	**K**	☐ **longitude** 276
☐ intense 129		☐ longitudinal 276
☐ intensify 129	☐ keep fit 741	☐ **low atmospheric pressure** 247
☐ intension 129	☐ **kidney failure** 426	
☐ **intensity** 493, 129	☐ **kidney stone** 425	☐ low blood pressure 423
☐ **intensive** 129	☐ **kindergarten** 623	☐ low latitudes 277
☐ **interact** 034	☐ **kinetic energy** 474	☐ **lubricant** 298

☐ lubricate 298	☐ **metamorphosis** 351	☐ mutuality 131
☐ **lucrative** 754	☐ metaphorical 689	☐ myth 681
☐ lunar eclipse 227	☐ **meteorite** 228	☐ **mythic** 681
☐ **lyric** 687	☐ **meteorologist** 231	☐ mythical 681
☐ lyric poetry 687	☐ meteorology 231	☐ mythicism 681
	☐ meter 206	☐ mythology 681

M

N

☐ **magma** 269	☐ **metric** 206	☐ **namely** 179
☐ magnet 484	☐ metric system 206	☐ **narcotic** 464, 461
☐ **magnetic pole** 484	☐ **microbe** 428	☐ narcoticism 464
☐ **majority** 078, 530	☐ microbiology 428	☐ **natural resources** 291
☐ **majority rule** 530	☐ **microscope** 203	☐ **naturalization** 527
☐ make progress 086	☐ migrate 080	☐ naturalize 527
☐ **mammal** 333	☐ **migration** 080	☐ **navel** 385
☐ Mammalia 333	☐ milk tooth 388	☐ navel string 385
☐ mammalian 333	☐ **mineral** 302, 457	☐ **nearly** 180
☐ **manslaughter** 614	☐ mineral water 457	☐ **nebula** 220
☐ **mantle** 271	☐ minor planet 226	☐ **necessarily** 181
☐ **marijuana** 468	☐ minority 078	☐ nephritic 424
☐ **marsupial** 403	☐ **mirage** 500	☐ **nephritis** 424
☐ masculine 569	☐ **mixed media** 775	☐ nervous 370
☐ **masculinity** 569	☐ mobile 588	☐ **nervous system** 370
☐ **mass** 079	☐ modification 035	☐ **network** 770
☐ mass media 756	☐ **modify** 035	☐ **neurosis** 662
☐ **mass production** 546	☐ **molecule** 442	☐ neurotic 662
☐ massive 079	☐ molt 363	☐ **neuroticism** 663
☐ matriarch 583	☐ **molting** 363	☐ **nicotine** 470
☐ matriarchal 583	☐ **momentum** 478	☐ nicotinism 470
☐ matriarchy 583	☐ monarch 501	☐ **nitrogen** 450
☐ **maximize** 639	☐ monopolist 538	☐ **nonmetallic substance** 295
☐ **media** 756	☐ monopolize 538	
☐ **Medicaid** 558	☐ **monopoly** 538	☐ **nonrenewable resource** 293
☐ **Medicare** 557	☐ **mores** 571	
☐ meditate 670	☐ **motion picture** 787	☐ **norm** 566
☐ **meditation** 670	☐ **motivate** 635	☐ **notably** 182
☐ **medulla** 439	☐ motivation 635	☐ **nova** 222
☐ medulla oblongata 439	☐ motive 635	☐ **novel** 690
☐ **mercantilism** 716	☐ movie 787	☐ novelist 690
☐ merge 539	☐ **moviegoer** 790	☐ novelize 690
☐ **merger** 539	☐ moviegoing 790	☐ nuclear 311
☐ merit system 581	☐ moving picture 787	☐ nuclear bomb 311
☐ **meritocracy** 581	☐ murder 614	☐ nuclear family 582
☐ meritocrat 581	☐ **musical** 784	☐ **nuclear reactor** 311
☐ **metabolism** 409	☐ mutant 402	☐ nursery school 623
☐ metallic substance 294	☐ **mutation** 402	
	☐ mutual 131	

☐ **nutrient**	356	
☐ nutrition	356	

O

- ☐ objective 765
- ☐ **objectivity** 765
- ☐ oblivion 132
- ☐ **oblivious** 132
- ☐ **obscure** 133
- ☐ obscurity 133
- ☐ **observatory** 205
- ☐ obsess 666
- ☐ **obsession** 666
- ☐ obsessional 666
- ☐ obsessional neurosis 666
- ☐ **obsolete** 134
- ☐ **obvious** 135
- ☐ obviously 135
- ☐ occupational school 623
- ☐ **oceanographer** 265
- ☐ oceanography 265
- ☐ **oil field** 306
- ☐ **oil well** 305
- ☐ old age pension 737
- ☐ omnivora 336
- ☐ **omnivore** 336
- ☐ omnivorous 336
- ☐ on parole 619
- ☐ only 747
- ☐ **op art** 777
- ☐ operant 656
- ☐ **operant conditioning** 656
- ☐ optical art 777
- ☐ **oral literature** 698
- ☐ **orbit** 214
- ☐ **ordeal** 081
- ☐ **orderly** 640, 053
- ☐ **ore** 297, 302
- ☐ **organ** 322
- ☐ **organized crime** 731
- ☐ **originally** 183
- ☐ outdoor 748
- ☐ **overgraze** 312
- ☐ **ozone** 314

- ☐ ozone layer 314
- ☐ ozonosphere 314

P

- ☐ **paleontologist** 404
- ☐ paleontology 404
- ☐ **pancreas** 406
- ☐ pancreatic juice 406
- ☐ pancreatitis 406
- ☐ **parody** 700
- ☐ **parole** 619
- ☐ **particularly** 184
- ☐ **parts of speech** 701
- ☐ patriarch 583
- ☐ **patriarchal** 583
- ☐ patriarchy 583
- ☐ pay down 549
- ☐ pay in monthly installments 548
- ☐ **peer** 647
- ☐ peer group 647
- ☐ **pension** 737
- ☐ pensioner 737
- ☐ **perennial** 346
- ☐ **performance art** 778
- ☐ **periodical** 758
- ☐ periodically 758
- ☐ permanent tooth 388
- ☐ petit jury 601
- ☐ **petroleum** 301
- ☐ **phenotype** 398
- ☐ **phobia** 667
- ☐ **photosynthesis** 348
- ☐ **phototropism** 347
- ☐ **physical science** 471
- ☐ pistil 395
- ☐ **pitch** 496
- ☐ plaintiff 596
- ☐ **planet** 211
- ☐ **plausible** 136
- ☐ **play-off** 743
- ☐ **pneumonia** 419
- ☐ pneumonic 419
- ☐ poem 684
- ☐ poet 684

- ☐ poetic 684
- ☐ **poetry** 684
- ☐ poll 725
- ☐ **poll tax** 725
- ☐ pollen 355
- ☐ pollination 355
- ☐ **pollinator** 355
- ☐ **pollutants** 315
- ☐ pollute 315
- ☐ pollution 315
- ☐ poor soil 262
- ☐ **pop art** 776
- ☐ **population** 329
- ☐ portrait 036, 793
- ☐ **portray** 036, 793
- ☐ portrayal 036, 793
- ☐ **potential** 137
- ☐ **potential energy** 473
- ☐ potentiality 137
- ☐ pouch 371
- ☐ **pouched** 371
- ☐ pouched animal 371
- ☐ practical 101
- ☐ **precaution** 082
- ☐ **precede** 037
- ☐ precedent 037
- ☐ preceding 037
- ☐ **precept** 083
- ☐ preceptor 083
- ☐ **precipitation** 243
- ☐ **precisely** 185
- ☐ **predator** 337
- ☐ **predominantly** 186
- ☐ **prejudice** 084
- ☐ **premises** 750
- ☐ **premium** 555
- ☐ prerequisite 630
- ☐ **prescribe** 570
- ☐ **prescription** 570
- ☐ preservative 432
- ☐ **presumably** 187
- ☐ **prevail** 038
- ☐ prevailing 038
- ☐ prevalence 038
- ☐ prevalent 038

☐ **previously** 188	☐ psychoanalyst 661	☐ **reduce** 042
☐ **prey** 338	☐ psychoanalytic 661	☐ reduction 042
☐ **primarily** 189	☐ psychological 651	☐ reef 266
☐ primate 372	☐ psychologist 651	☐ **refill** 318
☐ **primates** 372	☐ **psychology** 651	☐ refine 308
☐ primatology 372	☐ psychopath 664	☐ **refinery** 308
☐ **prime meridian** 279	☐ psychopathic 664	☐ **reflection** 489, 376
☐ **principle** 085	☐ psychopathy 664	☐ reflective 376, 489
☐ **prism** 208	☐ **psychosis** 664	☐ **reflex** 376
☐ private detective 696	☐ psychotherapeutic 672	☐ **refraction** 490
☐ **produce** 039	☐ **psychotherapy** 672	☐ refractive 490
☐ product 039	☐ psychotic 664	☐ **region** 090
☐ production 039	☐ **public utilities** 541	☐ regional 090
☐ productive 039	☐ **publication** 762	☐ **relatively** 191
☐ profitable 754	☐ punctual 646	☐ reluctance 139
☐ **progress** 086	☐ **punctuality** 646	☐ **reluctant** 139
☐ progression 086	☐ **punctuation** 702	☐ **remain** 043
☐ progressive 086	☐ pupa 352	☐ **remarkable** 140
☐ progressive education 644	☐ **Puritan** 714	☐ **remarkably** 192, 140
☐ **progressivism** 644	☐ **pursue** 745	☐ **renewable resource** 292
☐ Prohibition 729	☐ pursuit 745	☐ representational 101
☐ **prolific** 138	**Q**	☐ representative 518
☐ **property** 087, 533	☐ **quota** 528	☐ **representative democracy** 504
☐ proprietor 542	**R**	☐ **reproach** 044
☐ **proprietorship** 542	☐ racial discrimination 724	☐ reproachful 044
☐ proscribe 570	☐ radiate 221	☐ reproduce 394
☐ proscription 570	☐ **radiation** 221	☐ **reproductive organs** 394
☐ **prose** 685	☐ radio broadcasting 753	☐ **reptile** 332
☐ **prospect** 088	☐ **radioactive** 287	☐ Reptilia 332
☐ prospective 088	☐ radioactive rays 287	☐ reptilian 332
☐ prospectively 088	☐ **ragtime** 779	☐ republic 504
☐ prosper 733	☐ **range** 089	☐ Republican 525
☐ **prosperity** 733	☐ **rapidly** 190	☐ **reputable** 628
☐ prosperous 733	☐ **ratification** 517	☐ reputation 628
☐ **protein** 448	☐ ratify 517	☐ required course 630
☐ **Protestant** 715	☐ **readership** 759	☐ **reservation** 728
☐ Protestant ethic 715	☐ **reasoning** 654	☐ **reservoir** 263
☐ Protestantism 715	☐ **recession** 559	☐ **resonance** 497
☐ provocative 040	☐ recessive 398	☐ resonant 497
☐ **provoke** 040	☐ **reconcile** 041	☐ **resource** 264
☐ psychiatrist 651	☐ reconciliation 041	☐ **respectively** 193
☐ psychiatry 651	☐ **Reconstruction** 723	☐ respiration 368
☐ psycho 664	☐ red blood cell 410	
☐ **psychoanalysis** 661		

☐ **respiratory system** 368	☐ **seismograph** 272	☐ **species** 324
☐ respire 368	☐ seismography 272	☐ **spectator** 752
☐ **respond** 045	☐ seismology 272	☐ spectator sport 752
☐ **response** 374, 045	☐ self-examination 671	☐ **spectroscope** 210
☐ **restrain** 046	☐ **self-reliance** 738	☐ **spectrum** 209
☐ restrain from ... 046	☐ senator 520	☐ **spinal cord** 440
☐ restraint 046	☐ senile dementia 674	☐ **spiral** 223
☐ retail 547	☐ **sense organ** 435	☐ **spontaneity** 095
☐ retailer 547	☐ **separate but equal** 726	☐ spontaneous 095
☐ **retain** 794	☐ **separation of powers** 507	☐ sport analyst 742
☐ return a verdict of guilty 602	☐ settle 092, 712	☐ **sports analyst** 742
☐ return a verdict of not guilty 602	☐ **settlement** 092, 712	☐ sportscast 742
☐ **revolve** 215	☐ settler 712	☐ **stamen** 395
☐ **rhetoric** 710	☐ **sewage** 320	☐ **standard of living** 531
☐ rhetorical 710	☐ sewage disposal 320	☐ static 485
☐ rich soil 262	☐ sewage works 320	☐ **static electricity** 485
☐ **rotate** 229	☐ short-term memory 679	☐ statutory 592
☐ rotation 229	☐ **significance** 093	☐ **statutory law** 592
☐ rugged 788	☐ significant 093	☐ stay fit 741
☐ **rugged individualism** 788	☐ significantly 093	☐ **stereotype** 589
	☐ signify 093	☐ **stimulant** 462
S	☐ **site** 094	☐ stimulate 373
☐ **salinity** 267	☐ **skeletal system** 369	☐ stimulation 373
☐ sand dune 285	☐ skeleton 369	☐ stimulative 373
☐ SAT 641	☐ **skyscraper** 795	☐ **stimulus** 373
☐ **satellite** 230	☐ slave 718	☐ **stock** 543
☐ **satire** 699	☐ **slavery** 718	☐ stock company 543
☐ satirical 699	☐ **slightly** 194	☐ Stock Exchange 543
☐ satirist 699	☐ slump 559	☐ stock exchange 543
☐ schizo 665	☐ **social insurance** 556	☐ stockholder 543
☐ **schizophrenia** 665	☐ **social stratification** 578	☐ **strain** 096
☐ schizophrenic 665	☐ socialization 587	☐ strained 096
☐ **Scholastic Assessment Test** 641	☐ **socialize** 587	☐ stratify 578
☐ scrutinize 091	☐ sodium 455	☐ **stress** 668
☐ **scrutiny** 091	☐ **sodium chloride** 455	☐ **strive** 047
☐ sculptor 773	☐ **soil** 262	☐ **stroke** 422
☐ **sculpture** 773	☐ solar eclipse 227	☐ subjective 765
☐ seascape 792	☐ solar energy 290	☐ **subscribe** 764
☐ segregate 724	☐ **solar system** 217	☐ subsequence 142
☐ **segregation** 724	☐ **solely** 195, 747	☐ **subsequent** 142
	☐ soluble 451	☐ subsequently 142
	☐ **solution** 451	☐ **substance** 097
	☐ **sophisticated** 141	☐ substantial 097
		☐ substantially 097
		☐ substantiate 097

☐ **substitute** 048	☐ **the Bill of Rights** 514	☐ **totalitarian**
☐ substitution 048	☐ **the Civil War** 721	**government** 502
☐ **suffrage** 516	☐ **the Democratic Party**	☐ totalitarianism 502
☐ suffragist 516	526	☐ **totally** 196
☐ **sulfur** 453	☐ **the Emancipation**	☐ **toxic** 319
☐ **sulfur dioxide** 454	**Proclamation** 722	☐ toxicant 319
☐ sulfuric acid 453	☐ **the Equal Rights**	☐ toxication 319
☐ sunlight 290	**Amendment** 740	☐ toxin 319
☐ supremacy 143	☐ **the Great Depression**	☐ tracking 648
☐ **supreme** 143	734	☐ **traditionally** 197
☐ **surface** 098	☐ the House 518	☐ tragedy 789
☐ survival 049	☐ **the House of**	☐ **trait** 391
☐ **survive** 049	**Representatives** 518	☐ transact 099
☐ **suspect** 610	☐ **the Ku Klux Klan** 732	☐ **transaction** 099
☐ symbol 565	☐ the large intestine 407	☐ **trauma** 673
☐ **symbolic** 565	☐ the Milky Way 219	☐ traumatic 673
☐ **sympathetic** 144	☐ **the New Deal** 735	☐ **trial** 100, 598
☐ sympathize 144	☐ the north latitudes 277	☐ **trial jury** 601
☐ sympathy 144	☐ The Origin of Species 324	☐ **trivial** 146
☐ **syndicate** 763	☐ **the Prohibition**	☐ tropical 254
☐ **synonym** 705	**movement** 729	☐ tropical zone 254
☐ synonymous 705	☐ **the Republican Party**	☐ Truth is stranger than
☐ synonymy 705	525	fiction. 688
☐ synthesis 207	☐ **the Senate** 520	☐ **turmoil** 739
	☐ the small intestine 407	☐ **typically** 198
T	☐ the south latitudes 277	
☐ take attendance 621	☐ **the Supreme Court**	**U**
☐ take the initiative (in	608	☐ **ulcer** 411
doing) 031	☐ the survival of the fittest	☐ ultrasonic 387
☐ **tardiness** 634	049, 401	☐ **ultrasound** 387
☐ tardy 634	☐ the White House 509	☐ **ultraviolet** 313
☐ teachers' union 629	☐ **theory of natural**	☐ ultraviolet rays 313
☐ **technology** 472	**selection** 401	☐ **umbilical cord**
☐ **telescope** 202	☐ thermometer 259	381, 385
☐ **temperate** 254	☐ thrift 145	☐ unalienable 529
☐ Temperate Zone 254	☐ **thrifty** 145	☐ unanimity 147
☐ temperature 254	☐ thriving 733	☐ **unanimous** 147
☐ testify 603	☐ **time deposit** 553	☐ **unconscious** 669
☐ testify against ... 603	☐ **topographic** 286	☐ unconsciously 669
☐ testify to ... 603	☐ topographic map 286	☐ under the influence of ...
☐ **testimony** 603	☐ topography 286	030
☐ the accused 596	☐ **tornado** 249	☐ **undoubtedly** 199
☐ the Amendments 513	☐ Torrid Zone 254	☐ uniform 638
☐ **the American**	☐ totalitarian 502	☐ **uniformity** 638
Revolution 717		☐ universal suffrage 516

☐ university	623
☐ **upward social mobility**	588
☐ uterine	384
☐ **uterus**	384

V

☐ vaccinate	430
☐ vaccination	430
☐ **vaccine**	430
☐ varied	713
☐ **velocity**	475
☐ **verdict**	602
☐ verifiable	050
☐ verification	050
☐ **verify**	050
☐ **vernacular**	791
☐ **versatile**	148
☐ versatility	148
☐ verse	685
☐ **veto**	512
☐ **vibrate**	492
☐ vibration	492
☐ viral disease	325
☐ **virtually**	200
☐ **virus**	325
☐ **vitamin**	458
☐ vocational school	623
☐ **volatile**	149
☐ volatility	149
☐ **volcanic**	275
☐ volcanic activity	275
☐ volcanic ash	275
☐ volcano	275
☐ **vulnerable**	150

W

☐ warm current	253
☐ warm latitudes	277
☐ **warm-blooded**	364
☐ water cycle	244
☐ **weather forecast**	248
☐ **weathering**	288
☐ **welfare**	736
☐ welfare state	736
☐ **white blood cell**	410
☐ **white-collar crime**	617
☐ wholesale	547
☐ wholesale prices	547
☐ **wholesaler**	547
☐ wind erosion	289
☐ with reluctance	139
☐ with unanimity	147
☐ women's suffrage	516

どれだけチェックできた？ 1 ☐ 2 ☐

聞いて覚える英単語
キクタン
TOEFL® TEST
【頻出編】

田中真紀子
Makiko Tanaka

神田外語大学外国語学部英米語学科教授。上智大学卒業後、上智大学大学院より MA（修士号）、カリフォルニア大学サンタバーバラ校より MA（修士号）、同大学より Ph.D.（博士号）を取得。教育学博士。専門は教育学（英語教育、児童英語教育）、応用言語学。著書に『TOEFL® ITP 完全攻略リーディング』（アルク）、『The Essential Guide for Academic Presentations』（マクミランランゲージハウス）などがある。NHK 教育テレビ 3 カ月トピック英会話「カリフォルニア縦断！シンプル会話術」講師。

書名	キクタン TOEFL® TEST【頻出編】
発行日	2009 年 3 月 31 日（初版） 2013 年 6 月 27 日（第 8 刷発行）
監修・解説	田中真紀子
編集	文教編集部
翻訳	鈴木美幸　田辺希久子
英文校正	Peter Branscombe、Owen Schaefer Joel Weinberg
アートディレクション	細山田 光宣
デザイン	若井夏澄（細山田デザイン事務所）
ナレーション	Jack Merluzzi、紗川じゅん
音楽制作	H. Akashi
録音・編集	幅 浩之（財団法人英語教育協議会）
CD プレス	株式会社 学研教育出版
DTP	株式会社 秀文社
印刷・製本	図書印刷株式会社
発行者	平本照麿
発行所	株式会社 アルク

〒168-8611　東京都杉並区永福 2-54-12
TEL：03-3327-1101　FAX：03-3327-1300
Email：csss@alc.co.jp
Website http://www.alc.co.jp/

地球人ネットワークを創る
アルクのシンボル
「地球人マーク」です。

・落丁本、乱丁本は弊社にてお取り替えいたしております。弊スタマーサービス部（電話：03-3327-1101　受付時間：平時〜17 時）までご相談ください。
・本書の全部または一部の無断転載を禁じます。
・著作権法上で認められた場合を除いて、本書からのコピーをます。
・定価はカバーに表示してあります。

©2009 Makiko Tanaka / ALC Press Inc. / H. Akashi Printed in Japan
PC：7009905
ISBN：978-4-7574-1565-2

アルクの書籍、通信講座の
ご注文はラクラク便利な…
アルク オンラインショップで！

24時間いつでもOK!

アルクのオンラインショップなら、24時間いつでもご注文できます。
初めてなのでちょっと不安…という方も、以下を参考に早速アクセス！

❶ まずはアルクのオンラインショップへアクセス。
http://shop.alc.co.jp/

❷ 画面左上の商品検索に、ご希望の商品名を入れて検索をクリック。

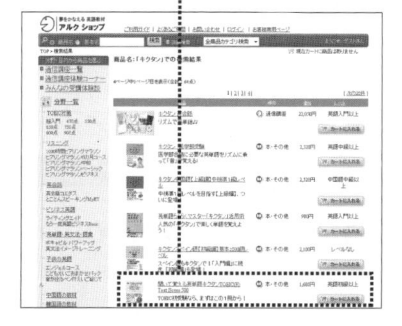

❸ ご希望の商品を選んで…

❹ あとはカートに入れて、レジへ進むだけ！

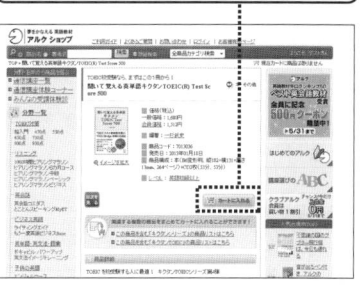

❺ 3営業日※以内に発送いたします。
※営業日は月～金、土日祝は休業日です。

お電話でも承ります。
アルク・お申し込み専用フリーダイヤル
0120-120-800
［携帯・PHSからもご利用いただけます／24時間受付］

※1回あたりのご購入金額が3,150円（税込）未満の場合には、発送手数料150円が加算されます。ご了承ください。

〒168-8611 東京都杉並区永福2-54-12　株式会社 アルク

目的・レベル別に選べる！
アルクの通信講座は充実のラインアップ

レベル	入門／初級			中級			上級
英 検	5級	4級	3級	準2級	2級	準1級	1級
TOEIC	−	−	350点	470点	600点	730点	860点
TOEFL	(iBT)		32点	46点	61点	80点	100点

聞く力をつけたい

- **ヒアリングマラソン・ベーシック kikuzo!** 英語聞き取りのコツをつかむ！
- 日常会話へステップアップ。 **ヒアリングマラソン中級コース**
- 120万人が受講した、人気ナンバーワン講座。 **1000時間ヒアリングマラソン**

話す力をつけたい

- **イングリッシュ キング** 1日20分×週3日の新英会話習慣！
- **英会話コエダス** 持ち歩ける英会話スクール。
- 決まり文句だけの英語から脱却！ **英会話コエダス・アドバンス**

ビジネス英語を学びたい

- **もう一度英語 ビジネス Basic** 1日15分！英語の基礎を総復習。
- 朝20分！脳科学に基づいた学習法。 **朝英語®Biz**
- 学校英語をビジネス仕様に磨き上げ！ **もう一度英語 ビジネス Chance**
- クリエイティブに会話を操る！ **ビジネス英会話 クリダス**
- プレゼン・会議・交渉の英語に自信を付けたい！ **ヒアリングマラソン ビジネス**

TOEIC®テストに備えたい

- **TOEIC®テスト 超入門キット** 1日15分、聞くだけで身に付く！
- **TOEIC®テスト 470点入門マラソン** 1日30分×週4日の学習で英語力の下地を作る。
- **奪取550点 TOEIC®テスト 解答テクニック講座** スコア直結の解答テクニックを手に入れる！
- 海外出張をこなせる力を養成。 **TOEIC®テスト 650点突破マラソン**
- TOEICのプロが奥義を伝授！ **奪取730点 TOEIC®テスト 攻略プログラム**
- 仕事で使える本物の英語力を。 **TOEIC®テスト 800点攻略プログラム**
- 目標はノンネイティブ最高レベル！ **挑戦900点 TOEIC®テスト攻略プログラム**

※各講座のレベルは目安です。

資料請求は無料です！下記フリーダイヤルまたはインターネットで

お電話 アルク・フリーダイヤル
0120-120-800
※携帯電話・PHSからもご利用いただけます。（24時間受付）

インターネット アルク・オンラインショップ
http://shop.alc.co.jp/
アルクの通信講座全ラインアップや講座の詳細もご覧いただけます。

※お知らせいただいた個人情報は、資料の発送および小社からの商品情報をお送りするために利用し、その目的以外での使用はいたしません。
また、お客様の個人情報に変更の必要がある場合は、カスタマーサービス部（TEL. 03-3327-1101）までご連絡をお願い申し上げます。